GOSPEL ALLEGIANCE

GOSPEL ALLEGIANCE

What Faith in Jesus Misses for Salvation in Christ

MATTHEW W. BATES

BrazosPress
a division of Baker Publishing Group
Grand Rapids, Michigan

Published by Brazos Press
a division of Baker Publishing Group
PO Box 6287, Grand Rapids, MI 49516-6287
www.brazospress.com

Printed in the United States of America

Library of Congress Cataloging-in-Publication Data

Names: Bates, Matthew W., author.
Title: Gospel allegiance : what faith in Jesus misses for salvation in Christ / Matthew W. Bates.
Description: Grand Rapids : Brazos Press, a division of Baker Publishing Group, [2019] | Includes bibliographical references and index.
Identifiers: LCCN 2019004659 | ISBN 9781587434297 (pbk.)
Subjects: LCSH: Christian life—Biblical teaching.
Classification: LCC BS2555.6.C48 B38 2019 | DDC 230—dc23
LC record available at https://lccn.loc.gov/2019004659

ISBN 978-1-58743-453-2 (casebound)

Scripture quotations labeled AT are the author's own translation, in order to highlight precise features of the Bible's original languages.

Bold or italics have been added to Scripture quotations by the author.

Some names have been changed to protect the privacy of those involved.

19 20 21 22 23 24 25 7 6 5 4 3 2 1

In keeping with biblical principles of creation stewardship, Baker Publishing Group advocates the responsible use of our natural resources. As a member of the Green Press Initiative, our company uses recycled paper when possible. The text paper of this book is composed in part of post-consumer waste.

For Jonathan Miles and Daniel Strudwick

In very different ways
your allegiance to Jesus the king
inspires me.

Contents

Acknowledgments

Let me express my gratitude.

Teresa Gorrell and Jonathan Miles gave extensive feedback as I finished each chapter, frequently reading several drafts. I am extraordinarily grateful.

Several people gave comments on a draft or a portion of it: Rod Bakker (a very good shepherd who has now retired), Aubrey Brady, Matthew Brady, Andrew Cashman, Daniel Strudwick, Joshua Jipp, Josiah Prenger, and Chuck Sackett. Chuck is another excellent shepherd. He gets a special shout-out for vetting my conversation-guide questions. Many thanks.

Sarah Bates, my amazing wife, helped me to process and commented on every chapter—and managed to do this while taking care of me and our seven children. To apply the word "saintly" is not hyperbole. For keeping me young and making me old simultaneously, I commend Tad, Zeke, Addie, Lydia, Evie, Anna, and Nate.

I am grateful to Renew.org, especially its director, Bobby Harrington. We share a common urgency to foster allegiant discipleship to Jesus the king. Not only did Bobby read for me and offer tremendous personal encouragement, he also orchestrated a partnership with Renew.org. His pastoral vision is helping the allegiance message reach a wider audience.

I want to thank Brazos Press for publishing *Gospel Allegiance*. A second book will follow, God willing. Specific individuals at Brazos deserve high praise. Bryan Dyer acquired this project. Bryan helped me to trim, reshape, and find consistency. Fantastic work. I'm grateful to Jeremy Wells, Mason Slater, Kara Day, and Shelley MacNaughton for their prowess in marketing and publicity. Eric Salo and his team were outstanding in production. Paula Gibson and her designers gave this book its striking public face.

This book is dedicated to Jonathan Miles (professor of philosophy) and Daniel Strudwick (professor of theology)—my closest colleagues at Quincy University. Permit me to offer a personal word: It is a delight to work alongside you. But that is not why I am dedicating this book to you. I see how you live each day. And the quality of your lives encourages me, in your own unique and quite different ways, to greater allegiance to King Jesus. More than you know.

Finally, I am grateful to any and every reader. Thanks for caring enough about the gospel to engage with this book. Would you be willing to help further? Please mention *Gospel Allegiance* on social media, on blogs, or in conversation. Rate or review it for others. Such things are incredibly important for spreading the word and creating energy in today's publishing world. Don't be shy about dropping me a note to let me know about reviews you post, how you are using it in your church, or discussions you are having. I am on social media. Or you can find my email address easily enough. Thanks.

May allegiance to Jesus the king increase!

Soli Deo gloria.

Introduction

Although ghostly in appearance, this was no wood spirit. The rifle he carried was solid and threatening. A soldier had emerged from the jungle and was rapidly advancing. The young adventure seeker, Norio Suzuki, ceased kneeling beside his campfire and stood while the soldier approached. Hands trembling, Suzuki saluted him.

Suzuki had traveled from Japan to the small Philippine island of Lubang for this very purpose. He hoped to find the legendary soldier Hiroo Onoda. The year was 1974.

Hiroo Onoda, a World War II Japanese intelligence officer, had been left on the island in 1945 by his commander with instructions to carry on a guerrilla battle without committing suicide—no matter what—until the Japanese forces returned for him and his troop. He had been told that he may need to wait many years.

Loyal unto death, Onoda was still fighting the Allied forces twenty-nine years later. He had recently lost his last four soldiers in a firefight with local police. Now, with no one left to command, he waged war alone. But then Suzuki, this strange Japanese adventurer, had appeared on the beach wearing rubber sandals and socks, something no native islander would do.

In his autobiography, *No Surrender*, Onoda recounts that monumental beachfront exchange. Onoda's first impulse had been to shoot Suzuki. But since Suzuki was unarmed and unusually dressed, Onoda decided to risk everything. He called out to him from the jungle. Suzuki responded on the beach with a proper Japanese salute. Onoda was astonished. Then Suzuki squealed in a high-pitched voice, "I'm Japanese," several times.

So Onoda, gun in hand, emerged from the undergrowth, asking pointed questions: "Did you come from the Japanese government?" "Are you from the Foreign Youth Cooperation?" Suzuki replied that he was a tourist. Onoda did not believe him. Then Suzuki asked, "Are you Onoda-san?" "Yes, I'm Onoda," he replied. "Really, Lieutenant Onoda?" Onoda nodded. Suzuki continued, "I know you've had a long, hard time. The war's over. Won't you come back to Japan with me?"[1]

Onoda told Suzuki that he would surrender only if he received "proper orders" from his higher ranking Japanese officer, Major Taniguchi. About three weeks later Suzuki returned with Major Taniguchi. Wary of betrayal, Onoda crept out from the jungle wearing camouflage. He was reunited with Major Taniguchi, who read aloud a formal order commanding that Onoda surrender.[2]

If Onoda's superior, Major Taniguchi, had not given the definitive command, Onoda might still be fighting in the jungle today. And he was just one of hundreds of documented Japanese holdouts, those who continued fighting for years after Japan had surrendered. Influenced by the Bushido codes of honor that the Japanese emperor bent to serve his imperialistic ambitions, Onoda and his comrades were unswerving in their loyalty to the emperor, almost reflexively. Like the honed edge of a samurai sword, the meaning of life and death was singular. *Allegiance*.

When he was fifteen years old, he was tossing hay for mules near the barn on his family farm in Charlotte, North Carolina.

The young man had been baptized and confirmed, attended church regularly, and served as a peer leader at his church. But he was mainly interested in baseball. He heard singing coming from the barn and concluded disdainfully that his father must have allowed some religious fanatics to use the space. The boy did not attend the revival in his father's barn that night. But a salesman named Vernon Patterson did. And Patterson prayed that God would raise up a worldwide evangelist right there in Charlotte.

Several weeks later, Mordecai Ham, a traveling evangelist, rolled into town to conduct another revival for several weeks. The boy had zero interest. But when he heard that this evangelist was a fighter, identifying specific sinners in the local high school by name, he began to think it might prove entertaining to go. A local farmer bribed him to attend by allowing him the fun of driving his dairy truck to the meetings. At the meetings, the young man increasingly felt convicted of his sin and unsure that his baptism and confirmation were sufficient to save him: "Our family Bible reading, praying, psalm-singing and church-going—all these had left me restless and resentful. . . . I was spiritually dead."

Each night Ham would present an invitation. Each night the young man resisted. Finally, one evening the choir sang "Just As I Am" and then "Almost Persuaded, Now to Believe." As the choir belted out the final verses, he found that he had been persuaded and now believed. With leaden feet he went forward. He prayed a sinner's prayer, asking to receive Christ. When he returned home, he threw his arms around his mother, jubilantly reporting, "I am a changed boy!"[3]

Billy Graham would become the greatest evangelist of the twentieth century, proclaiming the same message he had heard from Ham: right now you can repent, believe, and receive Christ for eternal life. Millions came forward at his rallies. Graham was a straight-talking Southern preacher whose message was clear: Your sins condemn you. But there's good news of salvation in Jesus. *Repent and believe.*

Introducing Gospel Allegiance

If you love the gospel, this book is for you. It aims to describe the gospel and saving faith with greater clarity and precision than other popular Christian resources. But it may prove disruptive. I've come to the following conclusions:

The true biblical gospel can never change.
The gospel must change.

These seemingly contradictory statements crackle with electric tension. The sparks flying between them ignite this book, which is but one of many efforts going on worldwide to add to the blaze. My prayer is that allegiance to Jesus the king will spread like fire.

Nothing matters more to the individual Christian, the church, and ultimately the world than the gospel. When it seizes us, its goodness becomes a volcanic pressure in our hearts. Praise erupts. "Your love, O Lord, reaches to the heavens!" When you finish this book, I hope you'll have a more precise understanding of the gospel and its relationship to faith, grace, and works. My desire is that this will bring you to new heights of praise. I pray it will also equip you for the church's disciple-making mission.

But let's be real. There are obstacles. A correct retrieval of the gospel, faith, and salvation is lacking in the church. We all know that there are bad teachers—slicksters like Jim Bakker and Creflo Dollar. But it's not just bad teachers that are the problem. It's the good ones too. This is why the gospel must change.

Misunderstandings about what the Bible teaches about the gospel and faith are widespread across the full spectrum of the church. This is a strong claim, but I think its truth can be shown. These misunderstandings are present in standard resources written by pastor-scholars such as Matt Chandler, Greg Gilbert, John MacArthur, John Piper, and R. C. Sproul. I mention these because they are all well-known authors who have written books about the gospel. They are also highly respected for their fidelity to the Bible. Rightly so. They are among the best teachers the church has.

So when we discover they are *all* slightly misrepresenting what the Bible teaches about the gospel, it demonstrates that problems are pervasive. It shows that the gospel must change in our churches.

There are extensive misunderstandings of the gospel today. I think this has happened because present salvation models such as lordship salvation, free grace, TULIP, and the Catholic model are inadequate. I do not pretend to have all the answers about how salvation works. It is a rich, extensive conversation that Christians have been carrying out for millennia. But as I join with others in reaching toward solutions, I hope I am at least asking the right questions. Trying to answer them has led to this conviction: we need better language and a new model to more accurately convey what Scripture teaches about salvation. My prayer is that this will lead to enhanced evangelism and discipleship and a greater capacity to praise God. The model I am proposing is *gospel allegiance*.

Concerning Furrowed Brows

More than a few brows have furrowed after reading these first pages. The claim of widespread errors with regard to essential Christian teachings may seem far-fetched or alarmist. In fact, even as I write these words, I can imagine some readers slamming this book closed in disgust, thinking: The church doesn't need a new model for salvation—the church needs to *preserve* the unchanging gospel of faith in Jesus alone, not reevaluate it.

Still others may be too timid to explore, finding the prospects too risky. After all, false preachers have been peddling pseudo-gospel messages from the very beginning (see Gal. 1:6–7). Today the church must contend with false gospels announcing that God wants to make us rich, or physically healthy, or psychologically balanced, or well connected, or militarily powerful, or tolerant of others. One especially wacky Episcopal priest in San Francisco recently made headlines for hosting a Beyoncé-inspired Eucharistic celebration. The choir sang popular Beyoncé songs rather than offering praise to God![4] I'm not sure what kind of false gospel to call this. The good news that God wants us all to be pop-music, sex icons? We live in strange times.

Unlike these false gospels, the true gospel addresses the human sin problem. It also has implications for the whole social order and for creation itself. The gospel must change us.

I need to say a further word to the reluctant, because I sympathize. In the wake of my previous book, *Salvation by Allegiance Alone*, I have had many conversations about faith and the gospel. So I can say with some confidence that those who consider it a false and risky quest to rethink the gospel usually do so because they regard the true gospel as pure and simple.

For the reluctant, the gospel can easily be summarized in a variety of ways: believe that Jesus died for your sins and you will be saved; trust in Jesus's righteousness alone, not in your own works; have faith in Jesus's sacrifice for your sins and in his resurrection power. And surely no biblically informed Christian can question the necessity of grace and faith and the problematic nature of works. After all, the apostle Paul says, "For it is by grace you have been saved through faith . . . not by works, so that no one can boast" (Eph. 2:8–9 AT).[5] The true church is in little danger of losing sight of these central truths—so it is thought. The conclusion: the proposed journey will lead us astray or nowhere new.

Is a New Model Necessary?

But this is precisely the problem. When the Bible presents the gospel, it is not "believe Jesus died for your sins and you will be saved." Nor is it "trust in Jesus's righteousness alone, not in your works." Neither is it "have faith in Jesus's sacrifice for your sins and in his resurrection power." And contrary to the claims of MacArthur, Piper, and others, the heart of the gospel is certainly not justification by faith (see chap. 1). The gospel presented in the Bible is quite specific. While the Bible does say that Jesus's death for sins and his resurrection are part of the gospel—and obviously central facts to be believed—this is only a portion of the true gospel. And even to frame it in this way puts the focus in the wrong place. The consequences of these misarticulations are serious.

Furthermore, while we affirm faith and grace, are we sure we know what these words actually meant when the apostle Paul and others wrote them? After all, Paul used the Greek words *pistis* and *charis*, words that meant something different in his time and culture than what "faith" and "grace" mean in ours. Moreover, Jesus, Paul, and other New Testament writers say again and again that we'll be judged on the basis of our deeds (e.g., Matt. 16:27; John 5:28–29; Rom. 2:6–16; see chap. 5 below for further discussion), so the role of works in salvation is more complex than first meets the eye. While we may agree that the Bible's vision of salvation manifests a beautiful simplicity, it is not simplistic.

The gospel given to the church by Jesus and the apostles can never change. The problem is that the church as a whole—including many pastors, authors, and churches that loudly proclaim themselves biblical—have embraced distorted understandings of the gospel, faith, grace, works, and salvation.

As imprecisions ripple outward, distortions are magnified. Problems emerge for the church. This is why our gospel must change. We need a new biblical paradigm so that the saving good news can be heralded forth in all its truth and power. The gospel-allegiance structure allows us to more accurately capture what the Bible teaches about salvation. Presenting it is our task in this book.

The Gospel through a Window, Darkly

It is not that the true gospel is entirely missing or that people are not entering salvation. Far from it. The gospel is still being preached with saving effect. Rather, the current situation is like standing in a cluttered garage with a lone, dusty window. A rosebush can be seen growing outside—an appreciable amount of goodness and beauty—but the view of the roses is obscured.

Once you recognize the need, you begin to sweep, dust, and remove boxes. And when you look out again, you see vibrant lilies, orchids, tulips, and poppies as well as more roses than you ever could have imagined—in a hundred vibrant colors. You hadn't realized that the rosebush was part of a flower garden. This book attempts to move boxes and clean the windowpanes so we can see the whole garden in all its radiant beauty—the saving gospel of Jesus the king.

I want to show that the gospel and our faith response must not be reduced to the cross, or even to the cross and resurrection. The gospel is bigger than that. Why does our gospel need to change? Because the climax of the biblical gospel is not the cross but something frequently not considered part of the gospel at all: the enthronement of Jesus. And when we see this, we might begin to see why saving faith in the Bible intends not just belief or interior trust in God's promises but *bodily allegiance* to a king. Seeing this compels us to rethink how faith, grace, and works fit together.

What Was, Is, and Will Be

This book stands on its own. You need not have read *Salvation by Allegiance Alone* first. But it is helpful to understand how my earlier book relates to this one. I keep receiving two basic questions about saving allegiance, one theological and the other pastoral: (1) How can we deepen our understanding of salvation by allegiance alone? (2) What can we do to foster an allegiance culture in our churches and personal lives?

These are huge questions that can never be exhaustively answered. *Gospel Allegiance* attempts a beginning by going beyond my previous work in the following ways:

1. *It is gospel first.* The gospel itself is defined more precisely and explored more thoroughly.
2. *It is more practical and pastoral.* This book is aimed, first, at church leaders, everyday Christians, small group

studies, and church education programs. Students and scholars are second. There are plenty of stories and examples. My principal dialogue partners are standard pastoral resources by John MacArthur, John Piper, and the like. My work is informed by scholarship and seeks to advance that conversation too, but the priority is pastoral. To maximize the book's practical and experiential aims, it should be read with the guide for further conversation in appendix 2, which gives suggested questions and activities for individuals or groups.

3. *It goes deeper*. Readers have asked for more on the gospel, faith as allegiance, grace, and works. This book moves along the trajectories established in my previous work but gives additional nuance, detail, and supporting evidence.
4. *It reframes*. Nobody wants a rehash. The principal gospel passages in the Bible will always remain principal, so some overlap in presentation is unavoidable. Yet different lenses and angles of approach can generate new insights. To minimize repetition, all the biblical texts are approached afresh and new ones are added to the discussion.
5. *It is more focused*. This is a deeper but narrower study. *Gospel Allegiance* treats the gospel, grace, and works more thoroughly. It places a premium on the apostle Paul's theology since this has been the main focus of debate regarding these topics—although it seeks to integrate and contextualize Paul's theology within the whole biblical vision.

The chapters in this book develop themes suggested by Ephesians 2:8–10, the passage frequently regarded as the premier statement of salvation theory in the Bible:

> For by grace you have been saved through faith. And this is not from yourselves—it is the gift of God—not by works, in order that no

> one may boast. For we are his workmanship, created in the Christ, Jesus, for good works, which God prepared beforehand, that we should walk in them. (AT)

The body of this book will seek to problematize and then refine our understanding of key topics: the gospel, faith, grace, works, and how these relate to the Catholic-Protestant division. In the final chapter, we will bring it all together by applying it experientially: Can you take what you've learned and explain Ephesians 2:8–10 from within the gospel-allegiance framework? You'll be able to test yourself by comparing your attempt with this book's answer. No peeking at the last pages!

For those seeking more, *Salvation by Allegiance Alone* covers many pertinent topics that could not fit here. If you are disappointed that I don't treat a specific issue pertaining to salvation here—like the order of salvation, justification's relationship to sanctification, or imputed versus imparted righteousness—check there.

I am also presently writing a book that will extend the core gospel-allegiance model to issues that lie beyond it. I'm excited! Stay tuned.

Traveling Together

The journey into gospel allegiance mirrors my own intellectual and spiritual pilgrimage. This is a journey that I believe has been "further up and further in," as C. S. Lewis might put it. As you've begun to travel with me, you may be interested to hear a small portion of my story.

If you are a sleuth, you've already got this figured out. I completed my doctoral work at the University of Notre Dame. I teach in a Catholic-Franciscan university. I have seven children. (You could probably even discover that we drive a huge church van to accommodate all these kids.) I pray the Catholic morning office and attend Mass on occasion. And this book argues that we are saved by allegiance. Even if there is no incense burning, it smells Catholic.

But the clues are misleading. I am a Protestant. Although I appreciate Catholic values and have many Catholic friends, I find that uniquely Catholic doctrines do not accord with the Bible, earliest Christian history, or the truth. I was raised in a conservative independent Bible church. As a college student and adult, I moved frequently in pursuit of various educational opportunities. I have regularly attended or held membership in independent, Presbyterian, Baptist, Mennonite, and Evangelical Free churches. My formal training was at a university situated in the Reformed tradition for my undergraduate degree (Whitworth), a multidenominational Protestant seminary for my master's degree (Regent College), and a Catholic university for my doctorate (Notre Dame).

The overall result? I am a theological mutt—a traditionally minded Christian who is pro-church but not associated with any particular denomination. I am grateful for this diversity of training and experience, as I think it has helped me appreciate the strengths and weaknesses of various Christian traditions. As for my contention that we are saved by allegiance alone, some virulently anti-Catholic readers may insist that surely I *must* have made a secret pact with the devil and the pope during my time at Notre Dame. But, in fact, nearly all my influences in arriving at this conclusion are Protestant. (Ironically, my dissertation director at Notre Dame, who bears no responsibility for my views, is a Lutheran.) I am not Catholic, Orthodox, Lutheran, Anglican, Reformed, Arminian, or Baptist. I do not write from or for any official theological system. Apart from Christian and Protestant, I reject all such labels.

It is fair to say, though, that I am an unusual Protestant. This is because I do not think that my Catholic or Orthodox brothers and sisters have rejected or compromised the content of the gospel. This is why I consider them my full brothers and sisters in the Christ. This doesn't mean that our ongoing disagreements aren't serious and substantive. But we are all *full members* of the one Christian family. If you don't think this could possibly be true, then keep reading.

Why must our gospel change? Because nonbiblical versions of the gospel are wrongly splitting the one true church. Despite improved relations between Catholics, Orthodox, and Protestants, the fact remains that in present circumstances I as a Protestant would be happy to receive communion with the pope, but as a member of the Catholic church he is not willing to receive it with me—even though we confess the same gospel and have both been baptized as Christians. On the other side, too many Protestants love to spit venom at Catholics. This grieves me. Consider me an advocate of what C. S. Lewis called "mere Christianity," a vision of the church that celebrates its common ground. Common, yes, but not at the expense of the gospel truth—rather because of it.

Ultimately, *Gospel Allegiance* cuts across traditional denominational accounts of what the Bible teaches about salvation, offering a new model. Do not allow precut labels that others have created predetermine what you find. Let Scripture—not "Reformed," "Arminian," or "Catholic"—be your guide. If you read with care, you'll find that such labels do not accurately describe the gospel-allegiance model. Consider this an opportunity to reassess where the biblical boundaries lie apart from such labels.

On our journey we should bear in mind that the Bible was written by and for real ancient people. It was God's word to them as much as it is God's word to us. This means we must attend to ancient word meanings and cultures, as well as to our present context. Accordingly, I sometimes cite ancient sources (such as Josephus, Philo, and the Catholic Apocrypha/Deuterocanon), not as authoritative Scripture, but in order to show how certain words were being used when the New Testament was written. Practicing gospel allegiance involves learning to negotiate between ancient and modern meanings and applications.

Toward a More Allegiant Future

I opened this book by juxtaposing the stories of Hiroo Onoda and Billy Graham. It might be obvious by now that I am suggesting that the story of Onoda's allegiance, even though it was not properly aimed, can help us correct deficiencies in Graham's evangelistic model. I admire Graham. Who would dare to suggest that he didn't achieve mountains of good?

Yet Graham's model promotes a divorce between a salvation decision and discipleship. Accordingly, Graham has been accused of encouraging what some call "easy believe-ism" or what is known today, less pejoratively, as the "free grace" position. John MacArthur and his supporters have attempted to refute so-called free grace by advocating for "lordship salvation." This has been a productive conversation for the church. But gospel allegiance provides an even more holistic vision for evangelism and discipleship. More on this later.

I have a further purpose in opening with stories about Onoda and Graham. Stories take us deeper than raw facts. They help us to experience the texture of life's fabric, to understand with both the head and the heart. So I'm going to tell a third story, one that is both true and ancient. It happened near the end of the New Testament era. It helps us both to know and to experience why allegiance mattered for salvation back then—and why it still should today.

Pliny was troubled. He was a non-Christian governor in the Roman Empire in the early second century. Certain individuals in his region had been denounced as Christians. Although he knew Christianity was illegal, he was uncertain what to do. So he sent an urgent letter to Emperor Trajan requesting direction.

In the meantime, he needed to act quickly because the "contagion" and "superstition," as he himself described Christianity, had already penetrated city, village, and countryside alike. Thus, while awaiting the emperor's response, he settled on a personal interview to test the accused and dispatch the guilty: "I asked them whether they were Christians, and if they confessed, I asked them a second and third time with threats of punishment. If they kept to it, I ordered them for execution."[6] So Christians were given an opportunity to recant, but if they persisted they were summarily executed.

Yet while Pliny was attempting to deal with these pesky Christian troubles, his difficulties increased. When the state started giving credence to personal accusation, the finger pointing accelerated. In fact, Pliny was given a list with the names of numerous alleged "Christians," but the list was unsigned by specific accusers. Therefore Pliny was obliged to conduct even more interviews.

Pliny was forced to refine his interview procedure so that he could determine who was and who was not a true Christian. Some of its details may prove puzzling to contemporary readers: "As for those who said that they neither were nor ever had been Christians, I thought it right to let them go, since they recited a prayer to the gods at my dictation, made supplication with incense and wine *to your [Emperor Trajan's] statue, which I had ordered to be brought into court for the purpose* together with the images of the gods, and moreover cursed Christ—things which (so it is said) those who are really Christians cannot be made to do."

In assessing Pliny's test from our twenty-first-century vantage point, it probably does not surprise us to learn that true Christians would refuse to curse Christ or would decline to worship the pagan gods. But Pliny's very deliberate placement of Emperor Trajan's statue is odd. If we were to do some research, we would correctly conclude that the Roman emperors were increasingly receiving divine honors during this time period. So perhaps it is fine that Pliny felt it fitting to include Trajan's statue as a god among other gods. But why wasn't it sufficient simply to test whether the accused would worship pagan idols *in general*? What did Trajan's image *in particular* have that these others lacked? Pliny's description continues: "Others who were named by the informer said that they were Christians and then denied it, explaining that they had been, but had ceased to be such, some three years ago, some a good many years, and a few even twenty. All these too both *worshiped your statue and the images of the gods*, and cursed Christ."

Again, the emperor's image is given singular significance beyond the other idols in the test. Why? The other gods may rule, but the emperor's divine rule is visible, concrete, and immediate. For Pliny, Trajan is the *living* emperor-god, the one who rightfully demands the *ultimate yet practical loyalty* of his subjects. This allegiance would be expressed by their adulation as well as their pledged loyalty, support in war, and tax payments.

Faith as Allegiance to the King

Pliny grasped something we often miss. Even though allegiance is at the margins of Christian theology today, Pliny included obeisance to Trajan's statue as a litmus test because he had correctly discerned its absolute centrality. For Pliny, the true Christian does not merely recognize Jesus's divinity by worshiping him to the exclusion of all other gods. Nor does he or she simply have "faith alone" in Jesus's death for sins. Rather, Jesus as the resurrected, enthroned, and now *ever-living king* was felt to demand a similar sort of *ultimate yet practical allegiance* as did Emperor Trajan. The true Christian gave allegiance to Jesus the king, subverting the emperor's claims to be a god, the supreme ruler, and a savior.

The word "faith" itself needs to be reconsidered by Christians today. The word ordinarily translated as "faith" is *pistis* in the New Testament's original Greek. But *pistis* is a richer word than "faith." It can mean allegiance. For example, in Revelation 2:13, Jesus commends the church at Pergamum for remaining loyal to him even when they were under pressure to worship the emperor instead. Jesus says to them, "You did not deny *pistis* to me" (AT).[7]

Jesus does not mean, "You did not abandon your faith in me to forgive your sins," but rather, "You did not deny your allegiance to me as king." Just as allegiance was key for Emperor Trajan, so it is also for King Jesus. And as we reappraise Christian theological categories—the gospel, faith, grace, works, and justification—it might prove to be key for us as well.

PART 1

Discovering Gospel Allegiance

1

Getting the Gospel Right

It was one of the most awkward dinner situations I've experienced. Through it I learned why we need to get the gospel right.

We had invited three middle-aged Chinese men over for dinner in our basement suite. I had met them through my church as a volunteer English-language tutor. Anyone could get tutoring, whether they were interested in Christianity or not. Over several months our friendship had grown. So my wife and I wanted to extend hospitality.

When we opened our door, they entered with shy grins. They came bearing gifts—eight giant clusters of bananas and dozens of tiny clementines—more than my wife and I could ever eat. My wife had prepared a rich beef stew and rolls, and I had helped with a garden salad. They raved over the attractiveness of the food: "Your salad is too lovely to eat."

The stew was already in the bowls. I prayed. We began passing the salad. Before my wife and I realized what had happened, two of our guests had served their salad into their stew bowls! Lettuce, dressing, and chunks of parmesan were floating on hot broth, beef medallions, and red potatoes.

We were shocked and embarrassed for failing to inform our guests. We hastily retrieved new bowls from the cupboard. But they refused to accept clean bowls—even when we had ladled fresh stew into them. They were also enormously embarrassed, but preferred to help their hosts save face by minimizing our shame. (The West has much to learn from the East about humility for the sake of others in guest-host relations.) So they instead ate the stew-salad monstrosity, insisting, "This is just the way we prefer it! It is much better this way!"

Several weeks later they invited us to their basement and made us authentic noodle soup. We did not put salad on it—although we should have!—and we were able to laugh together about our previous dinner.

A Better Gospel?

As our friendship blossomed, I explained why I was at seminary. I had left a high-paying job as an electrical engineer to become a poor student in order to be better equipped to serve Jesus. This downward career trajectory puzzled them. We should never underestimate how intriguing Jesus's ways are to those with little experience.

As time went on, I shared the gospel directly with the three men. They were interested, but unsure what to make of Jesus. Did he truly heal people? Was he really raised from the dead? One of them, Mao, was wrestling with Christianity more fiercely than the others.

When I presented the gospel to Mao, I recall asking him to repent and believe that Jesus died for his sins. We spoke about the hardships he would face in China if he became a Christian. A month later Mao expressed faith in Jesus. A few weeks after that he returned to China. I have never been able to contact him, so I do not know if he still follows Jesus. Sometimes one or two brief moments is all we get. Getting the gospel right matters.

There is no such thing as a better gospel. The true gospel is more than good enough. But is that what I shared?

I know now that Mao heard only a rough approximation. After all, what more is needed if the gospel is that "you can't do anything for yourself, so repent and believe"? Why does it require discipleship? I attempted to sow seed. But was the gospel I presented able to dig deep enough into the soil? I trust the Spirit was working in spite of the deficiencies in my gospel presentation.

But it also motivated a quest to get the gospel right. If I were to present the gospel to Mao now, I think I could help him receive a firmer planting, one more likely to yield a harvest. I could help him holistically hold together salvation and continued discipleship within one framework: allegiance to Jesus the forgiving king.

Nothing is more vital than the pure gospel. The church must safeguard, display, and invite others to experience this treasure. When the church has come to grasp the biblical gospel imperfectly, it must change its gospel by refining toward the truth. God works to save despite our flaws. Yet it is not hyperbole to say that eternal lives are at stake. For God has entrusted the task of gospel preservation and proclamation to his church.

Gospel Matters

In this chapter we will begin examining in some detail what the Bible says about the gospel. As I have presented this material, I've found that many who think they thoroughly understand the gospel are surprised to learn that they hold substantial misconceptions. I think it can be shown that even popular books on the gospel by leading pastor-scholars like Matt Chandler, Greg Gilbert, John MacArthur, John Piper, and R. C. Sproul contain inaccuracies in their presentations of the gospel. These are authors who seek to be biblical. Yet I submit that the gospel they are presenting needs to be fine-tuned in light of what the Bible actually says. And these are the good ones! If their gospels need sharpening, how much more dubious are the gospels presented by Christian teachers like Benny Hinn, Kenneth Copeland, and Joel Osteen. This shows the degree to which the gospel in the church today needs to change, for gospel imprecision is a pervasive problem. My hope in presenting this material is that discipleship and evangelism will be reinvigorated.

The Gospel Is Not

We primarily learn by contrast. When we are children, we learn what the color blue is mostly by recognizing that blue is not green, red, or yellow. So if we are going to discuss what the gospel is, it can be helpful first to describe what the gospel is *not*. And it's no wonder there is widespread confusion in the church when we discover the wildly flexible ways in which the word "gospel" is used. When "gospel" comes to mean anything and everything, there is no defining contrast—no green, red, or yellow to help us identify blue. Gospel confusion ensues.

Not Vague Christian Activities

The word "gospel" has been co-opted to describe a whole host of Christian or quasi-Christian activities and projects that only loosely relate to its biblical description.

Gospel everything is nothing. When everything becomes the gospel, nothing is, because the word is meaningless. Or worse, it becomes a marketing scheme: gospel-driven this, gospel-centered that, and gospel "projects" abound. Many of these are first-rate Christian resources even when only loosely related to the gospel. But savvy marketers apply the gospel label because they know the gospel sells. This overly wide use of the term "gospel" as a marketing strategy causes confusion, for the church loses its gospel precision. The gospel is not the whole of Christianity or the entire Christian story. And it certainly shouldn't be a way to make more money.

Gospel actions? Other activities are confusingly called the gospel. The gospel is not loving others unconditionally. It is not the rule of God in your heart. It is not a style of music. Jesus heralds good news for the poor, the sick, and the oppressed (Luke 4:18–19), so some church traditions call activities aimed toward helping those groups the "social gospel." A more accurate way to state it might be that the gospel is a political statement with social implications. And the Bible exhorts and commands Christians to undertake such actions in the name of Jesus the king. But we must distinguish the gospel proper from the various kinds of benefits it brings (see chap. 3 and "Bridge" at the end of part 1).

There are numerous activities we adopt once we are changed by the gospel, but we only introduce confusion if we call these activities the gospel. So, the gospel is not extending forgiveness or grace toward others. It is not becoming more holy, self-controlled, or generous. The actual gospel is what God has done in and through Jesus the king, not what we are becoming or doing for others. Period.

Say it! There's a related problem: the gospel is not actions divorced from words. Saint Francis of Assisi is reported to have said, "Preach the gospel at all times; use words if necessary." We find this saying attractive because talking about Jesus and salvation to those outside the church can be intimidating. But the Bible describes the gospel as something that cannot be proclaimed purely through good deeds toward others. Our good deeds can amplify the gospel message, but the message itself must first be verbally proclaimed by someone in order for our actions to reinforce it. And actually there is no evidence Saint Francis said any such thing.

So the gospel is not the whole Christian story, a marketing slogan, helping out, feeding the poor, loving others, or extending grace or forgiveness toward others. And it must be proclaimed not merely through our actions but through our words that tell *what God has done through Jesus*. The gospel is not the Christian activities that we do. It is about Jesus's actions, not ours. To present the gospel we must describe his actions using our words.

Not the Romans Road

There are many who present the gospel as if it is equivalent to what has come to be known as the "Romans Road." In this system, verses from the book of Romans are used to explain salvation. The path begins with the recognition that all fall short of God's righteous standard (Rom. 3:23) and that none are righteous (3:10). Since God is just, he must pay us the wages we deserve for our sins: death (6:23). But even while we were sinners, Christ died for us (5:8) as a free gift for eternal life (6:23), so that anyone who believes and confesses that Jesus is Lord will be saved (10:9–10).

The Romans Road is presented in a variety of forms, including books, tracts, bookmarks, crafts, kits, banners, and flash cards. You can get a ruler, a bracelet, or even a pen with a pullout banner for a mere $2.24—you know, just in case you are doodling a cross, someone asks, and you require assistance in sharing the gospel. Two very popular recent books take this general approach.

In the first, Matt Chandler's *The Explicit Gospel*, the aim is announced in the title.[1] Chandler wants to present the biblical gospel in the plainest possible terms. The book is structured so as to expose the reader to the gospel from two directions—from the ground and from the air. The gospel from the ground presents basic biblical information about God's perfect righteousness, God's just wrath on fallen humans, Christ's substitutionary sacrifice that bears that wrath, and the way God's grace enables the human response of faith. So the first half of the book follows a traditional Romans Road approach—even if that is not made evident. In the second half, the gospel from the air takes an even wider view, focusing on how God's good creation was tainted by the fall but how God has reconciled *all things* in Christ, so that the whole creation is destined for renewal.

Greg Gilbert's *What Is the Gospel?* helpfully catalogues a vast number of evangelical statements that attempt to define the gospel.[2] His point is that there is surprising disagreement over the boundaries of the gospel. As a corrective, he suggests it might be prudent to look at what the Bible itself says. Indeed! But in the end he settles on a tour of Romans as the best way to define the gospel. Is it not predictable, then, that the gospel presentation in his book ends up traveling the well-worn ruts of the Romans Road? God is the righteous creator, humans are sinners, Jesus Christ is the Savior, and we must respond with faith and repentance.

The problem with the Romans Road approach is not that the verses it uses are devoid of pertinent salvation truths. Those verses contain saving truths. The problem is that a distorting framework is introduced through which these truths are presented. The Romans Road contributes to what Scot McKnight helpfully calls a "salvation culture"—the easy believe-ism associated with Billy Graham and other evangelists—but it does little to cultivate an authentic gospel culture.[3]

Why? The Romans Road approach superimposes *our ideas* about what the gospel must be as we seize upon prooftexts from the book of Romans and then arrange them into an artificial structure that we then call "the gospel." Instead, we can get closer to the truth by giving primacy to Bible passages that intentionally and directly address gospel content. These explicit passages give us an outline and framework. (So, ironically, Chandler's *The Explicit Gospel* is not nearly explicit enough.) When we grab a verse here and there—even when those verses contain core salvation truths—we introduce distortions to the gospel.

The Romans Road is not the gospel. If the Bible's own description of the gospel is the standard, the Romans Road entirely misses most of the gospel's true content—and it adds many ideas that aren't part of the gospel at all. This is why Chandler's and Gilbert's efforts to describe the gospel accurately fall short. The Romans Road is best regarded as the contemporary church's rearrangement of a few salvation-related facts. It is definitely not the gospel. After you finish this chapter, I think you'll see more fully why this is true and why it matters.

Not Our Justification by Faith

Among biblically informed pastors and scholars, this is the most common error: claiming that our justification by faith is the gospel or its center. As with the Romans Road approach, this view draws from the writings of Paul. The apostle Paul evokes an important metaphor to help us understand salvation: the law court. We see this especially in his deployment of words like "righteousness" and "justification." These words pertain to the quality of being legally just or innocent. God is the judge, and we are guilty before God for our sins. But in Christ we are justified—that is, our status changes from guilty to innocent.

Much of the dispute in the Reformation era pertained to how exactly this change in status comes about. Martin Luther argued that this declaration of innocence comes about through faith alone. The Catholic Church responded by maintaining that penance and absolution, among other things, were also necessary. Catholics contend that serious sins forfeit the grace attained at baptism. If a person sins seriously after baptism, they must be restored to a state of grace through the sacrament of reconciliation. We will enter further into the nuances of this debate in chapter 6. For our present purposes, it should be noted that Luther was so adamantly convinced of the doctrine of our justification by faith alone that he often called it "the gospel" or included it as part of the gospel.[4]

Justification by faith as the gospel's heart? Today many scholars still speak of our justification by faith as central to the gospel. For example, in his *God Is the Gospel*, John Piper declares, "I am thrilled to call justification the heart of the gospel." He goes on to clarify: "By 'heart' I mean that justification addresses the main problem between God and man most directly. . . . [It is] the sustaining source of all the other benefits of the gospel."[5]

Piper has made two questionable assertions about the gospel. One is claiming that justification by faith is the heart of the gospel. Sounds plausible. But do you have a concordance or an electronic version of the Bible? Search on every word occurrence of "gospel" or "good news." Try mixing it with various combinations of "faith" and "justification" or "righteousness." Do these searches in Greek if you know how. List the passages where justification by faith is explicitly said to be part of the gospel. This shouldn't take long. Done? If you are working in the original language of the New Testament, there aren't any.

If you were to *misinterpret* Romans 1:16–17 or Galatians 3:8—texts we'll discuss later—you might be tempted to equate the gospel and justification by faith. Acts 13:38–39 is part of a gospel text (see esp. v. 32) that, if you look at it with one squinted eye, almost speaks of justification by faith as part of the gospel. But not quite. The nearest we come to an equation between "gospel" and "justification by faith" is in Galatians, where Paul is appalled because the Galatians are abandoning the gospel in favor of a nongospel (1:6–7). Later, Paul details various gospel-compromising actions (2:5, 14), suggesting that some people are seeking justification by the law or works of the law (2:16; 3:11, 24; 5:4) rather than by faith. But Paul does not indicate that his gospel is justification by faith, even if many of Paul's interpreters from Luther onward have gone beyond Paul in arriving at this conclusion. If the Bible never once says that the gospel is justification by faith, perhaps we can at least agree that Piper's claim that it is the gospel's heart is suspect.

I am not claiming that justification by faith alone is untrue. It is absolutely true if justification (*dikaiosynē*) and faith (*pistis*) are rightly understood. My claim is different: our justification by faith is not part of the gospel. We need to work cautiously to ferret out exactly how justification and faith separately relate to each other and to the gospel. But when we begin saying that it *is* the gospel, or even part of the gospel, we seriously distort the Bible's presentation.

God is the gospel? In *God Is the Gospel*, Piper risks a misunderstanding of the gospel in another way. His error is similar to that of a pastor with whom I was corresponding last year. He asserted to me, "Jesus is the gospel." In reply I pressed him to reconsider—humbly, I hope—by reminding him that although the gospel is principally *about* Jesus, the Bible never says Jesus *is* the gospel. He accepted the pushback, appreciating how it forced him to be more specific in his preaching and teaching.

The title of Piper's book makes the same overgeneralization by saying that God *is* the gospel. We need to be careful not to nitpick. After all, Piper is more accurate between the book covers in describing the biblical gospel. He is keen to show that the gospel allows us to bask in the glory of God. For him, this is the ultimate good news even if the Bible doesn't call that *the* good news. We should allow Piper some poetic license. (And it is good to remember that the press rather than the author often chooses a book's title.) But at the same time, if we are on a quest for exactitude, we should bear in mind that neither Jesus nor God is ever said to *be* the gospel in the Bible.

I have featured John Piper in my discussion, but he is by no means alone in treating justification by faith as the heart of the gospel. The error is widespread. For example, in *Faith Alone*, R. C. Sproul asserts, "justification by faith alone is essential to the gospel."[6] Likewise in his *Getting the Gospel Right*, Sproul makes faith alone and trust in Jesus's righteousness alone part of the essential gospel message.[7] John MacArthur in *The Gospel according to Paul* says, "the doctrine of justification by faith is the linchpin of Paul's teaching on the gospel," and also calls it "the core and touchstone of the gospel according to Paul."[8] A multitude of others say the same.

Beware of the Gospel Pretzel

Why does it matter whether our justification by faith is the heart of the gospel or even part of it? First, the truth always matters. And it matters even more when dealing with the gospel.

Second, if we make our faith part of the gospel when it is not, we risk making it the object of gospel affirmation and evaluation in inappropriate ways. The gospel then pretzels so that it inappropriately faces the individual. It becomes about personal trust rather than the Christ's actions: "You can't earn it, but don't worry because *the good news is that all God wants is your trust that . . .*" When this happens, the good news depends on my having the correct psychological posture. Part of the good news becomes that trust alone can save me. But am I really trusting? Do I really have faith? The spiral inward toward the self proceeds, as does self-doubt. All of this contributes to a salvation culture rather than a gospel culture.

Do not misunderstand. We need to trust that the Messiah died for our sins. However, though our trust is related to the gospel, it is not actually part of it. Our faith is external to the gospel, not internal. This has definite ecumenical implications as it helps show why much of the Reformation-era polemics, echoed by Protestants and Catholics today, miss the target.

Third, something similar happens when our righteousness or justification is made central. The gospel becomes about us rather than Jesus. Although I'll develop these points in chapters 3 and 6, I introduce them here to begin to clarify what is at stake.

Is the Gospel Cross-Centered?

A great many writers—scholars and pastors alike—assert that the cross is the center of the gospel. For example, Gilbert's *What Is the Gospel?* has an entire chapter devoted to "keeping the cross at the center."[9] Similarly, in *The Future of Justification*, Piper states, "The gospel has as its center the events of the cross and resurrection."[10] What is intended here is the cross as the instrument by which Jesus died for our sins, vanquishing sin, death, and malevolent spiritual powers. Is the cross really at the center of the gospel? Yes. Sort of.

To say that the cross is the center of the gospel is true but misleading. What, after all, does "center" mean? And does the assertion that the cross is the center downplay other equally important gospel elements? I'm going to make a provocative claim that I invite you to test in light of the evidence as our study progresses: the cross is not presented as *the* theological center of the gospel in the Bible.

Jesus's death on the cross for our sins is a nonnegotiable gospel fact alongside other gospel facts. Arguably, the cross is the *dramatic* center of the gospel story, with the resurrection as the denouement. The cross is essential to the gospel and is theologically central. Yet the gospel climax, the theological point that receives the most emphasis in the Bible's own descriptions of the gospel, is that *Jesus is the Christ, the king.*

Gospel Basics

Given the gospel's pivotal importance, we might think the Bible speaks about it frequently. Yes and no. The Bible uses "gospel" language 162 times (the *euangel* word group), but many of these references are to "good news" in a wider sense than with reference specifically to Jesus. For example, the first reference to gospel language in the ancient Greek version of the Bible is in 1 Samuel. When Saul commits suicide in battle, his enemies, the Philistines, rejoice. They cut off Saul's head, strip him of armor, and dispatch messengers throughout the land of Philistia "to proclaim the gospel [*euangelizontes*] to the house of their idols and to the people" (1 Sam. 31:9).

Even if it is not about Jesus directly, this example teaches us something vital about "gospel"—namely, that it does not necessarily refer to Jesus at all but was used in the ancient world with regard to any message of glad tidings. In this case, the death of the Israelite king is "good news" for the Philistines. "Gospel" (*euangelion*) was the message itself—the proclaimed content. Meanwhile, the activity of "gospeling" or "proclaiming the gospel" (*euangelizō*) was about heralding that happy message, spreading it abroad. So the Bible uses gospel and gospeling language often.

Yet given its import, we may be surprised to discover that with reference to Jesus, the specific *content* of the gospel is detailed in only a few passages in the Bible. We will explore these together. They include Mark 1:14–15 (and parallels); Luke 4:18–19; Romans 1:3–4; 1 Corinthians 15:3–5; and 2 Timothy 2:8. Some others supplement (Rom. 1:16–17; 16:25–26; and Gal. 1:11–12). But these only augment the more detailed passages. Other passages—the speeches in Acts, Philippians 2:6–11, and others—can also, on the basis of these, be established as gospel texts. But if we are to aim for precision, there should be widespread agreement that the most solid starting place is to describe and synthesize those passages that explicitly intend to give the gospel message.

Jesus Proclaims the Gospel

It's always a good idea to begin with Jesus. When we are attempting to define the gospel, Jesus provides us with an orienting framework. In Mark, the earliest Gospel, after Jesus's baptism and testing, the very first thing he does is proclaim the gospel: "Now after John was arrested, Jesus came into Galilee, proclaiming the gospel of God, and saying, 'The time has been fulfilled, and the kingdom of God has drawn near; repent and believe in the gospel'" (Mark 1:14–15 AT).

Like a color contrast, the exact wording helps us delineate the boundaries of the gospel. Jesus says, "believe [*pisteuete*] in the gospel." This makes it clear that *the gospel itself is different and separate from the believing*, for the gospel is the thing to be believed. (In the next chapter we'll explore whether "believe" is a rich enough word.) Even though Piper, Sproul, MacArthur, and many others suggest that our justification by *faith* (*pistis*) is the center of the gospel, we immediately find evidence in Jesus's words that this is doubtful. Believing, the faith activity, the *pistis* action, is better understood as the required *response* to the gospel.

Although closely related to the gospel, the commands "repent and believe" are not technically part of the gospel. The distinction is subtle, but as this study progresses it will become increasingly clear why the separation is vital to maintain. *Repentance and faith are required for salvation but are external to the gospel, not internal.*

Jesus's Kingdom Gospel

Now to the content. Jesus is said to be proclaiming "the gospel of God." Fortunately, Mark immediately clarifies the substance of this gospel message: "The time has been fulfilled, and the kingdom of God has drawn near" (Mark 1:14–15 AT).

So what is the gospel according to Jesus in this opening scene of Mark? It pertains to a *completion of time* and the *imminent arrival of the kingdom of God*. Perhaps the most important thing to notice, however, is that Jesus himself is at the center of his own message—doubly so. As we read Mark, we discover that Jesus is the one bringing about this fullness of time through his climactic ministry. He is also the anointed king who will one day rule. Both themes come together in Mark's Gospel in, for instance, the parable of the son sent to the tenants (12:1–12) and the Olivet Discourse (chap. 13). In other words, *Jesus is both the primary herald of the gospel and its principal subject.*

A royal message. That Jesus will become the king is the primary theme of the Gospels even if this is sometimes missed by interpreters. For example, it is the first substantial thing we learn about Jesus in the Gospel of Luke: "He will be great and will be called the Son of the Most High. And the Lord God will give to him the throne of his father David, and he will reign over the house of Jacob forever, and of his kingdom there will be no end" (1:32–33). Luke tells us that Jesus will attain the kingship by steps: first he will be great and will be called God's Son (a title with royal connotations in Jesus's day—e.g., see Ps. 2), then he will attain the throne, and then he will begin his eternal rule.

Becoming king is a process. It is telling that Jesus begins to proclaim the gospel, the nearness of the kingdom, immediately after his baptism but not prior. For although chosen by God far in advance to be the Messiah, he technically only became the Messiah ("the anointed one," "the Christ") upon his reception of the Spirit at his baptism. He could boldly proclaim the gospel of the kingdom's nearness because he had now been anointed. He had become the Christ, the chosen-in-the-present-but-still-future king. Meanwhile his attainment of the throne as the official ruling Messiah would not happen until several years later, after his resurrection and ascension to the right hand of God.

When Jesus lived his earthly life, he was in the process of becoming fully king. Compare this situation to David, another man called "messiah" in the Bible. David was anointed by Samuel as king, becoming a Christ, years before he actually began to reign. Jesus's case, as the offspring of David, is similar. Jesus's becoming king involved a progression through stages: (1) election or being chosen, (2) anointing, (3) installation on the throne, and (4) sovereign rule. The good news in the Gospels is that this process is underway for Jesus of Nazareth—and it is soon to reach its culmination when he begins to rule officially on God's behalf.

A royal manifesto. After being tested in the wilderness, Jesus returned "in the power of the Spirit" to his hometown, Nazareth. He entered the synagogue, unrolled the scroll of Isaiah, and read: "The Spirit of the Lord is upon me, because he has anointed me to proclaim good news to the poor. He has sent me to proclaim liberty to the captives and recovering of sight to the blind, to set at liberty those who are oppressed, to proclaim the year of the Lord's favor" (Luke 4:18–19, citing Isa. 61:1–2 and 58:6). In this passage, sometimes called Jesus's Nazareth Manifesto, Jesus outlines his identity as well as the purpose of his public ministry. Bear in mind that any royal message is inherently political and social. He identifies himself as God's anointed one—that is, as the Christ. He does not view this as a mere water or oil anointing. The Spirit is upon him. We are reminded of the Spirit's arrival during his baptism. The purpose of this anointing is to proclaim good news (*euangelisasthai*) to the poor. And this proclamation is good news also for prisoners, the blind, and those oppressed with bondage. Jesus proclaims the year of the Lord's favor.

The day of restoration—now! This year of the Lord's favor was connected to release and restoration. It has associations of erasure of debt and release from enslavement (Lev. 25). Yet it is combined with images of restoration after exile (Isa. 61:3–4). From Dead Sea Scroll texts like 11QMelchizedek, we know that Jews in Jesus's day saw Isaiah 61:1–2 as announcing a future era of divine restoration. Jesus's intention to speak of a future release and restoration would have been transparent to his audience. His proclamation itself makes it clear that some of the gospel's social benefits are immediate and for anyone—especially for the poor and oppressed. As we shall see, other benefits pertain to ultimate salvation in a future era that he is in the process of inaugurating. These final-salvation benefits are only for those who respond to the good news by acknowledging Jesus as Lord.

Nevertheless, we can imagine that the crowd gathered at the synagogue must have gasped when Jesus applied these words to himself in the present moment. After reading, he climactically declared, "Today this Scripture has been fulfilled in your hearing" (Luke 4:21). Jesus was claiming that he was the anointed one, the Messiah. The restoration was beginning right then. Stunned, all spoke well of him at first. Then they remembered he was just a local. Jesus speaks hard words of truth to an increasingly hostile crowd.

But the mob is unable to kill Jesus, and he begins to herald this gospel widely: "I must preach the good news of the kingdom of God to the other towns as well; for I was sent for this purpose" (Luke 4:43). *Jesus's fundamental life purpose was to herald the gospel of the kingdom of God—namely, that he had already been anointed by God as king, so his formal rule would inexorably follow.*

Gospel as kingly becoming. Once we realize that the gospel is a proclamation of the kingdom of God, the floodgates open. For every time Jesus teaches or speaks about the kingdom of God (or, as Matthew prefers, the kingdom of heaven), he is heralding the gospel. In fact, I could spend the remainder of this book exploring how Jesus's own proclamation of the kingdom of God was really an announcement that he was in the process of becoming king. Fortunately, this isn't necessary, as Scot McKnight, N. T. Wright, and others have written accessibly on this topic already.[11]

Indeed, not just Jesus's formal teachings but his healings and controversies as well are gospel announcements. For they were signs that the kingdom was erupting around and through Jesus. Luke and Matthew intentionally associate Jesus's gospel proclamation with his healing ministry (e.g., Matt. 11:5; Luke 7:22; 8:1–2; 9:6). Matthew in particular emphasizes this through repetition by using nearly the same words in two separate passages: "And Jesus went throughout all the cities and villages, teaching in their synagogues and proclaiming the gospel of the kingdom and healing every disease and every affliction" (9:35; cf. 4:23). Given that each kingdom parable, action, or mighty deed of Jesus in the Gospels helps explicate the gospel, we can't examine all the relevant passages.

Yet we can mention a few. A couple of these passages are especially pertinent because they explicitly reference the gospel, rounding out the picture. Taking up the cross for Jesus and for the gospel results in life after the judgment when we follow Jesus (Mark 8:34–38). Those who lose possessions and family for the sake of the gospel will receive them back in superabundance (10:29). The disciples assist Jesus in gospel proclamation (Luke 8:1; 9:6). The gospel will be proclaimed to all nations (Matt. 24:14; 26:13; Mark 13:10; 14:9). These passages supplement our understanding of the gospel.

What gospel did Jesus proclaim? The four Gospels in the Bible are really four different testimonies describing the single gospel—the good news of how Jesus became the saving king. We can summarize the gospel message that Jesus heralds about himself as follows: As the servant-king, the Son sent by the Father, Jesus would become king through suffering crucifixion in order to be a ransom for others. His blood would ratify a new covenant. Since Jesus was the righteous suffering servant, the king who represented his people as a substitute, God would vindicate him after this suffering, raise him from the dead, and seat him at his own right hand—all of this in fulfillment of the Old Testament. As the glorified king, he would ultimately judge the world. For Jesus, the gospel is that the kingdom of God has drawn near. He has been anointed as king but does not yet officially reign. The cross and resurrection are necessary steps on the path by which he is to become the ruling king.[12]

The Gospel according to Paul

In looking at Jesus's proclamation of the gospel, we have already seen evidence that the Romans Road and our own justification by faith may not be the gospel after all. Neither highlight the nearness of the kingdom of God or sufficiently front Jesus's kingship.

Although it is wise to start with Jesus, we turn now to the apostle Paul, whose more detailed gospel has usually been taken as its classic expression. The vital texts are Romans 1:1–4; 1:16–17; 1 Corinthians 15:3–5; and 2 Timothy 2:8 because they explicitly describe the gospel's content. Here we will enter into Romans 1:1–4 and 2 Timothy 2:8. It will be more profitable to examine Romans 1:16–17 and 1 Corinthians 15:1–5 in a subsequent chapter, after we have discussed faith as allegiance. You may be surprised by what is and is not the gospel in these texts.

The Abbreviated Gospel

The simplest passage expressing the gospel's content is 2 Timothy 2:8. While exhorting Timothy to share in sufferings valiantly as a good soldier of Jesus the Christ, Paul encourages Timothy to "remember Jesus the Christ, raised from among the dead ones, of the seed of David, according to my gospel" (2 Tim. 2:8 AT). This gospel has resulted in Paul being put in chains. But despite this circumstance,

Paul exclaims, "the word of God is not chained" (v. 9 AT), which suggests that the gospel has power (cf. Rom. 1:16). What does Paul emphasize in this brief description of the gospel's content?

A title of honor. We must not rush past the obvious: the title. The content of the gospel pertains to Jesus *the Christ*—that is, Jesus *the Messiah*, the long-awaited Jewish (but universally significant) *king*.[13] I would strongly urge the reader to resist seeing "Jesus Christ" in the Bible as merely a name or a singular referent. Above all, when you see "Jesus Christ," do not allow yourself to think in terms of a person with the first name Jesus and the last name Christ. The title "Christ" is absolutely vital to grasp because it keeps front and center the Bible's consistent emphasis on Jesus's *kingship* as the most essential gospel fact. "Christ" is not a last name nor merely a way to refer to a specific person. It is an honorific title.[14]

It is like the term "doctor" in our contemporary society. If we were introduced, you might say, "It's delightful to meet you, Dr. Bates." If you opted to call me Dr. Bates, it would be because you recognize that I've earned that honor by completing a PhD (although I'd probably say, "Please call me Matt," because I'm not very formal). A similar honorific is in view in the New Testament. It means something far different to refer to "Jesus of Nazareth" than to refer to "Jesus Christ." The "of Nazareth" is closer to our contemporary ideas of a last name, and it is generally spoken by those who do not yet recognize him as the Messiah or when it otherwise needs to be specified precisely which "Jesus" is in view (e.g., Matt. 21:11; 26:71; Luke 18:37; John 1:45; 18:5–7). Meanwhile, he is "Jesus Christ" throughout our early Christian literature because authors want to stress his royal office.

When I am teaching and writing, I typically say "Jesus the Christ" or "Jesus the Messiah" or "King Jesus" rather than "Jesus Christ," in an effort to compel the audience to linger over the title. Consider doing the same when talking with others about Jesus. It's a small change that helps bolster the royal gospel.

Raised from among the dead ones. It is significant that Paul's summary highlights the resurrection, that King Jesus "was raised from the dead"—or even better: "having been raised from among the dead ones" (2 Tim. 2:8 AT). The word "dead" in Greek is plural here, so more than one person is in view. Paul's point is not merely that Jesus as a solitary man was dead. It is that the anointed king was in a state of death amid others who were likewise. This hints that God's resurrection power has implications not just for Jesus but potentially for all the dead. It also accords with what Paul says elsewhere about Jesus's resurrection as the firstfruit that anticipates a full resurrection harvest when others are raised too (1 Cor. 15:20–23).

Additionally, when Paul says Jesus the Christ "has been raised," he uses a verb form that stresses the ongoing significance of this action. The verb (*egēgermenon*) emphasizes completed action and its continued effects. An apt translation is, "Remember Jesus the Messiah-king, *who has been raised and still is raised from among those who are dead*, of the seed of David, according to my gospel" (2 Tim. 2:8).

A royal prophecy. Finally, for Paul, the significance of this "of the seed of David" or alternatively "by the seed of David" is threefold. First, it implicitly asserts *prophetic fulfillment* of the Old Testament. God made promises to David, especially the promise of an offspring in conjunction with an eternal throne (2 Sam. 7:12–16; Ps. 89:29). Second, it reinforces Jesus's royal status, emphasizing his *kingly lineage*. Third, it stresses Jesus's true *humanity*. Paul recognizes Jesus as the Son of God but nevertheless also sees that Jesus took on human flesh. In a closely related gospel text, Romans 1:3–4, Paul again touches on these three themes—prophetic fulfillment, kingly lineage, and putting on human flesh.

In summary, Paul focuses on kingship and resurrection in his brief gospel summary in 2 Timothy 2:8. Yet Paul does not include the cross or forgiveness of sins. This does not mean, as we shall see, that the gospel does not include them. The cross and forgiveness are essential to the full gospel. But their absence from Paul's brief gospel description here should help us realize that the gospel's center of gravity might be elsewhere.

Humble Flesh, Rules with Power

Romans 1:1–4 is one of the most vital gospel texts in the Bible, but it is not always well understood. It is also stunningly neglected given its prominence at the beginning of Paul's most famous letter. Consider that neither Matt Chandler's *The Explicit Gospel* nor Greg Gilbert's *What Is the Gospel?* even mention it (nor do they mention 2 Tim. 2:8). Even John MacArthur's *Gospel according to Paul* never discusses it. This is extremely odd given that Paul's gospel is MacArthur's subject.

Let's read Romans 1:1–4 with care in order to learn what others might be missing. This passage must be integrated if we are to gain a full view of the gospel.

> Paul, slave of the Messiah, Jesus. A called apostle, having been set apart for the gospel of God that he promised beforehand through his prophets in the holy Scriptures concerning his Son, who as it pertains to the flesh came into being by means of the seed of David; who as it pertains to the Spirit of Holiness was appointed Son-of-God-in-Power by means of the resurrection from among the dead ones—Jesus the Christ our Lord. (Rom. 1:1–4 AT)

Paul begins by clarifying his relationship to Jesus. Even this is instructive for understanding the gospel. Jesus is the Messiah, *the Christ*, the universal Jewish-style king. Paul is a *doulos*, a servant-slave of this king. But not only is he a servant-slave; he is also an emissary, a delegate, an ambassador. For this is what it means to be an apostle. An "apostle" is someone who is dispatched, usually by a powerful leader, in order to deliver a message or negotiate political affairs.

In other words, even before Paul begins to unpack the details of the gospel, he has already stated that Jesus is the king and that he, Paul, is this king's servant-ambassador, dispatched to herald God's good news. Thus, he has intimated that the gospel message is a *kingly proclamation* about Jesus.

Promised in Advance

Lest there be any confusion about the details of this good news, Paul immediately clarifies: it is the gospel that God "promised beforehand through his prophets in the holy Scriptures" (Rom. 1:2). Here we learn that for God's people, the gospel is not an unanticipated eruption into human history. Yet it was not simply predicted—as if God's prophets were merely clairvoyants who could foresee the future. God had invested himself.

God imprisoned himself within the confines of his own word. God is absolutely sovereign, free to do anything with his creation that accords with his nature (e.g., Ps. 135:6; Dan. 4:35; Acts 17:24–28). But his sovereignty includes the right to limit his own freedom for the sake of love for the other. He obligated himself by entering into covenants. And he further obligated himself by giving his ancient prophets—Isaiah and others—true words to speak about future obligations, such as judgment and rescue.

He had made a promise to bring about good news for his damaged creatures and indeed for the whole created order. And since, as Hebrews reminds us, "it is impossible for God to lie" (6:18), his promise unshakably bound him. Moreover, because these promises were specific—for example, the promise to David of an eternal throne (e.g., 2 Sam. 7:12–16) and the promise through Isaiah of a new-exodus rescue (e.g., Isa. 35; 52)—they were not willy-nilly. They had to conform to specific Old Testament parameters and patterns (see Gal. 3:17). In other words, the absolutely free God became "unfree" by taking on specific historical responsibilities. Above all, Paul emphasizes, he had specifically promised *the gospel* through these Old Testament prophets. This gospel concerns God's Son.

Taking On Human Flesh

Romans 1:2–4 is gospel in the raw. It is notoriously difficult to translate because Paul's language is so compressed.[15] Yet the truth of the gospel burns most brightly in the details, so I've supplied appropriate formatting and a terse translation to help the English reader see how Romans 1:2–4 is structured in the original Greek:

The gospel . . . concerning his Son
euangelion . . . peri tou huiou autou
  who came into being
  tou genomenou
    (a) by means of the seed of David
      ek spermatos Dauid
    (b) as it pertains to the flesh
      kata sarka
  who was appointed Son-of-God-in-Power
  tou horisthentos huiou Theou en dynamei
    (b) as it pertains to the Spirit of Holiness
      kata pneuma hagiōsynēs
    (a) by means of the resurrection from the dead
      ex anastaseōs nekrōn
Jesus the Christ our Lord . . .
Iēsou Christou tou kyriou hēmōn

The most vital thing to observe is that Paul is expressly articulating the gospel, even if this passage is strangely excluded from popular books on the gospel. Second, we should not lose sight of the fact that Paul has asserted in 1:2 that Jesus is the Son of God, as this is a bedrock gospel fact for Paul.

Gospel in two movements. But next, notice the structure of 1:3–4. It falls into two parts. We know that two activities are the premier gospel facts, because the rest of the information is structured to explain these activities. The two activities are (1) coming into being and (2) being appointed Son-of-God-in-Power.

How do other structural details help us? Notice the balanced pairing, so that each of the two activities is qualified in a similar fashion. The *scope* of each activity is specified by describing what it "pertains to" (Greek: *kata*). And the *means* by which each activity came about is also given (Greek: *ek* / *ex*). This deserves further explanation.

Coming into Being Bodily

Paul says that the Son "came into being by means of the seed of David." This should not be translated "descended from David" (ESV) or even "was born of a descendent of David" (NASB), neither of which is precise enough. When Paul speaks about normal human procreation, he prefers *gennaō*, as this is the ordinary word (e.g., Rom. 9:11; Gal. 4:23, 24, 29). But when a change from preexistence to human existence is in view for God's Son, he opts instead for *ginomai*—as he has done in Romans 1:3. For example, Paul selects *ginomai* when he says that Jesus "*came into being* by means of a woman" (Gal. 4:4 AT). Or when he affirms that Jesus was equal to God but "*came into being* in the likeness of humankind" (Phil. 2:7 AT). So it is best to translate the reference to the Son in Romans 1:3 as "came into being" rather than "descended" or "was born."

Only regarding the flesh. But in Romans 1:3 this "came into being" is qualified to clarify that this was only "as it pertains to the flesh." This qualification is crucial, because without it Jesus did not preexist as the Son alongside the Father but only started to exist when he was created at some later time. This is a heresy that would later be called Arianism (and is associated particularly with Jehovah's Witnesses today). Paul's description indicates that the Son did *not* come into existence entirely when he was born. Rather, the preexisting Son of God took on human flesh at that moment (see also Rom. 8:3).

Mary as seed of David. When Paul explains the method by which this transpired, he makes it doubly clear that Jesus divinely preexisted and was now coming into human existence. He states, "who came into being *by means of the seed of David.*" Similar language elsewhere in Paul's Letters suggests that this most likely refers to Jesus's birth *by means of Mary*. For example, Paul says that Jesus "came into being *by means of a woman*" (Gal. 4:4). Mary is specifically called the "seed of David" in other very early

Christian texts (e.g., Ignatius, *To the Ephesians* 18.2; Irenaeus, *Demonstration of the Apostolic Preaching* 36).[16] Tellingly, this is also how our earliest explicit interpreter of Romans 1:3–4, Irenaeus, understands it. He affirms that "by the seed of David" refers to the virgin birth (*Against Heresies* 3.16.3).

Incarnation. Jesus was already the divine Son before taking on human flesh. But when he took on flesh he became fully human too. As John describes it, "The Word became flesh and pitched his tent among us" (1:14 AT). In other words, Paul appears to be describing the same thing as John but with different language—what later theologians would call the incarnation.

Appointed Heavenly King

The second primary gospel activity emphasized by Paul is Jesus's appointment to a new office. The Son is appointed Son-of-God-in-Power. As with the first action, Paul likewise qualifies the scope of the second.

Only regarding the Spirit. Paul says that this appointment as Son-of-God-in-Power "pertains to the Spirit of Holiness." On the basis of Old Testament evidence and the Dead Sea Scrolls, most scholars agree that "Spirit of Holiness" was a Hebraic way of referring to the Holy Spirit.[17] This probably intends the sphere or domain of the Holy Spirit's presence and work, the point of which seems to be that Jesus's present reign is coextensive with the Spirit's indwelling presence.

A new heavenly office as reigning king. During his earthly life Jesus was the Son of God and the anointed Messiah. But he did not yet actively rule. After his resurrection, this all changed because he was appointed Son-of-God-in-Power. This office, a new position of sovereign power, is one that Jesus came to hold when he was seated at the right hand of God.

We can arrive securely at this conclusion because Paul describes Jesus's activities similarly in Philippians 2:6–11. In that passage Jesus is initially described as "existing in the form of God" and being "equal to God" (v. 6 AT). But after Jesus humbles himself even to the point of death, God exalts him to the place of highest sovereignty. The Greek text doesn't say that Jesus was exalted but rather that he was super- or hyperexalted (*hyperupsōsen*), making it clear that he is now positioned *even higher* than previously (v. 9). Prior to the incarnation, he was with God in glory as the nonfleshly Son of God. Now he is the hyperexalted Son of God, the absolute sovereign God in human form. There is a movement from Son to enthroned Son.

We see the same basic idea in Philippians 2:6–11 as in Romans 1:3–4: the preexistent Son takes on human form, but after humbling himself, he is eventually hyperexalted. Then he is no longer just the Son. He is the *actively ruling* Son of God, the absolute Lord, the Son-of-God-in-Power. He is the one to whom knee-bowing, tongue-confessing allegiance is universally owed.

Incarnation and enthronement. In sum, when Paul details the content of the gospel in Romans 1:3–4, he has two activities in view: the Son's coming from divine preexistence into divine-human existence and his being appointed ruler at God's right hand. Other supporting gospel facts are mentioned as well: royal Davidic lineage, resurrection from among the dead ones, and the way in which Jesus's rule correlates with the Spirit's presence. Here the gospel is above all about God's ancient promises reaching fulfillment in the Son's *incarnation* and *enthronement*.

In Romans 1:1–4, the principal gospel fact is that Jesus has become the absolutely sovereign king of the universe. Paul stresses this in four ways: (1) his own relationship as servant-slave and apostle of the king; (2) his use of the title "Christ"; (3) his emphasis on Jesus's installation as Son-of-God-in-Power; and (4) his declaration that this Son is "Jesus *the Christ* our *Lord*." The gospel is a royal proclamation.

Presenting the Purified Gospel

In light of dilutions and distortions to the biblical gospel, even by some of our best scholar-pastors, this chapter began a quest for the pure gospel. The goal is truer, better gospel proclamation. Our task is partially complete.

The gospel is not vague Christian activities, the Romans Road, or justification by faith. The cross is theologically central to the gospel, but it should not be described as its unqualified theological center. The gospel Jesus preached was the arrival of the kingdom of God. That is, Jesus's gospel was fundamentally about his attainment of universal sovereignty at the right hand of God the Father.

Two of the three passages in which Paul most explicitly articulates the gospel, 2 Timothy 2:8 and Romans 1:3–4, reinforce this claim. The gospel announces that Jesus is the Christ. But both also mention his ruling office, his Davidic birth, and his resurrection from among the dead ones.

Yet also take note of what is *not* mentioned in these two gospel passages. No human sin, God's righteous standard, cross, death for sins, or return of Jesus. Nothing about heaven. Nor is the gospel said to be purposed toward helping a person get there. In fact, nothing has been said about our salvation at all. There is no mention of trust, repentance, or the like as part of the gospel. Neither is there any indication that justification by faith is part of the gospel.

In the next chapter we will see how the cross and Jesus's death for sins do fit into the full gospel sequence. We will also discover why the gospel is the power of God for salvation. The best way to do this will be to rethink how the overarching gospel message—Jesus has become the king!—compels us to reconsider the meaning of faith.

This chapter opened with a story of how an awkward dinner led to a life-changing conversation with Mao. I trust that you already agree that getting the gospel right matters. Yet we fail even more miserably if we don't share the good news with our neighbors, friends, coworkers, strangers—whoever is willing to listen.

How do we help others come to experience the gospel's power? It is not in the first instance by telling them "only trust" (although they do need to trust). It is by telling them that Jesus is the king and by sharing the rest of the gospel. When we do this, those who have ears to hear may begin to hear.

If you are uncertain how to begin this task for your church, organization, friends, or neighbors, then realize that this book was written to help you live and proclaim gospel allegiance. The guide for further conversation in appendix 2 contains suggested questions and activities for small groups or personal reflection. Dig in, spread the word, and invite others to join this conversation about the gospel.

2

Not Faith but Allegiance

Carrying the flag into battle in the Civil War was extraordinarily risky. While cannons roared and slugs whistled through the air, flag-bearers walked defenselessly into the fray, usually ahead of the front line. Then the common soldiers would follow their respective flags into battle. It is not surprising that flag-bearers often met a grim death.

In the Battle of Gettysburg, the Union flag-bearers were killed in rapid succession. When one reads an account of their fate, the swift demise of the first flag-bearer is not what grabs attention. Nor is it the sheer number of casualties, even though eight men die in succession while attempting to carry just one of the flags. What really arrests is the courage and tenacity of each man as he eagerly *volunteers* to loft the flag, knowing full well that death almost certainly awaits.[1]

What motivated such reckless boldness? The flags representing the Union and the Confederacy were not just arbitrary scraps of cloth; they were symbols of great and momentous causes—preservation of national unity, the right of states to political self-determination, regional pride, attitudes toward slavery—to which the North and South had resolutely committed. Any soldier brave

Published in *Harper's Weekly*, September 20, 1862

"A Gallant Color-Bearer" by Thomas Nast. This sketch depicts a wounded soldier in the Civil War of the United States. With blood spurting out, he attempts to march onward, unwilling to relinquish the colors.

enough to take up the flag knew the meaning of loyalty to leaders, comrades, and country.

I am not suggesting that today's church should rally around the flag or revive nationalist zeal. But the sensibilities of *allegiance* in this Civil War anecdote may assist us in rethinking the heart of the Christian tradition—salvation, faith, works, and the gospel. We need to begin practicing *gospel allegiance*.

If Christianity is to remain healthy, the pure gospel must remain its lifeblood. In the previous chapter we discovered there is widespread gospel confusion. The gospel we are teaching and preaching needs to change. So we launched a search for the true gospel. We did this by looking at key passages that explicitly describe the content of the gospel (*euangelion*) or speak about proclaiming (*euangelizō*) in such a way that the gospel message is transparent.

Yet several crucial gospel passages have not yet been discussed. I deliberately refrained from treating these in the previous chapter because they are better discussed in light of faith as allegiance.

In this chapter I suggest that "allegiance" is the best term to use when talking about a saving response to the gospel. This does not mean that faith is simply allegiance. Yet if the gospel can best be summarized as "Jesus now rules as the forgiving king," then the saving response God requires becomes clear. Jesus the king ultimately requires one and only one thing from his subjects: loyalty. In responding to the gospel, we are saved by allegiance alone.

Faith Problems

English translations of the Bible have always favored the words "faith" and "believe"—from John Wycliffe's Bible (1382–1395) and the King James Version (1611) onward. English speakers have powerful emotional attachments to these words. Even when we suspect them of being inadequate, we may nonetheless *feel* that the words "faith" and "believe" are unimpeachable—as if they were given to us by Jesus and the apostles themselves to explain what we need to do to be saved. Many speak about the necessity of "faith alone." Alternatively, you might hear the Latin *sola fide* ("by faith alone").

But we must remember that the English word "faith" is not inspired. It didn't even exist at the time of Jesus. The Latin *fides* was in use, but the New Testament was written in Greek, not Latin. The Greek word is *pistis*. No one in Jesus's day talked about "believing" in Jesus or the gospel for eternal life. They used the verb *pisteuō*, which is related to the noun *pistis*. These Greek words relate imprecisely to our contemporary "faith" and "believing." Ancient words have their own meanings that do not map perfectly onto medieval, Reformation-era, or modern words or definitions.

Meanwhile the word "faith" itself has changed over the last five hundred years of English-language usage. This is one reason we need to consider new words—like "allegiance"—that might better convey the meaning of *pistis*. Contrary to current ideas about faith, as far as the Bible is concerned, faith (*pistis*) is not a blind leap. It is not mere optimism about the future or keeping a positive mindset. *Pistis* is embodied and outward facing—topics we'll discuss more in the second part of this book.

Moreover, modern skepticism and the emergence of naturalistic worldviews have given "faith" an anti-evidentialist connotation in contemporary discourse. For example, atheist Richard Dawkins is famous for saying, "Faith is the great cop-out, the great excuse to evade the need to think and evaluate evidence. Faith is belief in spite of, even perhaps because of, the lack of evidence."[2] For many today like Dawkins, faith is the opposite of evidence.

These faith-is-the-opposite-of-evidence ideas are superimposed on the Bible today. After all, the Bible says, "Faith is being sure of what we hope for and certain of what we do not see" (Heb. 11:1 AT).[3] Those influenced by anti-evidentialist sensibilities about faith seize upon the "certain of what we do not see" in this verse and think that the Bible supports the idea that faith is believing without any evidence. This wrongly makes people think that Christian faith is irrational and arbitrary.

But in the letter to the Hebrews, taking "faith" (*pistis*) as the opposite of evidence is contrary to the point. The actual point is that what we externally see points to the invisible certainty associated with God's word and promises. For example, we look outward to see the created universe, which is evidence for the creative power of God's word (11:3). When we see it, our faith in God's word is confirmed. Seeing the physical evidence leads toward the judgment that God's creative word is indeed powerful. Despite cultural narratives that paint faith as contrary to evidence, in Hebrews faith actually involves following evidence in order to confirm God's powerful word. Biblical faith is not anti-evidential.

In short, neither "faith" nor "believe" are inspired words. Their applied meaning today is frequently distant from the real meaning of *pistis* and *pisteuō* in the Bible. So we must consider other words.

Faith as Allegiance

There is more to say about how misunderstandings of faith have obscured the Bible's teachings about salvation. But we need to secure a firmer understanding of *pistis* (traditionally "faith") before moving forward. Here I want to make three points: (1) *pistis* can mean allegiance; (2) but *pistis* does not usually mean allegiance; and (3) how words mean things matters to this discussion. In what follows we will look at why "allegiance" is the best, most holistic term we can use to describe faith (*pistis*) when speaking about a saving response to the gospel.

Pistis Can Mean Allegiance

When we look up the word *pistis* in the most authoritative dictionary that covers the New Testament era, we find something interesting. The glosses under the first definition do not mention faith *in* something at all; rather, they pertain to the quality someone possesses that evokes faith or trust in another: *faithfulness*, *reliability*, *fidelity*, and *commitment*.[4]

Translators and scholars have long been aware of *pistis* as faithfulness, but its pertinence for salvation has not been sufficiently appreciated. For example, Paul says that slaves should not steal but should "display all good *pistis*" toward their masters (Titus 2:10 AT). Paul is not saying that slaves should entirely trust in their masters but rather that they should show complete faithfulness or loyalty to them. In Matthew's Gospel, while discussing tithing, Jesus calls down woes on the Pharisees for neglecting more important matters of the law: "justice, mercy, and *pistis*" (23:23 AT). Jesus is not suggesting that they have insufficient faith in God; he is saying they are demonstrating in their behavior a lack of faithfulness or fidelity to God and to his law.

Other examples are even more pertinent to gospel allegiance. Consider Paul, who writes to the Thessalonians, "We boast about your steadfastness and *pistis* in all the persecutions and trials you are enduring" (2 Thess. 1:4 AT). The immediate context associates *pistis* with remaining steadfast and indicates that it pertains to persevering through trials. This suggests that the correct translation of *pistis* here is "loyalty," "faithfulness," or "allegiance" rather than "faith." Thus, Paul says, "We boast about your steadfastness and *loyalty*."

This informs our understanding of the relationship between *pistis* and the gospel. The presence or absence of loyalty (*pistis*) during these trials (2 Thess. 1:4) is specifically the criterion for whether one is helped or harmed by the Lord Jesus's judgment when these difficulties continue (v. 7). The Lord Jesus will be revealed from heaven and will take "vengeance on those who do not know God and on those who do not *obey the gospel* of our Lord Jesus" (v. 8). Contextually, *loyalty* (*pistis*) *to the Lord Jesus* when experiencing difficulties has been equated with *obedience to the gospel.*

In other words, in 2 Thessalonians 1:4–8, maintaining *pistis* while enduring trials is equivalent to saving obedience to the gospel. Context demands that this *pistis* with respect to the gospel is not merely trust in Jesus as Savior but obedient allegiance to Jesus as the heavenly Lord. The royal gospel demands loyalty in response. In 2 Thessalonians 1:4, *pistis* can fairly be translated as "allegiance" and is the saving response to the gospel.

Pistis involves saving allegiance in other passages too. For example, Paul tells the Colossians: I rejoice to see "your orderliness and the firmness of your *pistis* unto the Messiah" (2:5 AT). The association of "your orderliness" with "the firmness of your *pistis*" suggests that *pistis* is a character quality here, like faithfulness. But since in context this faithfulness is with respect to the Messiah (the king), then "loyalty" or "allegiance" is the better gloss: "your *allegiance* unto the Messiah."

This is confirmed as Paul continues: "Therefore as you have received the Messiah, Jesus the Lord, continue to walk in him, being rooted and built up in him, being strengthened in *pistis* even as you were taught, abounding in thanksgiving" (Col. 2:6–7 AT). Paul doubles down in his emphasis on Jesus's sovereign authority by calling him the Messiah and the Lord. Furthermore, when he mentions *pistis*, Paul is talking about how the Colossians should conduct themselves in their behavior toward this king, not about how they should trust in him as Savior or the like. Context suggests this should be translated, "being strengthened in *allegiance* even as you were taught" (v. 7).

Examples abound throughout the Bible of *pistis* meaning loyalty or allegiance. When Paul tells the Philippian jailer, "*Pisteuson* on the Lord Jesus and you will be saved, both you and your household" (Acts 16:31 AT), context demands that this involve an embodied switch in the jailer's loyalty, no longer to the emperor's magistrates but now to Jesus as the ultimate sovereign. The jailer stops serving the magistrates, the emperor's ambassadors, and starts serving Paul and Barnabas, the ambassadors of Jesus.

Pistis signals allegiance in other sources too. For example, the Jewish historian Josephus, Paul's contemporary, often speaks of *pistis* as allegiance.[5] Josephus brags that King Antiochus was so impressed with the loyalty of the Jewish people that the king specially noted it when writing to his governor. Josephus states, "The king also testified in writing to our piety and loyalty [*pistis*] when . . . he learned of the revolts in Phrygia and Lydia" (*Antiquities of the Jews* 12.147). The context is loyalty to a king during a revolt, so here *pistis* means allegiance.

In 1 Maccabees, a book that is in the Catholic Bible but not the Protestant, King Demetrius writes a letter to the Jews, trying to persuade them to side with him rather than his rival: "Since you have kept the compact with us and have maintained our friendship, and have not gone over to our enemies, we have heard this and we rejoiced. Now continue to maintain *pistis* with us, and we will reward you with good for what you do for us" (10:26–27 AT). Given the king's efforts to convince the people to join him and not his opponent, it should be obvious that allegiance or loyalty is intended for *pistis*. Similarly, the king later declares, "Let some of the Jews be put in posts in which *pistis* is necessary" (v. 37 AT).

In the book of Revelation, Jesus, "the ruler of kings on earth" (1:5), commends the church at Pergamum for its allegiance even when a Christian named Antipas was martyred: "You did not deny your *pistis* unto me" (2:13 AT). Later, when suffering violently at the hands of those who worship the beast, the church is instructed not to receive a mark on the forehead or hand. Judgment is coming. The author states, "Here is a call for the steadfastness of the saints, those who keep the commandments of God and *pistis* unto Jesus" (14:12 AT).[6] Since the saints are described as having steadfastness, their further description as those who keep the commandments and who display *pistis* unto Jesus suggests that *pistis* is akin to steadfastness and commandment-keeping. Thus, it is best read as faithfulness or allegiance to Jesus the king.

Other examples of *pistis* as allegiance can be found in key passages about salvation. More will be discussed in the chapters that follow in this book, and they could be multiplied.[7] But this is not to say that *pistis* always or even usually should be translated "allegiance."

Pistis Does Not Usually Mean Allegiance

I'm not arguing that faith simply means allegiance without remainder. Nor am I denying that *pistis* primarily means "faith/faithfulness" or "trust/trustworthiness." My point is that the Greek word *pistis* has a meaning potential that can be actualized in different ways in context. One such way is allegiance. In fact, trust in or faithfulness toward a leader that endures through trials over the course of time is probably best termed "loyalty" or "allegiance." But this is not to say that *pistis* or the related verb *pisteuō* consistently intend allegiance. They do not.

Let me give three examples to explain why *pistis* and *pisteuō* do not always intend allegiance. First, when speaking of believing in Jesus's healing power or his other mighty deeds, Jesus and others use the word *pistis*, but it should not be translated "allegiance." For example, when Jesus says to the Canaanite woman, "Great is your *pistis*," and we hear that her daughter was healed instantly (Matt. 15:28), what is stressed is her trust in Jesus's ability, not her loyalty to him as a ruler.

Yet prior to her daughter's healing, the woman cried out for assistance: "Lord, Son of David, have mercy on me" (v. 22 AT), which points to her recognition of his royal authority. We need to be cautious because often in such episodes shades of allegiance are present alongside faith and trust. Nevertheless, in light of the context, "Great is your *pistis*" should be translated here as "Great is your *faith*" or "Great is your *trust*." In many other similar texts, *pistis* and related words are best translated as "faith," not "allegiance" (e.g., Matt. 8:10; 9:2, 22, 29; 14:31; 16:8). *Pistis* can refer to confidence displayed in something external or in someone, rather than loyalty toward something or someone—although these are often bound together. So when Jesus says that "if you have *pistis* like a grain of mustard seed" then you can move a mountain (Matt. 17:20), "allegiance" is not an apt translation. "Faith" is.

Second, *pistis* occasionally refers to objects or abstract ideas that relate only tangentially to allegiance. For example, it can intend proof or assurance. "[God] has fixed a day on which he will judge the world in righteousness by a man whom he has appointed; and of this he has given *pistis* [proof or assurance] to all by raising him from the dead" (Acts 17:31). It can also mean an oath or pledge. Paul says that young widows should remarry, for if they take a vow to remain widows in the Messiah but then are overcome by desire, they "incur condemnation for having abandoned their former *pistis*" (1 Tim. 5:12)—that is, their oath or pledge.

Third, the verb *pisteuō* sometimes refers to matters to be believed or affirmed, not allegiance. When speaking to the blind men, Jesus says, "Do you *pisteuete* that I am able to do this?" Jesus is asking whether they believe a specific proposition about a state of affairs: "I am able to do this." He is certainly *not* saying, "Do you give allegiance that I am able to do this?" That would be nonsense. This use of *pisteuō* ("to believe") followed by *hoti* ("that") is very common and refers not to giving allegiance but to affirming a statement's trustworthiness or accuracy.

In sum, although the words ordinarily translated "faith" and "to believe" (*pistis* or *pisteuō*) can mean or intend allegiance, this is not the root meaning. Why then should we think that allegiance is particularly important when the gospel and salvation are in view? The answer has to do with how words mean things.

How Words Mean Things

Because we are influenced by dictionaries, we tend to think of them as valid deposits of word meanings. Yet scientific studies strongly suggest that a dictionary approach is not how we create or decode meaning.[8] The important point is this: the majority of words have a *singular* conventional meaning as that word points at a specific prototypical object, type of object, or schematic mental representation. This is true even when the word has multiple definitions in a dictionary. While it's true that some words have several distinct conventional meanings, mental economy pressures us toward one central meaning.

We know this because specific neuron groups fire in the brain in association with specific word representations, and that firing spreads to related conceptual categories. Most images and words do not initially cause multiple sets of neuron groups to fire because we tend to have a bias toward a single prototypical meaning. Some words that have two or more very strong and distinct prototypical meanings (like "bank," which can be both a financial institution and the side of a river) do cause multiple sites to fire initially. But most words—like "goat," "inflate," and "sneeze"—are not like this.[9] On the level of initial brain chemistry, they have a single prototypical meaning, even though a dictionary may list multiple meanings. We are adept at coding and decoding that single mental representation in diverse contexts because a word's prototypical meaning prompts access to vast reservoirs of social and cultural knowledge. This allows us to select and apply the correct *social frame* when participating in the meaning-making process.

For example, when we hear or see the word "sheep," on the level of initial brain chemistry, because of our bias for singularity, the prototype we think of is *a wooly animal* (dictionary definition #1). We do not think of *a weak, helpless person who is easily led* (dictionary definition #2). The word "sheep" has one conventional meaning in terms of initial brain activity, even though it, like all words, cascades to evoke related associations in the brain (e.g., "sheep" might cascade to "animal," "farm," "goat," "docile person," etc.). We use our social and cultural knowledge to apply that one meaning to many different situations by identifying the best social frame. Yet if we were to use a dictionary, we might think definition #2 of "sheep" is equally valid to definition #1 in sorting out how word meaning is created and decoded. It isn't. Why is this a concern for our discussion of faith, allegiance, and *pistis*?

Due to our bias for single meaning, it is probable that Paul, Jesus, and others during the New Testament time period had only one basic image-concept in mind with regard to the *pistis* word family. It was not allegiance per se. What was it? It was trustworthiness (faithfulness) or trust (faith). Study after study has affirmed that such ideas are the core meaning potential for the *pistis* word family. This has recently been confirmed yet again by Teresa Morgan's marvelous and comprehensive monograph *Roman Faith and Christian Faith*.[10]

This does not suggest that *pistis* means faithfulness or faith without remainder, as this single concept could be actualized in a wild variety of ways in the New Testament era—that is, it was applied within diverse social frames. We discover that *pistis* is used to describe relationships between generals and soldiers, kings and subjects, patrons and clients, masters and slaves, friends, family members, and lovers, and even one's relationship with the self. Its purview includes politics, economics, law, philosophy, logic, tradition, and everyday life. It also describes divine-human relationships. This wide-ranging word was given applied meanings in nearly every sphere of personal, social, and institutional life.

Yet when speaking about how to respond to a messiah or to good news about a king, a *royal frame* is present, so "allegiance" is the obvious actualization for *pistis*. And we have firm evidence that *pistis* intends allegiance in royal and imperial contexts, even if Roman paranoia about tyranny makes it less common than we might otherwise expect.[11]

In fact, Morgan indicates that *pistis* (and *fides*, its rough Latin equivalent) as loyalty or allegiance to military commanders and kings/emperors was so common that it is attested across a wider range of sources than any other category! This loyalty was reinforced by a military oath of allegiance. This *pistis* was not described as a one-time decision; rather, its duration is consistently stressed—allegiance that was genuine endured over the course of a full campaign or military career.[12]

How words mean matters. The gospel is fundamentally a *royal* proclamation. Data proving this has already been advanced in chapter 1, and this conclusion will be reinforced as this study continues. The core meaning potential of *pistis* is faithfulness or faith, but when a royal social frame is present, this potential can be actualized as allegiance. In other words, we should expect allegiance to be a prominent applied meaning for *pistis* or *pisteuō* when we are talking about the Christ, the gospel, or saving benefits that a king bestows. And this is precisely what we discovered to be true above. *Pistis* can mean allegiance as the saving response to the gospel. Yet an even tighter link between the gospel and allegiance emerges when we inspect passages that relate to the *purpose* of the gospel.

Gospel Purpose

What is the purpose or goal of the gospel? Because such things are felt to be self-evident within salvation culture, the purpose of the gospel is all too often assumed rather than demonstrated. To generalize, the purpose of the gospel within salvation culture is to get us to trust in Jesus's atoning and priestly work for us rather than in our own deeds so that we can be forgiven and go to heaven. This is not, however, what Scripture teaches about the gospel's purpose. Not even close.

There are Bible passages that speak overtly of the purpose of the gospel, but they are strangely ignored by those who champion a salvation culture. For example, in their analyses of the gospel, neither R. C. Sproul (*Getting the Gospel Right*) nor John Piper (*God Is the Gospel*; *The Future of Justification*) ever discuss or reference *any* of the three passages that most clearly state the purpose of the gospel in the Bible. Leading books about the gospel do not incorporate what the Bible most explicitly says about its purpose! We will look at these three passages immediately below.

As a corrective to salvation culture, J. D. Greear's treatment of the gospel gets nearer to the mark because he recognizes that the gospel pertains to various facts about Jesus. But he looks wider: "The goal of the gospel is to produce a type of people consumed with passion for God and love for others."[13] Although Greear helpfully places emphasis on how facts about Jesus affect life today, he leans heavily on Jesus's words about the greatest commandments (Matt. 22:37–40) rather than what the Bible says about the gospel.

There is some truth in these wide generalizations about the purpose of the gospel, but only at the level of a loose synthesis of biblical themes. If we stay on that broad field, we might miss each beautiful gospel bud, blade of grass, and leaf that God intends for us. Generalizations lack a grounding in the Bible's own explanations of the gospel's purpose.

For Allegiance in All Nations

The Bible's most explicit statement of the gospel's purpose is given in the doxology at the end of Romans. Paul is praising

God. God is the one who is able to strengthen the Romans, so he deserves all the glory as the only wise God. Although Paul makes several intriguing statements about the gospel, the most vital thing he describes is its purpose. I've translated the central portion and arranged it to help the English reader appreciate some aspects of its structure in Greek:

> *my gospel and the preaching about Jesus the Messiah*
>
> which has been made manifest
>
> according to the revelation of mystery that was kept silent for eternal ages
>
> but which now has been made known through the prophetic writings
>
> according to the command of the eternal God
>
> *for the obedience of pistis in all the nations* (Rom. 16:25–26 AT)

The structure helps us to see what we might otherwise miss. Paul is directly describing the gospel.

The gospel is placed alongside the activity of preaching about Jesus the Messiah so as to indicate that this is the gospel's main content (cf. Acts 5:42). Here, as elsewhere, the gospel is fundamentally about Jesus the king, his story. In Romans 1:2 Paul spoke of the gospel as "promised in advance" (AT). Here Paul reaffirms that the gospel was God's plan all along—although now he stresses its once-hidden-but-now-revealed quality. And we learn something striking and vital: *the purpose of the gospel is the "obedience of faith" (pistis) among all people groups*. What does this mean?

The phrase traditionally translated "the obedience of faith" is *hypakoēn pisteōs* in Greek. We know what obedience involves: when an authority figure issues a directive or command, obedience means following the order (e.g., Rom. 6:16). "Faith" (*pistis*) is a more difficult word because it has so much baggage in our contemporary culture.

In light of the evidence already gathered that the gospel centers on Jesus's kingship and that *pistis* can mean loyalty, I submit that the basic meaning of "the obedience of *pistis*" in Romans 16:26 is most likely "the obedience characterized by *pistis*," or "faithful obedience," or even better, "allegiant obedience." A few details might help you better weigh this claim.

This is so crucial to a proper understanding of the gospel that we need to get technical for a moment. The phrase in Greek, *hypakoēn pisteōs*, traditionally "the obedience of faith," is a head noun followed by a genitive noun. The basic force of the genitive is qualitative, that of an emphatic adjective.[14] For example, if I were to say, "the knight wore armor of silver," this is an alternative way of saying, "the knight wore silver armor." By "of silver," I mean that the armor can somehow be described as silver, has the quality of silver, is characterized by silver, or is made of silver. "Of silver" functions as an adjective describing the armor.

Likewise, when Paul describes the purpose of the gospel as "the obedience of *pistis* in all the nations" with respect to the Jewish king, he probably means "the obedience characterized by *pistis*"—that is, "loyal obedience" or "allegiant obedience." Since in English *obedience* is presupposed as part of genuine loyalty to a king and vice versa, allegiant obedience can fairly be summarized by one word in English: allegiance. What then does the Bible say is the primary purpose of the gospel? The allegiance of the nations to Jesus the king.

For Allegiance, Again

Now for a second passage. Even if the gospel has other minor purposes, we can be confident that the major purpose is allegiance to Jesus the king. Paul's statement about the purpose of the gospel in Romans 16:26 is expressed nearly identically in Romans 1 when, immediately after giving the content of the gospel (1:2–4), he speaks about the identity of the Son: "Jesus the Christ our Lord, through whom we received grace and apostleship *for the obedience of pistis in all the nations* in behalf of his name" (vv. 4–5 AT). He calls Jesus not only "Son-of-God-in-Power" (v. 4) but also "the Christ" and "Lord." Jesus's sovereignty is foregrounded in every conceivable way. Paul then speaks about the commissioning of the apostles, the ambassadors of the good news, with respect to this powerful king. The heralding of this gospel message is to be done "in behalf of" or "for the sake of" the name of Jesus, the Messiah-king.

The reason the apostles received grace and were commissioned as heralds of the gospel is "for the obedience of faith [*hypakoēn pisteōs*] in all the nations." Paul uses the same expression in Romans 1:5 that he uses in 16:26. Given all the contextual signals, we must locate the meaning of "the obedience of *pistis*" within a royal social frame. Once again the purpose of the gospel is explicit: to bring about loyal obedience or allegiance to Jesus the king in every nation.

For Loyal Obedience

The phrase "obedience of *pistis*" is not used elsewhere by Paul or by any other New Testament writer. But a third passage speaks to the purpose of the gospel directly. In Romans 15:15–16, Paul indicates why he has written to the churches in Rome. Although he was not actually a priest (he belonged to the tribe of Benjamin, not Levi), he uses a sacrificial metaphor, suggesting that his ministry has been priestly. His goal as a "priest" has been to see to it that the Gentiles are an acceptable offering, having been sanctified by the Holy Spirit. His work is "to bring the Gentiles to obedience" (v. 18), and in so doing he has "fulfilled the ministry of the gospel of Christ" (v. 19). Although here Paul has said nothing about faith, once again it is evident that the aim of Paul's gospel proclamation is allegiance. The loyal obedience of the nations to King Jesus is the purpose of the gospel.

Other Purpose Passages

Although not as explicit in declaring the purpose of the gospel, other passages speak about the gospel in ways that suggest allegiant obedience to the Messiah as its purpose. Paul states, "For this very reason the Messiah died and returned to life, in order that he might be the *Lord* of both the dead and the living" (Rom. 14:9 AT). Earlier in Romans, Paul laments that "they have not all *obeyed the gospel*" (10:16), meaning that not all have confessed Jesus as royal Lord. Paul says that the Lord Jesus will inflict vengeance on all who do not know God or "obey the gospel of our Lord Jesus" (2 Thess. 1:8). Peter echoes this, indicating that judgment will begin within the household of God, so that the outcome for those who do not "*obey the gospel* of God" will be incalculably more severe (1 Pet. 4:17). If the gospel, above all, is that Jesus has become the King of kings, then failure to obey the gospel most likely intends failure to show allegiance to him as the sovereign.

Meanwhile, the gospel is also purposed toward salvation. In Ephesians, the word of truth is called "the gospel of your salvation" (1:13). Perseverance in the gospel results in glory (2 Thess. 2:14). Jesus is the Savior who has "abolished death and brought life and immortality to light through the gospel" (2 Tim. 1:10). Accordingly, we can infer that allegiance to Jesus the king determines salvation. Paul speaks about the gospel as the power of God for salvation in a key gospel text that brings together topics central to this book—Romans 1:16–17.

The Gospel Is God's Saving Power

The gospel in Romans 1:1–5 is about the incarnation and enthronement. It is purposed toward the allegiance of the nations to Jesus the king. When Paul speaks again about the gospel in Romans 1:16–17, we have every reason to believe that he has in view the gospel content of 1:1–5. Yet we discover something new—namely, that the gospel itself is God's saving power, and much more:

> For I am not ashamed of the gospel, for it is the power of God for salvation for everyone who gives *pistis*, to the Jew first and also to the Greek. For in it the righteousness of God is revealed by *pistis*, for *pistis*, as it is written, "But the righteous [one] shall live by *pistis*." (Rom. 1:16–17 AT, citing Hab. 2:4)

There are five puzzles in this important text: (1) How is the gospel God's saving power? (2) What does the "righteousness of God" mean? (3) What proof did Paul think the quote from Habakkuk offers? (4) Why did Paul use the cumbersome expression "by *pistis*, for *pistis*"? (5) Who is intended with "the righteous" or "the righteous one"? It is worthwhile to work through these puzzles, challenging though they are, because they offer much-needed insight into the inner workings of the relationship between the gospel, faith, and salvation.

1. How Is the Gospel God's Saving Power?

In speaking about the gospel as God's saving power, N. T. Wright puts it well: the gospel "not merely 'possesses' God's power or 'is accompanied by' God's power but simply *is* God's power." How could this be if the gospel is not a system of salvation per se but the story of how Jesus has become king? Wright continues, "Paul has discovered in practice, in city after city, that announcing the good news—that there is one God who now claims the world as his own through the crucified and risen Jesus—is in itself powerful and that power is all God's."[15] The gospel is about Jesus's royal career, but it is a saving career that provides us with *benefits* once we are united to him through allegiance.

Our receipt of these saving benefits is principally the Holy Spirit's work. We have already discovered in Paul's articulation of the gospel in Romans 1:4 that Jesus's office as Son-of-God-in-

Power is coextensive with the domain of the Holy Spirit. Although the gospel is about Jesus's saving career, his sovereign rule at God's right hand corresponds functionally to the Spirit's enactment of that rule. Part of the gospel is that the Spirit is responsible for Jesus's reign as king.

This is confirmed by other gospel passages. For example, Paul relates the gospel's purpose and the Spirit's power in Romans 15. He says that in the Messiah the Gentiles have been brought to obedience "by the power of the Spirit," and the result has been to fulfill "the ministry of the gospel of Christ" (v. 19). Thus, when we wonder how it is that the gospel is "the power of God for salvation" (1:16), we are justified in seeing the Holy Spirit's work as what Paul predominately has in view (cf. 15:13).

The gospel of Jesus resonates within, yet subverts, its Roman imperial context. When citizens of the Roman Empire hear Paul's message about Jesus the heavenly king, they are changing allegiance by repenting of their former sinful ways of life, joining the Spirit-filled community, and proceeding to live new lives as citizens under the rule of King Jesus. With the Spirit's assistance, they are finding that they are no longer enslaved by sin but have come under the banner of a new master (Rom. 8:1–17). The gospel is the power of God for salvation because it announces that Jesus's reign at God's right hand is enacted by the Spirit being sent to dwell in the midst of his people.

2. What Does the "Righteousness of God" Mean?

The gospel may be God's power for salvation through the Holy Spirit, but Paul doesn't stop there. He offers a further explanation for why he is not ashamed of the gospel as God's saving power: "for in it [the gospel] the righteousness of God is revealed" (Rom. 1:17). The righteousness of God is one of the benefits unveiled in the gospel.

An important clue to the meaning of the righteousness of God is frequently missed by English translations of the Bible. Headings and translations tend to separate Romans 1:17 from 1:18, omitting the word "for" in verse 18 (in bold below). But they must not be separated. In the Greek text, verse 17 is explained by verse 18.

> For I am not ashamed of the gospel, for it is the power of God for salvation for everyone who gives allegiance, to the Jew first and also to the Greek. For in it the righteousness of God is revealed by allegiance, for allegiance, as it is written, "But the righteous [one] shall live by allegiance." **For** the wrath of God is revealed from heaven against all ungodliness and unrighteousness of men, who by their unrighteousness suppress the truth. (Rom. 1:16–18 AT)

Each new "for" (Greek: *gar*) in this text attempts to explain why the previous portion is reasonable. So when Paul speaks about *the revelation of the wrath of God* from heaven against human unrighteousness in 1:18, we must recognize that he believes this somehow begins to explain *the revelation of the righteousness of God* in 1:17.

We learn that the revelation of the righteousness of God is bound up with the revelation of God's wrath against unrighteous humans (cf. Rom. 1:32; 2:5; and esp. 3:5). That is, if we see the righteousness of God as having a strictly pleasant *saving* function—like a status of "justification" or "innocence" that we receive—totally apart from weighing its *condemning* function, then we have oversimplified and are off the mark. At the same time, if we miss seeing its positive aspects as a standing we can enjoy (cf. Rom. 3:21–22; 2 Cor. 5:21; Phil. 3:9), we likewise go astray. The righteousness of God relates to judging wrath but is also a gospel benefit. Working through the remaining puzzles will add information about the righteousness of God.

3. What Proof Does Habakkuk Offer?

We receive additional hints about the meaning of the righteousness of God in Romans 1:17. Paul says that in the gospel the righteousness of God is revealed "by *pistis*, for *pistis*," and then he clarifies by citing Habakkuk 2:4: "as it is written, 'But the righteous [one] shall live by *pistis*.'" So the best way to discover what Paul means with "by *pistis*" and to learn more about the righteousness of God is to inspect Habakkuk 2:4.

The prophet Habakkuk had a problem. He had been crying out to God for help for a long time. His fellow Judeans were disobeying God's law, justice was lacking, and the wicked far outnumbered the righteous. God answers: "Behold, I am raising up the Chaldeans" (1:6) to execute judgment on Judah on his behalf. Habakkuk took little comfort in this news. It only caused him to ask a new question: How could it possibly be fair to use even more unrighteous Babylon to judge unrighteous Judah (v. 13)? He awaits God's answer.

In reply, God promises to judge the arrogant Babylonians, but in the midst of this judgment affirms, "But the righteous man will live by *his faithfulness* [*ʾĕmûnâ*]" (Hab. 2:4 AT). The Hebrew word *ʾĕmûnâ* in the Old Testament is best translated as "steadfastness," "trustworthiness," "faithfulness," or "honesty," not "faith" or "belief" in something.[16] So Habakkuk affirms that the righteous man will live by his fidelity—that is, by remaining loyal to God and the covenant during the crisis of God's judgment on Babylon.

When we get to Paul's use of Habakkuk 2:4, we find that he does not follow either the Hebrew or the Greek Old Testament exactly. Paul does not say "his" *pistis* (the righteous man's loyalty to God) or "my" *pistis* (God's own loyalty); instead, he omits pronouns, leaving just a bare *pistis*: "but the righteous [one] shall live by *pistis*." Paul has left it ambivalent whose *pistis* is in view, whether the righteous man's or God's own. Perhaps his omission is deliberate because he intends both human and divine *pistis*—as we shall see.

What is highly probable in any case is that for Paul *pistis* means fidelity or loyalty here, not "trusting in." This is true because in Habakkuk 2:4 *pistis* or *ʾĕmûnâ* does not primarily mean trusting in someone or something; rather, it means fidelity or loyalty toward someone or something. So, on the basis of both the Hebrew and the Greek Old Testament traditions, it must be regarded as strongly probable that with *pistis* Paul intends fidelity or loyalty. Paul understands Habakkuk 2:4 to mean, "The righteous one will live *by loyalty*," or something very close to that. Moreover, Paul's understanding of the noun *pistis* as loyalty that results in righteousness in Habakkuk ("the righteous one will live by *pistis*") is reconfigured by Paul in verbal form in key salvation passages (e.g., Rom. 3:22; Gal. 2:16; 3:22). This shows that for Paul the verb *pisteuō* can carry overtones of loyalty or allegiance too.

The righteous man in Habakkuk is the one who can pass through the crisis of judgment by loyalty. We can infer that the righteousness of God should have a similar valence in Romans 1:17, where "the righteousness of God" is probably the status that results when one is vindicated by loyalty when judged by God (cf. Rom. 3:21–26). It connects negatively to wrath but positively to rescue because Jesus is the substitutionary sacrifice that bears the wrath and then is raised.[17] Having become a curse for us, he bore that curse by suffering in his body on the cross, but then he was justified or vindicated unto new life (see Gal. 3:10–13, in which Paul cites Hab. 2:4; cf. Col. 2:14).

4. *What Does "by Pistis, for Pistis" Mean?*

Paul uses an odd phrase to describe the revelation of the righteousness of God. He says, "In it [the gospel] the righteousness of God is revealed by *pistis*, for *pistis*" (Rom. 1:17). It is so strange, in fact, that some translations simply make it a rhetorical flourish, saying that our becoming right with God is all about faith "from first to last" (NIV), or "from start to finish" (NLT). But this is inaccurate. Paul's language is cumbersome because it is part of his thesis statement in Romans, and hence hypercompressed. A better translation is, "In it the righteousness of God is revealed by fidelity, for fidelity." Or, since a king is in view, "*by allegiance, for allegiance*."

Habakkuk helps illuminate the first part of the phrase—"by *pistis*"—as meaning something like "by acting in a loyal fashion during a time of testing." Yet the second part—"for *pistis*"—must still be clarified. Let's go back to Romans 1:5, where Paul states the gospel and its purpose: "for the obedience of *pistis* in all the nations in behalf of Jesus's name" (AT). Since the topic in both verses is the gospel, the most likely meaning of "for *pistis*" in 1:17 is "for allegiance to Jesus the Messiah in all the nations."

Putting both parts together, in Romans 1:17 "by *pistis*, for *pistis*" means "by the Christ's allegiant actions, for the purpose of fostering allegiance to the Christ in all the nations." This meaning is confirmed subsequently in the letter when Paul says that the righteousness of God has been revealed "*through* the *pistis* of Jesus the Christ, *for* all who give *pistis*" (3:22 AT). Hence, in both Romans 1:17 and 3:21–22, the righteousness of God is revealed *by* (or *through*) the allegiant actions of the Messiah, and it is *for* all humans who perform the allegiance action. When Paul says that the righteousness of God is revealed "by *pistis*, for *pistis*" in Romans 1:17, he intends "*by* Jesus the king's *allegiance* to God, *for* the purpose of cultivating *allegiance* to Jesus the king in all the nations of the world."

5. *Who Is the "Righteous One"?*

There is a final mystery. Paul says, "As it is written, 'But the righteous [one] shall live by *pistis*'" (Rom. 1:17 AT, citing Hab. 2:4). Who, then, is the righteous man or righteous one? Anticipating my conclusion, it is first of all Jesus the king who lives because of his *pistis* (loyalty) in going the way of the cross, and it is secondarily anyone who gives *pistis* (loyalty) to him.

The Christ is the righteous one. In the Hebrew of Habakkuk and in the Greek of Romans, the righteous individual is in the masculine singular, a single man. Although this can sometimes be a way to generalize and could refer to any righteous person, the phrase "the righteous [one]" (Greek: *ho dikaios*) is suggestive, for Jesus the Christ was frequently given this title in the New Testament and in early Christian literature.[18] For example, in his gospel proclamation at Solomon's portico in the book of Acts, Peter laments, "You denied the Holy and Righteous One, and asked for a murderer to be granted to you" (3:14). Peter calls Jesus the "Righteous One."

As for Paul, he is reported to have called Jesus the "Righteous One" in Acts 22:14, and indisputably identifies Jesus as the uniquely righteous one elsewhere. In fact, Paul associates righteousness, obedience, and life in a passage that focuses on the contrast between Adam's action and Jesus's:

> If, because of one man's trespass, death reigned through that one man, much more will those who receive the abundance of grace and the free gift of *righteousness* reign in *life* through *the one man* Jesus Christ. Therefore, as one trespass led to condemnation for all men, so *one act of righteousness leads to justification and life for all men.* For as by the one man's disobedience the many were made sinners, so *by the one man's obedience the many will be made righteous.* (Rom. 5:17–19)

If we remember that the purpose of the gospel is "the obedience of *pistis*" or allegiance, we see how close Romans 1:17 is to Romans 5:17–19. In each, the righteous man lives in a way that reflects *pistis* or obedience, which results in life for others when they are joined to him. In Romans 5 it is explicit that the Messiah is this righteous man, suggesting that this is probably also true for Romans 1. Furthermore, it is clear from context in 5:20–21 that Paul has in view the Christ's resurrection *life*—life that he can share with others, much as the righteous one *lives* in 1:17.

Bringing it all together, when Paul interprets Habakkuk—"The *righteous* [one] shall *live* by *allegiance*" (Rom. 1:17 AT)—he is saying that Habakkuk anticipated the Christ's *allegiance* to God the Father in his obedient life, which climaxed in his death on the cross. Paul declares this righteous deed singularly effective. The result was that God, in his capacity as judge, declared Jesus to be what he clearly already was: *the righteous one*. In other words, Jesus was justified. God certified this by raising Jesus from the dead, so that now he *lives*. And he lives forevermore, as he has defeated death and is now installed at the right hand of God as the Christ.

The allegiant are the righteous. Beyond Jesus, there is a group of righteous ones secondarily in view. In Romans 1:17 Paul indicates that this righteous man, Jesus, lived *by* allegiance, but this was also *for* allegiance. The king's allegiant action was purposed to bring about our allegiance to him as the king, so that through Spirit-union with him we might be righteous and live too. Therefore, when Paul says, "as it is written, 'But the *righteous* [one] shall *live* by *allegiance*,'" he has in view Jesus as the *righteous* one who *lives* by *allegiance*. But he also has in mind us, because all of this was for the purpose of our allegiance, so that we might become *righteous* by *allegiance* too, and so that we might also *live*.

In sum, the following makes the most sense of Romans 1:16–17. This is not an attempt at an exact translation but an expanded paraphrase—an interpretation designed to draw out Paul's intention:

> For I am not ashamed of the gospel, for it is the power of God for salvation *for everyone who gives allegiance to Jesus as the Messiah*, to the Jew first and also to the Greek. For in the gospel, vindication from God as righteous on the other side of judgment is revealed by means of Jesus's *allegiance* in going to the cross; this vindication becomes ours through *allegiance* to Jesus as the Messiah-king. For both Jesus and us now, all of this accords with the prophetic word, "The vindicated one will live by *allegiance*." (Rom. 1:16–17)

We come to share in the vindication of righteousness and resurrection-life in the exact same way that Jesus did—by allegiance alone. Yet there is a vital difference. Jesus's allegiance was uniquely effective. His act of righteousness, a sinless life culminating in the crucifixion, resulted in a perfect vindication—resurrection from the dead. Our allegiance is imperfect, but since Jesus is the forgiving king whose allegiance was *for us*, our imperfect allegiance is sufficient to create a union with the Christ's allegiance-unto-death and his vindication-unto-life.

The gospel is the good news about Jesus the saving king. We are saved by allegiance alone. Jesus's singularly effective allegiance comes first. Our imperfect allegiance follows and depends on his. The result is saving vindication, resurrection unto new life.

Moving from Faith to Allegiance

This book strives to be biblical, theological, and practical. I am convinced that these are not competing goals. Careful attention to the Bible and its theology leads naturally to fresh application. My hope is that this chapter will prove practical for the church in a sneaky way. A common question I receive is, How can I best help my church become more allegiant?

Allegiance culture begins with a change in how Christians preach, teach, and converse about the gospel, faith, and salvation. How do we do that? This chapter and the preceding one have been structured to show one way this can be done. In working through the Bible's explicit gospel passages, I opted for a specific sequence: first Mark, then 2 Timothy, and finally the two passages from the first chapter of Romans. Why did I choose this order? You may also have noticed that I have not yet discussed the most obvious gospel passage in the Bible, 1 Corinthians 15:3–5. This passage is pure gospel, and it is essential that we integrate it in order to appreciate the gospel fully. Why do you think I have delayed discussing it? See the guide for further conversation in appendix 2 for discussion questions and practical exercises.

Might other sequences be better? Perhaps. But my own experience has been that if you want to move your church or those around you from a salvation culture to a gospel-allegiance culture, certain sequences of encounters with the Bible's explicit gospel passages are better than others.

We'll explore other ways to foster allegiance subsequently. Yet I think we can all agree that how we preach, teach, and talk about the gospel and faith is the foundational beginning point. Toward that end, the next chapter is the mountaintop toward which we have been climbing. It seeks to present the gospel-allegiance model in the boldest possible relief and to answer John Piper's primary objection to the royal gospel.

3

The Full Gospel of the King

How would you define the gospel in a phrase or a couple sentences? What words would you use or avoid in your definition? Are there specific Bible passages you'd have in mind? Consider writing down your answer.

In July 2003 a well-known pastor-scholar preached a sermon titled "Jesus Our Substitute" that was so popular it was subsequently published. In it he attempted to define the gospel in short compass: "Here's the gospel in a phrase. Because Christ died for us, those who trust in him may know that their guilt has been pardoned once and for all. What will we have to say before the bar of God's judgment? Only one thing. Christ died in my place. That's the gospel."[1] I hope by this stage of the book that your gospel-in-a-phrase is more accurate than this one. Although "Christ died in my place" expresses why substitution is essential to the gospel, it is narrow in view and blurry in focus. What is the effect for the individual, church, and world if this is proclaimed rather than the complete gospel?

Nothing matters more than the gospel. It is imperative that we master the gospel by allowing it to master us—for our own sake and the world's. We have been gathering steam toward the heart of the gospel-allegiance proposal in the last few chapters. It's time to bring it together.

The gospel of Jesus the saving king consists of certain core events. After exploring these, we will weigh the validity of the leading objections to the royal gospel and consider implications for church unity. The gospel proper will be distinguished from closely related topics that are frequently confused with the gospel, such as purpose, response, and benefits.

The Gospel Itself

There can only ever be one true gospel. In a simple sentence: Jesus is the saving king. A more expansive summary brings out its trinitarian structure: The gospel is the true story of how Jesus the Son was sent by God the Father to become the saving king who now rules forever at his right hand through the sending of the Holy Spirit, fulfilling God's promises in Scripture.

The Bible's own explicit presentation of the gospel suggests that it consists of ten events. Together they constitute the core gospel.[2] The most accurate definition of the gospel locates these ten events within a royal framework.

The gospel is that Jesus the king

1. preexisted as God the Son,
2. was sent by the Father,
3. took on human flesh in fulfillment of God's promises to David,
4. died for our sins in accordance with the Scriptures,
5. was buried,
6. was raised on the third day in accordance with the Scriptures,
7. appeared to many witnesses,
8. *is enthroned at the right hand of God as the ruling Christ,*

9. has sent the Holy Spirit to his people to effect his rule, and
10. will come again as final judge to rule.

In this list the enthronement is italicized to give it special emphasis. This is because, as we shall see, it is repeatedly presented in the Bible as the climax of the gospel. Yet, when you read summaries of the gospel in popular literature or hear the gospel preached, it is all about Jesus's death on the cross for our sins. The resurrection sometimes gets tacked on. Meanwhile Jesus's enthronement is rarely (if ever) mentioned. This must change if we are to get the gospel right.

Expanding on the Gospel Content

The gospel is the saving career of Jesus the Messiah-king. It is best divided into ten stages or events. To prove this, I will show that each of the ten is repeatedly exemplified either in verses that use explicit "gospel" language or in biblical passages that indisputably proclaim the essence of the gospel. These include texts that we've already examined in chapters 1–2, as well as passages such as Acts 2:14–36; 3:11–26; 5:27–32; 10:34–43; 13:16–47; and 17:22–31, speeches that no one doubts are gospel proclamations, even though only two of them use "gospel" language in Greek (Acts 10:36 and 13:32). No single proclamation has all ten stages or events, but when collectively considered, all ten frequently appear.

The purpose of this expanded treatment is to enter more deeply into these ten events, so that we can better proclaim the gospel today. We should memorize these events and be able to explain them from Scripture. The overarching framework for the ten, you'll recall, is that *Jesus is the saving king*.

1. The king preexisted as God the Son.

When we speak of the preexistence of the Messiah, we mean that he was personally with God in glory before taking on human flesh. This is the starting point of the good news.

When preaching the gospel at Solomon's portico, Peter ironically states, "You killed the Author of life" (Acts 3:15). In so doing Peter definitively affirms Jesus's preexistence as the creator God. The preexistence of the Son alongside God the Father is also implied in Paul's gospel description in Romans 1:3: "who came into being . . . as it pertains to the flesh" (AT).

The identification of the Messiah as the ultimate speaker or addressee of certain psalms, written long before Jesus's birth, likewise attests to Jesus's preexistence. For example, in Peter's Pentecost sermon in Acts 2:25–28 and 2:34–35, the Messiah is identified as the true speaker of Old Testament words concerning his incorruptible body and future ascension to the right hand of God (cf. 2:30–31 for the explanation that David is speaking only as a prophet, which means the ultimate speaker must be the preexistent Christ). The implication is that the Messiah personally preexisted long before he took on human flesh as the man Jesus. Paul's gospel proclamation in Acts 13:33–37 also involves assumptions that the preexistent Christ is the true speaker of passages written long prior in the Old Testament.[3]

2. The king was sent by the Father.

When speaking about the gospel, Jesus himself stresses that he was sent: "I must preach *the good news* [*gospel*] of the kingdom of God to the other towns as well; for I was *sent* for this purpose" (Luke 4:43). The "sent" nature of his overall gospel mission was reinforced by Jesus in parables about the kingdom (e.g., Matt. 21:31). In the parable of the tenants, God the landowner sends many servants, all of whom are killed. Then, "finally he *sent his son* to them" (v. 37). Of course, the wicked tenants kill the son too, anticipating Jesus the Son's crucifixion.

In John's Gospel, Jesus makes numerous statements pertaining to salvation, affirming that he was sent.[4] Consider just one example. In John 5:24, Jesus says, "Truly, truly, I say to you, whoever hears my word and *believes* [*pisteuōn*] him who *sent* me has eternal life. He does not come into judgment, but has passed from death to life." Jesus is sent, and believing results in eternal life. Yet in assessing such statements, we must bear in mind that in John the *pistis* action intends more than simply believing (e.g., 2:23–24). It cannot be separated from obedience: "Whoever *believes* [*pisteuōn*] in the Son has eternal life; whoever *does not obey* the Son shall not see life, but the wrath of God remains on him" (3:36). That Jesus was sent by God the Father for our salvation is demonstrated by Jesus's own witness as reported in the Gospels.

Meanwhile, beyond the four Gospels, other New Testament passages indicate that the Son was sent. In the gospel proclamations in Acts, God's overall agency in sending Jesus is affirmed by Peter (Acts 3:26). And in a slight variation on this language, Paul affirms that God "brought to Israel a Savior, Jesus" (Acts 13:23). Several passages that do not mention "gospel" explicitly (but are replete with gospel themes) indicate that Jesus preexisted and was sent:

> For God has done what the law, weakened by the flesh, could not do. By *sending* his own Son in the likeness of sinful flesh and for sin, he condemned sin in the flesh. (Rom. 8:3)

> But when the fullness of time had come, God *sent* forth his Son, having come into being by woman, having come into being under the law, to redeem those who were under the law, so that we might receive adoption as sons. (Gal. 4:4–5 AT)

> In this the love of God was made manifest among us, that God *sent* his only Son into the world, so that we might live through him. In this is love, not that we have loved God but that he loved us and *sent* his Son to be the propitiation for our sins. (1 John 4:9–10)

It is a secure gospel fact that the Father sent the preexistent Son as the beginning of the good news for humanity. This sending connected to the Old Testament promise.

3. The king took on human flesh in fulfillment of God's promises to David.

The preexistence of the Messiah is a prerequisite for his incarnation, so the passages mentioned in the first subsection are pertinent here too. We've already seen that incarnation, undergirded by the Davidic promise, is one of the main points of the gospel message in Romans 1:3–4 and 2 Timothy 2:8.

Through the prophet Nathan, God had made firm promises to David regarding an eternal kingdom through his offspring: "When your days are fulfilled and you lie down with your fathers, I will raise up your offspring after you. . . . I will establish the throne of his kingdom forever. I will be to him a father, and he shall be to me a son. . . . And your house and your kingdom shall be made sure forever before me. Your throne shall be established forever" (2 Sam. 7:12–14, 16).

These promises to David pertaining to an eternal kingdom are celebrated throughout the psalter (e.g., Pss. 2; 18:50; 89; 132:10–12). They became a source of hope for future national renewal in the subsequent prophetic literature: "In that day the Root of Jesse will stand as a banner for the peoples; the nations will rally to him. . . . He will assemble the scattered people of Judah from the four quarters of the earth" (Isa. 11:10, 12 NIV). Isaiah, David, and others anticipated a future king in the line of David who would restore Israel, gather the faithful from among the nations, and judge the wicked.

For example, Peter indicates that David knew that "God had sworn with an oath to him that he would set one of his descendants on his throne" (Acts 2:30). The promise to bring a royal Savior through David's line also features prominently in Acts 13:22–24. The gospel highlights the fulfillment of the Davidic promise in the royal incarnation of the Son.

The incarnation is theologically vital to the gospel. Jesus was sent to share in our humanity in every way (excluding sin), to be our sin offering, and to serve as our great high priest (Heb.

2:14–17; 4:15; 9:24–26). But there's more. To reign with the king we must become like him. God placed humans as his image in the midst of creation to rule it (Gen. 1:26–28). Yet our image-bearing and its attendant glory have become distorted through idolatry (2 Kings 17:15; Ps. 115:5–8; Rom. 1:22–23; 3:23).

Jesus the Christ was sent as the perfect image (2 Cor. 4:4; Col. 1:15) so that our image-bearing might be restored by gazing on his image as part of the necessary process of our salvation (1 Cor. 13:12; 2 Cor. 3:18; Col. 3:10; 1 John 3:2; cf. Rev. 22:4). Eastern Orthodox Christians helpfully emphasize this aspect of salvation, calling it *theosis*. Our image-restoration (and its glory) is a required salvation process, because God's final saving intention is that we rule the renewed creation along with King Jesus (Rom. 8:17–21; cf. Matt. 19:28; Col. 3:4; 2 Tim. 2:12; Rev. 20:6; 22:5). The incarnation is a vital component of the saving good news.

4. The king died for our sins in accordance with the Scriptures.

The death of Jesus as the king is indisputably essential to the gospel. This is made evident in the most famous gospel passage in the Bible—1 Corinthians 15:1–5. Paul begins by speaking broadly about how the Corinthians first received the gospel:

> Now, brothers and sisters, I bring to your attention the gospel [*euangelion*] that I gospeled [*euēngelisamēn*] to you, which you received, on which you stand, and through which also you are being saved—that is, if you hold fast to the word I gospeled to you; otherwise you have *given pistis* to no avail. (1 Cor. 15:1–2 AT)

The gospel may not be programmatic instructions for how to get saved, but it nevertheless truly is God's saving message.

Salvation in process. Here Paul emphasizes that salvation is a process ("being saved"), not a once-for-all-time faith decision. This is made clear by Paul's specific language in Greek. He says that we are "being saved," but only if we hold fast to the gospel proclamation. As Paul indicates, failure to hold fast means that initial *pistis* has been given to no avail (*eikē*)—that is, in a purposeless, empty fashion. This shows, as nearly all Christians agree, that perseverance in "faith" is required for final salvation. This gospel proclamation, the one that we must cling to tenaciously if we are to continue being saved, is further detailed by Paul:

> For as a matter of primary import I handed over to you that which also I received: that the Christ *died* in behalf of our sins in accordance with the Scriptures, and that he was *buried*, and that he has been *raised* on the third day in accordance with the Scriptures, and that he *appeared* to Cephas [Peter], then to the Twelve. . . . Then last of all, as if to a miscarried fetus, he appeared also to me. . . . Therefore whether I or those ones, thus we are preaching, and thus you believed. (1 Cor. 15:3–5, 8, 11 AT)

Paul received certain core elements of the gospel not from any human source but directly from the Lord Jesus himself (Gal. 1:11–12); nevertheless, the gospel that Paul received was already traditional in Paul's day and age.[5] This shows that Paul's gospel was not idiosyncratic but was the common property of the apostolic church.

Royal not individualistic substitution. In 1 Corinthians 15:3–5 Paul emphasizes four different events: (1) the Christ *died*, (2) was *buried*, (2) was *raised*, and (4) *appeared*. His death and resurrection are said to accord with Scripture. We'll expand on each of these as we continue to outline the ten core gospel events.

The gospel pertains to kingship. Notice that a *royal* framework in 1 Corinthians 15:1–5 is present too, much as it was in Romans 1:1–5, even if less obvious. Paul does not say, "*Jesus* died for *my* sins"—although individualistic salvation culture tends to make this the entire gospel! Jesus's name is not even mentioned, and the focus is not individualistic. Rather, 1 Corinthians 15:3 indicates, "*the Christ* died in behalf of *our* sins." Why does Paul emphasize the kingly title, "the Christ," rather than Jesus's personal name when discussing death for sins here? Probably because the royal framework of the gospel was paramount to its very essence.

The emphasis is on collective representation: *the king* as a substitute bears the penalty that *the whole people* deserve. Within the Christian tradition this has generally been called substitutionary atonement.

The Messiah's death *for our sins* is specifically said to accord with the Scriptures. This means it fulfilled prophecies and patterns in the Old Testament. In view are passages that feature the unjust punishment of a righteous sufferer who is then rescued by God for the benefit of others.[6] We know this because such texts are alluded to or cited in the New Testament in connection with prominent gospel themes or as part of gospel proclamation in Acts. We must never lose sight of the way in which the gospel is *for us*. It is good news because it brings possible or actual *benefits*. The Messiah's death *for our sins* is one such benefit.

Cross centered? The Messiah's death for our sins in 1 Corinthians 15:3 reminds us that the cross is indisputably essential to the gospel. The cross's irreducible centrality is reinforced because it is mentioned or strongly implied in a great many other gospel texts, such as Acts 2:23; 3:15; 5:30–31; 10:39; and 13:28–29 (cf. Rom. 8:3; Eph. 2:16; Phil. 2:8; Col. 1:20; 2:14). Other passages indicate that the Messiah's death on the cross is specially purposed toward the forgiveness of our sins (e.g., Matt. 26:28; Rom. 3:25; 6:6; Gal. 3:13; Heb. 2:17; 1 Pet. 2:24; 1 John 1:7; 2:2; 4:10). So the cross, where the Messiah died for our sins and won victory over death and evil spiritual powers, is definitely vital to the gospel.

There is another way in which the cross is central. In several passages, the message of the cross is *the central point of offense* in gospel proclamation—that which most severely shocks and repulses our sensibilities about what is appropriate.

> For Christ did not send me to baptize but to preach the gospel, and not with words of eloquent wisdom, lest the cross of Christ be emptied of its power. For the word of the cross is folly to those who are perishing, but to us who are being saved it is the power of God. (1 Cor. 1:17–18)

> But if I, brothers, still preach circumcision, why am I still being persecuted? In that case the offense of the cross has been removed. (Gal. 5:11)

The cross is indeed the central point of offense in the gospel.

But is the cross the center of the gospel? In chapter 1 we saw that the cross is central (essential) to the gospel and is, arguably, its dramatic center but it is not consistently presented in the Bible as its theological center. The conclusions of this chapter show that Jesus's kingship is the basic summarizing message and overall climax of the gospel. So Jesus's attainment of the royal office and reign has a centrality that goes beyond being an essential component.

The bottom line: The cross is theologically central to the gospel, but the focus is not individualistic forgiveness. Not even approximately. Proclaiming that "Jesus died for my/your personal sins" yields a salvation culture focused on individual belief in saving facts. We shouldn't be astonished if it is hard to build church community and encourage discipleship within such a culture. We must proclaim the fuller truth: "The king died for our collective sins, so that we could yield allegiance." When we do, we'll find a community of loyal disciples emerging.

5. The king was buried.

In Greek, "he was buried" is only one word, *etaphē*. This one word is spoken by Paul in 1 Corinthians 15:4 as he reminds the Corinthians of the gospel. Paul is stressing the reality of Jesus's death—that it was not a sham. In Acts, Paul's emphasis is much the same: "And when they had carried out all that was written of him, they took him down from the tree *and laid him in a tomb*" (13:29). Mention of burial serves to confirm that Jesus's death was genuine.

Peter's Pentecost sermon uses the tomb motif extensively. David said his body would not rot in the grave, but instead he would find life in the presence of God. Peter indicates that it doesn't make any sense for David to speak this way about *himself* since his body did in fact decay in the tomb. So David must have been speaking as a prophet from the vantage point of someone else—the preexistent Messiah (Acts 2:25–31, citing Ps. 16:8–11).

6. ***The king was raised on the third day in accordance with the Scriptures.***

A feature of the gospel is that the Messiah, Jesus, truly died a real death and truly came back to life in *the same body*. Albeit that body had been transformed and gloriously renewed. Since even among confessing Christians this can be confused with resuscitation (almost dead but not quite!), or with healing, revival, reincarnation, or the ascent of his soul to heaven, it needs to be said that such descriptions are not adequate. The physical reality of his resurrected body is emphasized in several accounts, especially when Jesus invites Thomas to touch his wounds (John 20:27) and when he eats fish with them (Luke 24:42; John 21:13).

Since there is a tendency in popular preaching to reduce the gospel to a transaction on the cross ("Jesus died for me"), it shocks many to discover that *resurrection is emphasized far more often than the Messiah's death for sins* in explicit gospel texts in the Bible (e.g., 2 Tim. 2:8; Rom. 1:3–4). Jesus's death on the cross is frequently mentioned in the speeches in Acts, but forgiveness is predicated on responding appropriately to the *entire* gospel message (not just to a forgiveness transaction on the cross)—a message that ordinarily climaxes with an announcement of Jesus's present enthronement. This suggests that forgiveness was linked especially to confessing loyalty to Jesus as king. Even in the four Gospels the claim that Jesus's heralding of the kingdom of God ultimately includes a proclamation of his death *for sins* is not self-evident but has to be argued for—although I am convinced that it does include this proclamation.[7]

My point is that the cross is significant, but resurrection and kingly rule are even more prominent in explicit gospel texts in the Bible. We must respond to the full gospel of Jesus the *raised*, *living king*. The gospel must not be reduced to the cross in our preaching and teaching. The good news is that the resurrected Jesus is now living in God's presence as the king. When we give allegiance, his resurrection power begins to work in our lives. *We live because he lives.*

7. *The king appeared to many witnesses.*

Jesus's resurrection appearances are well attested in explicit gospel passages. In Paul's narration of the gospel in 1 Corinthians 15:3–11, he lists an entire chain of witnesses who saw Jesus the Messiah after he had been raised from the dead: Peter, the Twelve, more than five hundred believers at the same time, James, additional apostles, and finally Paul himself. The theme of eyewitness attestation of the Messiah's resurrection is also prominent in Peter's Pentecost sermon (Acts 2:32), his sermon at Solomon's portico (3:15), the summary of the apostles' activities (4:33), the apostles' speech before the council (5:32), Peter's sermon to Cornelius's guests (10:40–41), and Paul's evangelization at Pisidian Antioch (13:31). It should be obvious why his appearance to many witnesses is essential to the gospel: it confirms that Jesus's physical body was truly raised from the dead within real history.

8. *The king is enthroned at the right hand of God as the ruling Christ.*

I place special emphasis on this stage of the gospel because we can demonstrate from the Bible that it is the gospel's climax and its best summary. We've discussed the importance of Jesus's ubiquitous title—"the Christ"—for understanding explicit gospel passages. Peter's entire evangelistic message to Cornelius's guests is prefaced by calling Jesus "the Christ" while asserting that "he is Lord of all" (Acts 10:36). Meanwhile, gospel activity is summarized as proving or proclaiming that "Jesus is the Messiah" (Acts 5:42; 8:5; 9:22; 17:3). The gospel's royal framework is everywhere apparent once we begin to look at our texts with fresh eyes.

Jesus's enthronement is the gospel climax. Jesus's appointment to the office of Son-of-God-in-Power is the culmination of the gospel's description in Romans 1:3–4; moreover, this connects to his authoritative titles and the gospel's purpose of allegiance in Romans 1:5. In Philippians we are reminded that Jesus has been super-exalted and has received "the name that is above every name" (2:9). Every knee will bow and every tongue confess, not that "Jesus died for my sins," but that "Jesus the Messiah is Lord" (2:11 AT).

This royal climax is found repeatedly in Acts. Peter's Pentecost sermon builds toward a finale with the declaration that Jesus has been "exalted at the right hand of God" in fulfillment of Psalm 110:1 (Acts 2:33). But it reaches a crescendo with the final words, "Let all the house of Israel therefore know for certain that God has made this Jesus whom you crucified both *Lord* and *Christ*!" (v. 36 AT). So as to not leave us in any doubt about the true climax of the gospel, Peter ends by doubling down on the sovereign titles—*Lord* and *Christ*—that describe Jesus's new position at God's right hand.

Meanwhile Peter's proclamation at Solomon's portico opens with the claim that the God of Abraham "glorified his servant Jesus" (Acts 3:13). Near the end of the sermon, Peter calls Jesus "the Christ appointed for you" (v. 20) and emphasizes his present location in heaven (v. 21). Thus the whole sermon is framed by an emphasis on Jesus as king, and the sermon peaks with a need for the audience to respond appropriately in light of his future royal visitation (vv. 22–23). Similarly, in the speech before the Sanhedrin, Peter and the apostles say, "God exalted him at his right hand as Leader [*archēgos*] and Savior, to give repentance to Israel and forgiveness of sins" (5:31). Mention of the right hand shows that Jesus's new heavenly position of authority is the key (see also Stephen's speech in 7:56). Likewise, in Acts 17:22–31, Paul's sermon concludes with an affirmation that God has established a day on which he will judge the world in righteousness by an appointed man. This man must himself be righteous since he has been raised from the dead (has been vindicated), now lives, and will execute God's righteous judgment (see also Rom. 1:17).

When the Bible presents the gospel, it consistently situates it within an overarching royal framework, which frequently climaxes with Jesus's appointment as the heavenly king at the right hand of God. The first seven stages of the gospel refer to *past* events that have ongoing saving significance. With the eighth, Jesus's kingly rule, we arrive at the *present* reality in the church age. This is another reason why it is the gospel's best summary.

Christianity's largest problem today. In light of this, it is not an overstatement to say that the largest problem within Christianity today is the exclusion of Jesus's kingship from the gospel. To show how widespread the neglect of the enthronement is *as gospel*, let's consider the definition of "gospel" in the Gospel Coalition's foundational documents. If anyone is going to get the gospel right, surely it should be the Gospel Coalition.

> We believe that the gospel is the good news of Jesus Christ—God's very wisdom. Utter folly to the world, even though it is the power of God to those who are being saved, this good news is christological, centering on the cross and resurrection: the gospel is not proclaimed if Christ is not proclaimed, and the authentic Christ has not been proclaimed if his death and resurrection are not central (the message is: "Christ died for our sins . . . [and] was raised").[8]

It is an unsurprising and in many ways helpful statement. But there are severe limitations. Christ is tacitly treated as a personal name rather than a kingly title. Death and resurrection are rightly put forward as central to the gospel, but this is painfully narrow. Why is the sending of the Son and incarnation into the line of David not central too? Or the sending of the Spirit? Most glaringly, *why not Jesus's kingship*? To be fair, in the next section of the foundational statement, titled "Christ's redemption," Jesus's incarnation and kingly rule are stressed. But they are not treated as if they are part of the gospel proper. When even the Gospel Coalition in its official definition has missed large portions of the biblical gospel, we know gospel imprecision has become an epidemic in the universal church.

Don't read this as a broadside attack against the Gospel Coalition. Folks associated with it are doing valuable work. I hope my actual point is clear. It may be readily acknowledged by Christians today that Jesus is Lord or King, but as with the Gospel Coalition's statement, Jesus's enthronement is treated as *external* to the gospel rather than *internal* to it. When Jesus's kingship is external to the gospel, it is easy to think responding to his kingship with allegiance is irrelevant for salvation. The opposite is true in the Bible, where *Jesus's kingship is so internal to the gospel that it is the gospel's summarizing content and climax*. The Gospel Coalition's official definition misses what the Bible emphasizes most about the gospel: Jesus's kingship. If TGC's gospel urgently needs refinement, how much more other church groups.

9. The king has sent the Holy Spirit to his people to effect his rule.

Jesus anticipated Pentecost by speaking of an allegiance declaration that would lead to Spirit empowerment. Jesus says that when he comes into his kingdom as the Son of Man (that is, as the ruler at the right hand of God; see Dan. 7:13–14), whoever "publicly acknowledges" him before others will be acknowledged by him before the angels (Luke 12:8–9). This "publicly acknowledges" (*homologēsē*) refers to a verbal confession and is a fitting way to describe swearing allegiance to Jesus as King of kings. (It is the same word Paul uses in Rom. 10:9 when he says that anyone who believes and *confesses* that "Jesus is *Lord*" will be saved.) Jesus indicates that those who make this confession will then be taught by the Holy Spirit what to say when bearing witness to Jesus's kingship (Luke 12:11–12).

The kingdom of God arrived with Jesus's ministry, since he was in the process of becoming king. He performed signs, healings, and exorcisms showing that the new era, the kingdom-of-God age, had arrived with him: "But if it is by the Spirit of God that I cast out demons, then the kingdom of God has come upon you" (Matt. 12:28). He is the anointed king; the Spirit came to rest on him at his baptism. This is why the kingdom has come upon the people. He has already been anointed as king and can already do kingly things as the prince in waiting. He will soon receive his throne. And when Jesus does receive his throne, he says, the gift of the Holy Spirit for his followers will come next (Acts 1:5; cf. 11:15–16).

Exaltation leads to the outpouring of the Spirit. It is no accident, then, that Pentecost, the giving of the Holy Spirit to the allegiant community, follows shortly after Jesus's ascension to the right hand of God in Acts. In case we are obtuse, Peter makes the connection for us: "Being therefore exalted to the right hand of God, and having received from the Father the promise of the Holy Spirit, he has poured out this that you yourselves are seeing and hearing" (Acts 2:33). Jesus's installation as sovereign leads to the outpouring of the Spirit. Those who acknowledge Jesus as exalted king give allegiance bodily (initially via baptism) and receive the Spirit, which is why the apostles can say God has given the Holy Spirit "to those who *obey* him" (5:32).

After the initial infilling at Pentecost, in Acts profession of allegiance ordinarily comes first and is followed by Spirit reception (e.g., Acts 2:38; 8:12–17; 19:4–6). Yet this is not always the case. In his sermon to the Gentiles (10:34–43), Peter preaches about Jesus as the Spirit-anointed king and about the cross and resurrection, future judgment, and forgiveness. But he doesn't call the Gentiles to repentance or mention the giving of the Spirit to those who obey. Nevertheless, the Spirit suddenly falls on all who hear (v. 44; cf. 11:15–16)! We hear nothing about their repentance, their belief/faith, or their confession of loyalty to King Jesus. Yet they receive the Holy Spirit, proving that their allegiance has been certified by God even before they have publicly confessed it or been baptized (cf. 15:8). Accordingly, baptism subsequently into the name of Jesus the Messiah cannot be withheld (10:44–48). The ordinary pattern of professed allegiance followed by Spirit reception is reversed when the Gentiles first enter the church, signifying God's desire to show that their inclusion is his will (11:17; 15:7–9).

The exaltation-outpouring sequence that we find in Acts is reinforced in John's Gospel, which has its own alternative timing for the giving of the Spirit. In Acts, the Spirit is given *after* Jesus's ascension. In John, it's *before*—even though John affirms that the Spirit is properly for those who give *pistis* after Jesus's glorification (7:38–39)! Why? For John, Jesus's being "lifted up" on the cross (3:14–15) is purposefully intermingled with his being "lifted up" in heavenly glory (8:28; 12:34). The crucifixion is Jesus's paradoxical exaltation to the right hand of the Father, where he will gather all nations under his banner: "And I, when I am lifted up from the earth, will draw all people to myself" (12:32). This is why John reports that the resurrected Jesus breathed on his disciples, saying, "Receive the Holy Spirit," in anticipation of his actual enthronement (20:22). Despite John's alternative sequence, just as in Acts, there is a firm link between Jesus's exaltation and the sending of the Spirit.

Spirit rule. When Paul articulates the gospel in Romans 1:4, he says that the Son has now been appointed Son-of-God-in-Power, but then qualifies the nature of Jesus's rule "according to the Spirit of Holiness." In other words, Jesus's reign is coextensive with the Spirit's empowering presence in the midst of his people. This is also why Paul can say that the Scripture preached the gospel in advance to Abraham (see Gal. 3:8, 14; see chap. 5 below for discussion). Likewise Paul can state, "Our gospel came to you not only in word, but also in power and in the Holy Spirit and with full conviction" (1 Thess. 1:5; cf. Eph. 1:13). The sending of the Holy Spirit is genuinely part of the gospel.

The receipt of the Holy Spirit as a gospel event is not the same as saying the kingdom of God is the rule of Jesus in each person's heart. This is a frequent misunderstanding of Jesus's teachings, fueled by mistranslation. When the Pharisees asked Jesus when the kingdom of God would come, Jesus answered, "The kingdom of God is not coming with signs to be observed, nor will they say, 'Look, here it is!' or 'There!' For behold, the kingdom of God *entos hymōn estin*" (Luke 17:21 AT). Some older translations, such as the KJV and NIV (1984) translate the last phrase as "the kingdom of God *is within you.*" But this is wrong. In Greek the "you" is plural, more than one person. So what is intended is that the kingdom of God is "in the midst of you who are standing here." Newer versions have corrected this. The NRSV has "among you"; the ESV, "in the midst of you"; and the current NIV, "in your midst." The kingdom is coextensive with the Spirit's corporate rule.

10. The king will come again as final judge to rule.

In Jesus's capacity as king, he will visit his people once again, exercising judgment. Jesus is magnificently described as "King of kings and Lord of lords" in Revelation, as he comes to judge and rule over the nations (19:15–16).

Jesus speaks of his kingship frequently in the Gospels. In fact, the title that Jesus most often used for himself—Son of Man—anticipates his future rule as king and judge. It derives principally from Daniel's vision:

> I saw in the night visions,
>
> and behold, with the clouds of heaven
> *there came one like a son of man*,
> and he came to the Ancient of Days
> and was presented before him.
> And to him was given dominion
> and glory and a *kingdom*,
> *that all peoples, nations, and languages*
> *should serve him*;
> his dominion is an everlasting dominion,
> which shall not pass away,
> and his kingdom one
> that shall not be destroyed. (Dan. 7:13–14)

In his capacity as Son of Man, Jesus is the everlasting king over an eternal kingdom. He is also appointed in his kingly capacity as the royal judge over the nations. Jesus calls himself the Son of Man and describes his future royal judgment: "When the Son of Man comes in his glory, and all the angels with him, then he will sit on his glorious throne. Before him will be gathered all the nations, and he will separate people one from another as a shepherd separates the sheep from the goats" (Matt. 25:31–32).[9] Not only will Jesus as the king serve as end-times judge, as in the vision in Daniel, but his people will join him in rendering royal judgment. "In the new world," Jesus says, "when the Son of Man will sit on his glorious throne, you who have followed me will also sit on twelve thrones, judging the twelve tribes of Israel" (Matt. 19:28; cf. Luke 22:30). It should not shock us, then, that Jesus invites others alongside him to assist in judging (e.g., Rev. 20:4). Nor should we be surprised when Paul says, "Do you not know that the saints will judge the world?" (1 Cor. 6:2).

In light of reluctance to consider Jesus's return as royal judge to be part of the good news in an unqualified fashion (see Piper's objection in the next section), its prominence in the Bible's explicit gospel proclamations needs to be established. Paul includes Jesus's final judgment on both the righteous and the wicked within the gospel in Romans 2:16, when he speaks of "the day when, according to my gospel, God judges the secrets of humankind by the Messiah, Jesus" (AT). The gospel also includes judgment by our Lord Jesus in 2 Thessalonians 1:8–10, and his judgment is perhaps also intended in Revelation 14:6–7.

Meanwhile, the proclamations in Acts usually include Jesus's coming judgment as part of the good news. At Solomon's portico, Peter calls for repentance, "that times of refreshing might come" and that "he might send the Messiah appointed for you, Jesus, whom heaven must receive until the time for restoring all things" (Acts 3:20–21 AT). In Cornelius's house, Peter declares, "He commanded us to preach to the people and to testify that he is the one appointed by God to be judge of the living and the dead" (10:42).

As Paul is addressing the Athenians, he declares, "[God] has fixed a day on which he will judge the world in righteousness by a man whom he has appointed" (17:31).

We should not be surprised that Jesus's judging function is included within the gospel if we realize that the gospel is not a program for how to get saved but a royal proclamation. Kings were responsible for administering justice in the ancient world—rendering judgment and seeing that sentences were carried out. Not everyone, however, is happy with this idea. Before offering concluding thoughts about the royal gospel, let's explore three possible objections.

Objections to the Royal Gospel

Objection 1: Royal Judgment Is Not Good News

John Piper has expressed a specific concern with the royal gospel. For Piper and others, Jesus as king cannot be the center of the gospel; rather, justification by faith must be (see chap. 1). According to Piper, apart from the declared innocence received via justification by faith, Jesus's kingship is not good news. It is appalling news, in fact, because it signals that judgment is coming. Piper says, "The announcement that Jesus is the Messiah, the imperial Lord of the universe, is not good news, but is an absolutely terrifying message to a sinner who has spent all his life ignoring or blaspheming the God and Father of the Lord Jesus Christ and is therefore guilty of treason and liable to execution."[10]

There are two problems with Piper's analysis. First, as we saw in chapter 1, the Bible never overtly says that *our* justification by faith is part of the gospel. Rather, the gospel proper is about *Jesus's* justification (vindication through resurrection and enthronement), and *pistis* is our response to the gospel.

Second, in seeking to defend justification by faith over against a royal gospel in relation to the quote above, Piper insists that there can be "no good news till I hear the terms of amnesty." But in so doing he has allowed the systematizing of an individualistic theology of salvation to trump first-century word meanings.[11] The word *euangelion* ("gospel") was used in the New Testament era to refer to an announcement of glad tidings associated with imperial rule with no real concern as to whether an emperor would rule well or not. For example, Paul's contemporary Josephus uses the word "gospel" to refer to news of the ascension of Vespasian to emperor.

> Fame carried [the news about Vespasian] abroad more suddenly than one could have thought, that he was emperor over the east, upon which every city kept festivals, and celebrated sacrifices and oblations for such *good news* [*euangelia*]. (*Jewish War* 4.618)

> And now, as Vespasian was come to Alexandria, this *good news* [*euangelia*] came from Rome, and at the same time came embassies from all his own habitable earth, to congratulate him upon his advancement. (*Jewish War* 4.656)[12]

The "good news" for Josephus is that Vespasian has become the new Roman emperor. It is gospel regardless of whether he has offered clemency to his enemies or will rule wisely in the future.

Even more important is the famous Priene Calendar Inscription, dated to 9 BC, for it speaks of Caesar Augustus (Octavian), the Roman emperor who was active during Jesus's upbringing. The inscription calls the emperor "savior" and "god," while speaking of the beginning of his reign as the gospel ("good tidings").

> Since Providence, which has ordered all things and is deeply interested in our life, has set in most perfect order by giving us Augustus, whom she filled with virtue that he might benefit humankind, sending him as a *savior* [*sōtēr*], both for us and for our descendants, that he might end war and arrange all things, and since he, Caesar, by his appearance . . . surpassing all previous benefactors, and not even leaving to posterity any hope of surpassing what he has done, and since the birthday of *the god* [*tou theou*] Augustus

> was the beginning of the *good tidings* [*euangelion*] for the world that came by reason of him. . . .

For the author of this inscription, the very day of Caesar Augustus's birth was the beginning of the gospel, the good tidings—before he had done anything, good or bad. This is true even though, for the author of this inscription, the gospel's full significance can only be discovered retroactively on the basis of the peace and benefactions Octavian proffered. This inscription was found in southwestern Turkey, ancient Asia Minor, which is the basic vicinity where Paul was active as a missionary. So it speaks to how Paul and his letters' audiences would have understood the word *euangelion* (gospel). The word "gospel" was (and is!) politically and socially loaded.

Contrary to Piper, when a first-century individual heard Paul say *euangelion*, he or she did not think: If Paul is not speaking about the good news of my personal salvation from sins, then Paul is misapplying the word, since my sins stand against me. Instead, a person heard that Jesus had been appointed as the ultimate saving king. Piper's objection puts artificial constraints around *euangelion* that would have been incomprehensible to a first-century audience.

Although Piper has wrongly forced *euangelion* to carry improbable meanings, he is correct to insist that Paul's gospel absolutely must include the good news of forgiveness from sins. This is part of the royal gospel proclamation in Scripture (e.g., 1 Cor. 15:3). The gospel is good news *for us*. But how can this be stated so that we capture the truth while avoiding the error? We should distinguish between the *possibility* of forgiveness and its *realization*.

The gospel in the Bible is an announcement of the *possibility* of the forgiveness of sins through Jesus the king—and this is amazingly good news indeed. Piper has wrongly concluded that the word "gospel" must include the *realization* of forgiveness in order for it to mean good news. The attempts of Piper, MacArthur, Sproul, and others to keep *our* justification by faith (*our* actualized forgiveness) at the center of the gospel is misguided and cannot be supported from Scripture. The good news is about Jesus's achievements, first, as established gospel fact; our personal saving benefits derive from and are contingent upon Jesus's achievements. They are not part of the gospel proper.

Objection 2: The Different Gospel in Galatia

Even though Paul never says that the gospel is justification by faith alone, many have concluded that it is the gospel's center. Since faith's unique role in justification was undoubtedly at risk in Galatia (see chap. 5 below), and because Paul warns about a "different gospel" in Galatians 1:6 (cf. 1:8–9; 2:5, 14), this conclusion is understandable. But it involves a questionable inference.

Paul is deadly serious in his warning about those who "distort the gospel of Christ" (Gal. 1:7). Yet there is no clear evidence that the false teachers or the Galatians were in danger of abandoning the ten Christ events that make up the royal gospel as Paul and others explicitly describe it elsewhere. What, then, does Paul intend? He is warning against twisting not the gospel's *content* but the only effective *response* to it (allegiance), its *result* (one new humanity), and one of its leading *benefits* (justification).

We frequently refer to a thing when intending its effects or other associations. (Linguists call this *metonymy*.) For example, if you arrive for tea, I might say, "The kettle is full," to tell you that it is nearly ready. I have referred only to the kettle. But I am really using *content language* to speak instead about *means*, *result*, and *benefit*. "The kettle is full" (content language) intends to say that water is being heated (means) and will boil (result) so we can enjoy tea (benefit). Mention of a thing can really be aimed at its results and other associations. This best explains Paul's warning in Galatians 1:6–9.

Later in Galatians, Paul uses the word "gospel" when speaking about its results again. Paul mentions "the gospel of foreskin" and "of circumcision" (Gal. 2:7). Yet in speaking this way he intends not the *content* of the gospel itself. Paul is not speaking about the gospel that consists of a portion of the penis nor a gospel that consists of a cutting action, but the gospel of the *result* of circumcision in marking off Jew and Gentile. So Paul sometimes uses "gospel" to point not to content but to results. That the results of the gospel (and other associations) can be intended by a reference to the gospel clarifies much. It explains why the content of Paul's gospel is the ten Christ events, not our justification by faith, but at the same time it shows why Paul's warning in Galatians not to deviate from the gospel is nevertheless urgent and appropriate.

Objection 3: The Thief at the Cross

When Jesus is dying on the cross between two thieves, one reviles him, but to the other Jesus says, "Today you will be with me in paradise" (Luke 23:43). Some have concluded that the thief (better translated as "criminal") is instantly saved by faith in Jesus's death on the cross apart from any acts of loyalty. Then they draw an implication: saving allegiance is invalid.

There are two problems with this conclusion. First, by staring solely at the cross, this conclusion is blind to the royal context. All around the criminal are people who fail to recognize Jesus's kingship despite the irony of a crucified Messiah. The people and rulers scoff, "He saved others; let him save himself, if he is *the Christ* of God" (Luke 23:35). The soldiers mock him, "If you are *the King* of the Jews, save yourself!" (v. 37). The inscription reads, "This is *the King* of the Jews" (v. 38). The first criminal mocks Jesus, "Are you not *the Christ*? Save yourself and us!" (v. 39). All of this suggests that *the criminal's salvation depends on genuine rather than mocking confession of Jesus as the king*.

Second, we have no indication that the criminal was specifically trusting in Jesus's death for his sins. Given that the crucifixion is in view, the story line probably encourages us to believe that he was, but the biblical text says nothing of the sort explicitly. Rather, the criminal encourages others to have an appropriate fear of God as the one who fairly judges the guilty and the innocent. The criminal does *not* say, "Jesus, I am trusting only in your sacrifice for me." Rather, he says, "Jesus, *remember me* when you come into *your kingdom*" (Luke 23:42).

In other words, the criminal publicly professes that this crucified Jesus is the true king and is about to receive his throne. He has heard the royal gospel (in summary form) and has responded with allegiance. Allegiance is in view because he thinks his personal confession ("remember me") of Jesus as *the king* ("your kingdom") has an enduring quality that will make him worthy of reward once Jesus begins his reign over him and all others in the coming age. Far from undermining the gospel-allegiance proposal, the salvation of the criminal at the cross supports it.

The Gospel and the Trinity

One advantage of summary statements is that they help us communicate effectively. Summaries structure and orient. Sometimes we need to be succinct and say, "The gospel is that Jesus is the saving king." At other times, especially when we are trying to combat gospel confusion in the church, we need to give the ten events in outline form, but nothing more. When preparing for evangelism we need to expand them, so that we are ready to share and support the good news fully from Scripture.

Following the Bible's lead, I think we can offer abridging summaries and still call these the gospel. Paul does this in Romans 1:3–4; 1 Corinthians 15:3–5; and 2 Timothy 2:8. Likewise, none of the proclamations in Acts have all ten elements. (Peter's sermon in Acts 2 only lacks #10, and perhaps #2.) But in our current climate of gospel imprecision, there is risk entailed in radically compressing its content but still calling it "the gospel." We are on safer ground if we give either the full ten-part gospel or summaries that highlight its trinitarian structure. This helps prevent the gospel from becoming some other story.

Although the doctrine of the Trinity did not receive its classic expression until the fourth century and beyond, it is a nonnegotiable biblical doctrine. This is true not only because the doctrine can be established from the Bible but also because *the gospel has a trinitarian shape*: The Father sends the preexistent Son to take on human flesh in the line of David. His death on the cross results in his resurrection and exaltation to a new position as Son-of-God-in-Power. That position's rule is coextensive with the Spirit's domain as the Spirit is sent. The *Father* and the *Son* send the *Spirit* so that the purpose of the gospel might reach fulfillment. The saving power of the gospel is actualized when, through the Spirit's empowering presence, the nations give allegiance to Jesus the king, who is seated at the Father's right hand.[13]

The gospel is not identical to the Trinity, nor is the Trinity identical to the gospel. But the doctrine of the Trinity bounds the gospel from the divine side, preventing it from becoming a false story about a nontriune God. It articulates eternal relationships of begetting and breathing forth between Father, Son, and Spirit. But these eternal relationships are known to us because the Trinity most clearly revealed its self-life historically in the gospel—by the Father sending the Son to become incarnate and by the sending of the Spirit. This is why when the doctrine of the Trinity is rejected—for example, by Jehovah's Witnesses and Mormons—the universal church says, if you deny the Trinity then you are not a Christian. The gospel has been rejected too.

One Gospel for All Christians

As we consider the actual gospel, one of the most important insights is that *no portion of the content of the true gospel is a matter of dispute among Catholic, Protestant, or Orthodox Christians*. The three great streams within Christianity are in complete agreement about the content of the gospel as the Bible presents it—even when representatives within these streams don't realize it. The church's gospel must change because the true gospel preserves the church's unity.

The biblical gospel's content is quite similar to outlines given by early church fathers,[14] as well as to the most widely embraced creed among Christians—the Apostles' Creed:

> I believe in God, the Father almighty, Creator of heaven and earth, and in Jesus Christ, his only Son, our Lord, who was conceived by the Holy Spirit, born of the Virgin Mary, suffered under Pontius Pilate, was crucified, died, and was buried; he descended into hell; on the third day he rose again from the dead; he ascended into heaven, and is seated at the right hand of God the Father almighty; from there he will come to judge the living and the dead. I believe in the Holy Spirit, the holy catholic church, the communion of saints, the forgiveness of sins, the resurrection of the body, and the life everlasting.

The similarities between the biblical gospel and the Apostles' Creed are no coincidence. Crafted by the early church, the creed was an attempt to summarize what the apostles preached about Jesus.

All three great streams must mutually recognize one another as fully Christian. Lack of full communion at the Lord's Supper between groups that uphold the one true gospel and share the Spirit is a scandal because it wrongly suggests that we are not fully brothers and sisters in the Christ. It contradicts Jesus's prayer for the church and radically compromises the church's mission (John 17:20–26). It also contradicts the apostle Paul's description of the Lord's Supper, which must *eliminate* divisions between Christians rather than *reinforce* them if it is to remain his actual supper (1 Cor. 11:17–22; cf. 10:17).

This is not to suggest that we should ignore important differences, false teachings, or the need for church discipline (i.e., biblically valid excommunication) within these streams as we work toward greater unity in the truth. Nor is it to suggest that unity must be hierarchical—that is, under the authority of the pope or some other governing body. (I am a Protestant for many reasons.) But it is to affirm that we agree about the one absolute essential and should be in communion. Catholics, Orthodox, and Protestants share the one true gospel and hence are all equally and fully Christian.

Bridge

Gospel Clarified—Gospel Mobilized

Bridges connect. If this book did not have one, it would be difficult to cross from the gospel-allegiance model in part 1 to its further development in part 2. While crossing this short bridge, you get a clarifying retrospective view of the gospel-allegiance model. But it is also forward looking, since the gospel-allegiance model will be more explicitly related to grace, faith, and works in part 2.

How must the gospel in our churches change? We must present the complete gospel—not just the death and resurrection bits of it—while relocating the whole within its true Jesus-is-king framework. We need to sharpen our ability to distinguish the gospel itself from its purpose, the required response, the benefits it brings, and its backdrop. We also need to show how these are different but interrelated. These distinctions hint at how saving allegiance can require good works without violating grace—all of which might assist Protestant-Catholic dialogue.

You've already started across, so don't stop. Because not only does this bridge make theological connections, it also helps the church advance its practical mission. It mobilizes the gospel. This bridge distinguishes the gospel proper from closely related concepts in order to facilitate better evangelism, discipleship, teaching, and preaching.

The gospel itself. Although the exact gospel proclamation varies in the Bible, its main lines can be detected securely. Ten distinct events are repeatedly mentioned, describing how Jesus became the saving king.

The gospel is that Jesus the king

1. preexisted as God the Son,
2. was sent by the Father,
3. took on human flesh in fulfillment of God's promises to David,
4. died for our sins in accordance with the Scriptures,
5. was buried,
6. was raised on the third day in accordance with the Scriptures,
7. appeared to many witnesses,
8. *is enthroned at the right hand of God as the ruling Christ*,
9. has sent the Holy Spirit to his people to effect his rule, and
10. will come again as final judge to rule.

Gospel purpose. The purpose of the gospel is saving allegiance to Jesus the king in all the nations. This was discussed extensively in chapter 2.

Required response. What response to the gospel is required for salvation? Allegiance alone. This is expressed in terms of repentance from sins, trusting allegiance (*pistis*) to him as the king described in the message of the gospel, and baptism. Repentance is best understood as turning away from other allegiances to give unique loyalty to Jesus as king. Baptism is best construed as the premier initial way to confess and embody allegiance to Jesus as king. Allegiance includes good deeds as empowered by the Holy Spirit (see chaps. 5–6). This is why it is accurate to say that salvation is by allegiance alone. Thus, the required response to the gospel and its chief purpose are the same: allegiance. But, even though the response and purpose are the same, distinguishing between the two reminds us that gospel allegiance is for all nations and has implications for all creation, not merely for individuals.

Other allegiances. Yet salvation by allegiance alone does *not* mean that we owe Jesus exclusive allegiance. It means that we give Jesus our unique, highest, and unconditional allegiance and that there are no other factors that determine our salvation. The allegiance we are called to give to other things is conditional. This is why it is true, but too simple, to say that "Jesus is king, so Caesar is not." It is true because we dare not think that the gospel is apolitical or nonsocial. Jesus is the king over these spheres of life and all others. As his citizens, we enact his kingdom principles no matter what governmental structure is in place. We can certainly never worship Caesar or his non-Jesus ways.

But to say that "Jesus is king, so Caesar is not" is at the same time too simple. Our allegiance to Jesus might in fact call us to support Caesar—as when we pay taxes (Rom. 13:6–7), pray for government leaders (1 Tim. 2:1–4), and live an orderly life amid non-Christians under the government's partial authority (Rom. 13:1; Titus 3:1; 1 Pet. 2:13–14). On the other hand, gospel allegiance might compel us to actively resist Caesar and his policies (Rev. 2:10–11, 13; 14:8–12; cf. Exod. 1–3). Jesus as the King of kings receives our *unconditional* allegiance. Mere earthly kings and governmental leaders receive our *qualified* allegiance, as long as it is not in conflict with our allegiance to the true king. Beyond government, we also must sort out how allegiance to family, employers, friends, and colleagues can all be ordered appropriately under allegiance to Jesus (see appendix 2 for activities).

Gospel benefits. In terms of final salvation, the gospel proper contains *potential* benefits, but not their realization. Only those who respond to the gospel by giving allegiance actualize the *special* benefits. These special benefits of final salvation are too numerous to mention, but they include forgiveness of sins, righteousness (justification), reconciliation, redemption, adoption, and glory. The gospel is also attended by *general* benefits—physical healings, assistance to the poor, and overall sociopolitical good—that are available even to the nonallegiant (e.g., Luke 4:18–19). These should not be confused with the special benefits of final salvation. Individually the special saving benefits are only received personally when we give allegiance and receive the Holy Spirit, as this unites us to others who have given allegiance and possess these benefits. The special benefits of the gospel belong only to the true church, but they and the general benefits have sociopolitical implications for all creation.

Gospel backdrop. The gospel assumes the Old Testament story as its backdrop. This includes creation, human disobedience with cosmic consequences, the promises to the patriarchs, the exodus, the giving of the law, entrance into the promised land, exile due to disobedience, and a return to the land. The backdrop places special emphasis on God's promises to Israel via the covenants with Abraham and David. But all of these background stories are not the gospel; rather, only their fulfillment in the saving career of Jesus is the gospel. The gospel is "promised in advance" (Rom. 1:2 AT), and the substitutionary death and then resurrection of the Messiah are said to "accord" with the Old Testament Scriptures (1 Cor. 15:3–5). The gospel should not be confused with the entire biblical story. It is good news that the stories and images in the Old Testament have reached a climax: Jesus is the saving king.

At this stage of the book, we've undertaken a reappraisal of the gospel and its allegiance requirements. I've attempted to show why standard ways of describing the gospel need to change. But faith as saving allegiance also raises challenging theological and practical questions. The next portion of the book seeks to show how grace and the gospel fit together within an allegiance model without falling into the error of thinking salvation can be earned by human effort or achievement. *Soli Deo gloria.*

PART 2

Advancing Gospel Allegiance

4

Grace in Six Dimensions

Philip Yancey, author of *What's So Amazing about Grace?*, was asked if anything recently had made him laugh aloud at God's grace. He told the following remarkable story:

> I met my friend Tom, whom I hadn't seen in fifteen years. Tom was a hard-drinking, lovable partygoer who stopped going to church soon after college. Last year his live-in girlfriend decided she wanted to attend church because of some crisis she was going through. Tom reluctantly agreed. That morning he sat down and started playing his guitar. Thinking of church, he resurrected three hymns from his distant memory. "Those are beautiful—what's the music?" his girlfriend asked. Tom explained the words to the hymns.
>
> They chose a church out of the phone book, and to Tom's utter astonishment, that Sunday the congregation sang all three of those hymns. It so rattled Tom that he completely turned his life around. Listening to him tell the story, I couldn't help laughing in surprised joy. I have a memory of Tom so drunk that he fell over while trying to roll a ball down a bowling alley. . . . Was that a miracle? It was certainly grace.[1]

Yancey calls this a story about grace. Why not a story about God's love? Or mercy? Or transforming power? All of these other dimensions are present, but I think we'll all agree that Yancey is right. Grace is the best rubric. We all have a sense of what grace involves, even if we struggle to offer a theological definition.

Tom didn't deserve grace. One facet of grace is its unmerited quality. His girlfriend's sudden desire to drag him to church was an undeserved gift from God. It conjured up memories of three hymns he used to sing. If only one of those hymns had been reprised at church, it would have been a rich gift. Two is absurdly lavish. We can only laugh with astonishment at a third. And yet, even while shaking our heads with wonder, Christians know that *the ridiculous* frequently characterizes God's grace.

Grace is not simply an important Christian doctrine. It is the hallmark of the Christian story's gospel climax. Our understanding of grace largely determines our theology of salvation. This chapter seeks both to enrich our understanding of grace and to correct misunderstandings by looking at the biblical evidence from six directions.

Grace Problems

There is disarray in popular Christian teaching and preaching about grace. The most blatant error is made by advocates of the free-grace movement—for example, Zane Hodges, Charles Ryrie, Chuck Swindoll, and Earl Radmacher, some of whom are deceased but whose teachings live on. These all teach that for grace to remain grace, behavior cannot factor into salvation at all.[2] Eternal salvation is reducible to believing or trusting that Jesus died for your sins. It does not depend on repentance from ongoing sins or obedience to Jesus the king. Repentance, in that system, merely means changing your mind about Jesus and trusting him to save you personally.

Free-gracers do not describe either the gospel or faith (*pistis*) accurately. For them, Jesus's death for sins is the entire gospel, so all that matters is believing or trusting that his death is effective. The free-grace position is roundly rejected by scholars today, certainly in part because of its naive view of linguistics.[3] At the popular level the free-grace position was combated by John MacArthur's lordship salvation. The free-grace position continues to decline, although it holds a firm purchase even still in some churches and circles.[4]

Meanwhile, beyond the free-grace error and its corrective lordship salvation, more subtle misconceptions about grace are widespread. Popular books by John Piper and R. C. Sproul, among others, also speak about grace in ways that lack biblical support. *Gospel allegiance* could provide a new path forward for the church by showing how faith (*pistis*) can include good works without violating grace.

Saving grace, far from an abstract idea in the New Testament, is thoroughly determined by the Christ events that constitute the gospel. *Saving grace is a specific, multidimensional gift with boundaries.* Saving grace is extensive, benevolent, and timely. It is unmerited and effective but not infinitely so. It also requires reciprocation. Salvation by allegiance alone is not a violation of grace because a gift or a grace must be accepted with a return gift. For Paul allegiance is the return gift that validates saving grace, the gospel, and allows its benefits to flow. To fail to give allegiance is to reject saving grace, the gospel, the particular gift that God chose to give us.

The Gospel Is Saving Grace

The gospel itself is God's saving grace. In Acts, Paul knows imprisonment looms in his near future as he journeys toward Jerusalem. He gathers the Ephesian elders and makes a speech: "I do not account my life of any value nor as precious to myself, if only I may finish my course and the ministry that I received from the Lord Jesus, to testify to *the gospel of the grace of God*" (Acts 20:24). The gospel is grace (*charis*), a specific gift from God.

I am trying to head off the idea that the Bible mainly treats saving grace as an abstract idea to be believed within a salvation culture, as if the gospel were God's system for how we get saved.

In this system, grace is, in the words of Carl Trueman, "the unmerited favor of God" and "the active outworking of God's unmerited favor in the life of the church and of the believer."[5] For Trueman and others, grace is mainly a *general concept* or *principle* that God gives to some of us beyond what we deserve.

When grace as a general concept is used to create a salvation system, something like the following narrative results: God wants to help certain chosen individuals attain eternal life. These individuals have been selected by divine decree for salvation long before they could do anything good or bad—before creation itself. As R. C. Sproul puts it:

> From all eternity God decided to save some members of the human race and to let the rest of the human race perish. God made a choice—he chose some individuals to be saved unto everlasting blessedness in heaven, and he chose others to pass over, allowing them to suffer the consequences of their own sins, eternal punishment in hell.[6]

These individuals were selected not because God foresaw any future goodness in them—or even because they would in the future have faith—but purely on the basis of God's inscrutable decree to save some and damn others. Nobody merits salvation—past, present, or future—for this would violate grace. These individuals cannot save themselves via good works but can only trust in Jesus the Savior. God graciously causes them to trust (which was inevitable since they were chosen by grace before time began) and then graciously makes them persevere unto final glory.

This narrative can be capably defended from Scripture by using philosophy. It may even be the truest way to speak about salvation. But from a biblical vantage point it involves questionable assumptions. Grace has been treated as a general principle by which God prefers to operate, but this is imprecise. When we treat saving grace as an abstract idea about God's consistent desire to act first or assist the undeserving, grace becomes putty that can be molded to fit to any moment in the salvation story—even if this is not how the Bible prefers to speak about it. We must let the Bible itself define saving grace more thoroughly.

In the Bible, "grace" (*charis*) can intend winsomeness or charm (Luke 4:22; Col. 4:6). It can mean favor toward, especially God's favor toward us (Rom. 5:15) or the resulting state (Rom. 5:2). It can also be a benefit received (Eph. 4:7) or transmitted to another (Eph. 4:29). Or it can intend gratitude (1 Cor. 10:30). It also was a greeting (Rom. 1:7; 1 Cor. 1:3).[7] Yet such categories do not deal adequately with saving grace as *the gospel gift given at a particular time in history*. Saving grace is gospel specific.

Paul is the great theologian of grace. Paul, when discussing human salvation, does not speak of *grace* as if *any* generic gift might be in view. The gospel is grace. Paul equates a turning from "the one who called you in *the grace of the Messiah*" with a turning to "a different *gospel*" (Gal. 1:6 AT). The good news of the king is the grace. The specific saving events of the gospel are *the definitive grace gift*, and thus references to saving grace in the New Testament tend to be specifically gospel-shaped, not generic.

Saving grace is often a way of describing the Christ events that constitute the gospel. For example, Paul identifies the gospel with "the grace of God" (Col. 1:6). And when Paul speaks of being "justified by his grace as a gift, through the redemption that is in Christ Jesus" (Rom. 3:24), grace is defined by specific Christ events. Proclamation of God's word, his gospel message, can be described as the "word of his grace" (Acts 14:3; 20:32). As John Barclay puts it, "This self-giving of Christ, 'the Christ-gift,' is an event."[8] Saving grace is Messiah-shaped and inextricably linked to the gospel. God's grace is saving through the very specific gospel process by which Jesus became king and is now ruling. *Saving grace is gospel defined.*

Six Dimensions of Grace

In his celebrated book *Paul and the Gift*, John Barclay disentangles six facets of grace. These six different ideas about grace have caused interpreters of the Bible to misunderstand and talk past one another. Many but not all of the Bible's ideas about grace align with those of the ancient and modern world. The six dimensions of grace are (1) merit, (2) size, (3) desire to benefit, (4) timing, (5) effectiveness, and (6) return-gifting.[9] Each will be explained and practically illustrated in what follows.

Because of our strong affection for grace, there has been a tendency throughout church history to extend each of these six dimensions of grace in our favor. Yet we've done this sometimes even more than the Bible itself does. We think, surely God must maximize grace to us in every conceivable way! But this is not true. In the end we must try to discover to what degree the Bible minimizes or maximizes each of these six dimensions of grace and adjust our understanding of salvation accordingly.

Merit

Let's say that while in school you are supplementing your finances by working at Tony's Fresh-Tossed Pizza. At Tony's you hand toss pizzas in front of customers in order to wow them with the quality. Your boss pays you every two weeks. She is legally required to pay you for the work you've performed, so this is not surprising.

A month ago you broke your wrist playing basketball with friends. You had to take a leave of absence from work without pay. You check the mail expecting to find more bills. Instead you are shocked to discover that your boss has just sent you a month's salary! She didn't owe it to you. You did nothing to deserve it. In fact, quite the opposite because you had been foolish to play basketball since you knew you could get hurt. This is what we mean by *unmerited* grace.

Everyone Agrees Grace Is Unmerited

The New Testament most emphasizes the *merit* dimension of grace. Saving grace is undeserved or unmerited. There is a lack of congruity between what we get and what we deserve.[10] As Paul puts it, "Now to the one who works, his wages are not credited according to *grace* but as an obligation. Yet to the one who does not work but *trusts* [*places pistis*] on him who justifies the ungodly, his faith [*pistis*] is counted as righteousness" (Rom. 4:4–5 AT). Grace is wages without work.

An *undeserved gift* is what nearly all contemporary theologians intend by grace. Louis Berkhof calls grace "the unmerited operation of God in the heart of man, effected through the agency of the Holy Spirit."[11] Whatever else grace might be, everyone agrees that it is *unmerited*.

Everyone Agrees Except the Ancients

Now for the surprise. While the New Testament generally teaches that grace is unmerited, this was highly unusual in the broader ancient world. *Merited* rather than unmerited grace was the "default assumption" in antiquity.[12] Although Jesus and Paul disagreed with them, their contemporaries thought a gift, a grace, should be given only to *the deserving*. For example, first-century Jewish philosopher Philo understands God's words, "I will be gracious to whom I will be gracious" (Exod. 33:19), to mean "I *give what is fitting* to the recipient, so to one who is *worthy of the grace*, I extend all that he is capable of receiving."[13] In other words, for Philo, God gives grace only to those who have proven themselves worthy of it. The surprise is that norms about grace in the New Testament era are nearly the opposite of today's. The ancients believed grace could only be *earned*. We tend to believe that grace can only be grace if it is *unearned*!

Merited Grace Today

As the surprise wears off, upon further reflection we can conclude that like the ancients, our own gift-giving often considers the worth of the recipient. You do not buy a four-year-old professional-quality art supplies. She will destroy the fine-tipped pens, blunt the brushes, and dump the paint on your favorite sofa.

You deem an aspiring fourteen-year-old artist worthy of such a fine gift. Many Christians do not give money directly to beggars, concluding that they will use it for drugs or alcohol. Homeless shelters deserve the gift. If we do not consider the merit or worth of the recipient to be part of grace today, this is because we treat grace as an abstract idea or general principle, disassociating it from the specific gifts (or graces) we actually give.

The Grace Revolution

How did the definition of grace change so that our sentiments about grace today are nearly the reverse of antiquity's? The answer, in short, is the triumph of Christianity—especially Jesus's teachings and Paul's theology.

Jesus had much to say about unmerited grace. "Give to the one who begs from you, and do not refuse the one who would borrow from you" (Matt. 5:42). "You received without paying; give without pay" (Matt. 10:8). In his parable about the unjust wages, in which some laborers receive more than they deserve, Jesus speaks about unmerited grace: "I want to give the one hired last the same as you" (Matt. 20:14 AT). Jesus says to invite the poor when giving a feast, "and you will be blessed, because they cannot repay you. For you will be repaid at the resurrection of the just" (Luke 14:14).

Jesus and the apostles generally extended grace to the undeserving, but they at times considered whether grace was merited. James says, "God opposes the proud but gives grace to the humble" (4:6). For James grace is not totally unmerited. The humble *deserve* God's grace. Moreover, Jesus and the apostles at times consider whether an individual or group *deserves* to hear the saving gospel (Acts 10:22–23) or to continue hearing it (Luke 10:10–11; Acts 13:46; 18:6). The unworthy do not get to hear the gospel, which is God's saving grace. Merit is also evaluated prior to healing (Luke 7:4–6; Acts 9:36–41). Even still, Jesus's ideas about grace as largely unmerited were unusual for his age. He launched a grace revolution that would be furthered by his apostles, especially Paul.

Like Jesus, Paul generally considers saving grace as unmerited. But not always. For example, he believes that he "received mercy" and that "the grace of our Lord overflowed" because he "acted ignorantly in unbelief" rather than intentionally in persecuting the church (1 Tim. 1:13–14). Paul felt that *the enhanced quality of his prior actions* affected God's grace at least a little in choosing him. For Paul, unintentional sin is better than intentional, and this affected God's choice to extend grace to him, even though he regarded himself a premier sinner nevertheless (1:15). Still, unmerited grace is strongly characteristic of Paul's teachings overall.

Unmerited, Specific Grace in Paul

Saving grace as unmerited is so widespread in Paul's theology that just a few among the many examples can illustrate:

> So too at the present time there is a remnant, chosen by grace. Now if it is by grace, it is no longer by works, since grace would no longer be grace. (Rom. 11:5–6 AT)

> I do not nullify the grace of God, for if righteousness were through the law, then Christ died for no purpose. (Gal. 2:21)

> Even when we were dead in our trespasses, [God] made us alive together with Christ—by grace you have been saved. (Eph. 2:5)

> [God] who saved us and called us to a holy calling, not according to our works but according to his own purpose and grace, which he gave us in the Christ, Jesus, before the ages began . . . (2 Tim. 1:9 AT)

Humans can do nothing to deserve this gospel-grace. Paul's conviction was that God's grace to humanity as a whole *in the specific gospel events* was unmerited.

A Specific Triumph Abstracted

Since Paul's time, saving grace moved from the specific to the general or abstract. The triumph of the heart of Paul's theology, *the specific gospel-grace for the undeserving*, reconfigured ancient ideas about grace so successfully in Western civilization that grace became abstracted away from the precise details of the Christ events that constitute the gospel. The result was that saving grace's gospel specificity faded from view while absolutely unmerited favor *in general* became the normal understanding. This abstraction persists today—in academic theology, among pastors, in the church, and in popular culture.

We need to recover grace's gospel specificity if we are going to stay true to the Bible's vision of salvation. We absolutely must keep emphasizing that the Christ-gift, the gospel, was given by God without regard to universal human merit or worth. Yet Paul promotes unmerited grace using the same strategy in all four passages cited above: by contrasting it with works or the law. This hints that there is more to say. Paul's specific historical context informed his theology of unmerited gospel-grace.

The relationship between unmerited grace and works of the law raises many questions. Did Paul have in view collective or individual worth? Did he oppose all works because he felt that no good deeds at all could be saving? Or was Paul more concerned with certain Jewish works of the law—like circumcision and a kosher table? How does this relate to boasting? This chapter will continue to view grace from multiple angles, so that we are in a stronger position to tackle such questions in chapter 6.

Size

We can separate grace's merit from its size. How would you feel if someone gave you a necklace made of copper? Of pure gold? What about a whole mountain of jewelry and gold? Whether you deserve it is not the question. Only the magnitude of the gift matters. This is what we mean when we speak about the *size* as an aspect of grace that can be measured independently of merit. All Christians agree that the gospel gift is enormous. How big is it?

Larger Than Adam's Trespass

The Bible emphasizes the size of God's grace by occasionally describing (and everywhere presupposing) the extent of the Christ events. Adam's trespass had a universal effect on all humanity—death—as well as decaying cosmic consequences for all creation (see Rom. 8:20–21). But grace *abounded* even more (Rom. 5:15). The extraordinary size of the Christ-gift makes Adam's transgression look pale in comparison:

> And the free gift is not like the result of that one man's sin. For the judgment following one trespass brought condemnation, *but the free gift following many trespasses brought justification.* For if, because of one man's trespass, death reigned through that one man, *much more will those who receive the abundance of grace and the free gift of righteousness* reign in life through the one man Jesus Christ. (Rom. 5:16–17)

The specific grace of the gospel is abundant. Despite the vast extent of the many trespasses, the Christ-gift is so large that it overwhelms with its justifying power.

Still Growing

Another example illustrating the size of grace is especially pertinent to gospel allegiance. Paul takes the Messiah to be the speaker of the psalmist's words, "I had trusting loyalty (*episteusa*), therefore I spoke" (2 Cor. 4:13 AT, citing Ps. 116:10; see chap. 5 for further discussion). Here Paul tells of the Christ's fidelity and his speech in calling on God for rescue. Since God delivered him, God will deliver us too when we follow the Christ's pattern (v. 14). When we enter into the Christ pattern (trusting loyalty that cries for deliverance, leading to life-giving rescue), the result is that grace grows: "For all this is for your sake, in order that as *grace expands to more and more people*, thanksgiving will increase, to the glory of God" (2 Cor. 4:15 AT). Paul defines grace in gospel-laden terms, indicating that grace increases as the pattern established by the Christ events is lived out. Grace is already enormous and getting larger.

Saving grace is growing. If we were to treat saving grace as a mere general principle—God always acts first in moving his elect along the road to personal salvation—it is hard to understand how it could be increasing in size. (If chosen before creation, the number of elect cannot grow.) Yet if, as the Bible indicates, the *specific* saving grace is the gospel, this makes sense. More and more people are embracing the gospel by giving allegiance, thus grace is expanding. Saving grace is increasing in size because it is inextricably linked with the gospel's purpose: the allegiance of the nations.

All Christians agree that the Christ-gift is large in size and extravagant beyond our wildest dreams. It gives unworthy humans eternal life in the presence of God.

Desire to Benefit

A third facet of grace is the *desire to benefit*. If desire to benefit is maximized, then a gift intends absolute benevolence to the recipient. There is no sordid motive. Barclay calls this the *singularity* of grace, meaning purely good intentions. Here *motive* looms large.

What if you were to receive a beautiful birthday present, a lustrously wrapped box with a shiny red bow on top? You are excited. You open it. The trigger your enemy wired to the flap turns the present into a dangerous fireball. A good gift? No! It's awful even to imagine. But a complete minimization, a total *lack* of desire to benefit in grace looks like that.

Grace could be extended with mixed or dishonorable intent. A man might take a woman out on a date, pay for everything—dinner, wine, the cute scarf in the shop, entertainment. All of these are unmerited graces freely given. Perhaps he is trying to win her heart for the honorable intent of marriage. Or perhaps he is trying to cultivate a feeling of obligation so that she is more likely to give sexual favors later that evening. Even good gifts are not always given in order to maximize the benefit to the recipient.

Limits to God's Desire to Benefit

As we ponder the benevolence of God's grace, we immediately tend to assume that God must *entirely will the good* for us in the Christ-gift. Does not God's perfection demand that he have only the best motives in sending Jesus as the Messiah for us? But the matter is not clear-cut. For the king-gift also holds the threat of judgment for disobedient humanity. Moreover, the Christ-gift can be perverted or received in an unproductive fashion.

Grace includes condemnation of the wicked. As part of the specific saving grace God has opted to give, the gospel, God has appointed Jesus the king to exercise end-times judgment. The day is coming, Paul reminds us, "when, with regard to my gospel, God will judge the secrets of humans by the Messiah, Jesus" (Rom. 2:16 AT). This includes the condemnation of the wicked. From the vantage point of the wicked, the specific kingly grace God has chosen is not benevolent but frightening.

Grace can be perverted. God's grace is capable of corruption by those who regard it as a license to sin all the more:

> What shall we say then? Are we *to continue in sin that grace may abound*? (Rom. 6:1)

> For certain people have crept in unnoticed who long ago were designated for this condemnation, ungodly people, *who pervert the grace of our God* into sensuality and deny our only Master and Lord, Jesus Christ. (Jude 4)

Grace can be corrupted. If God entirely wills the good in his grace, why did God not make it incorruptible? Perhaps God's very nature as a noncoercive lover demands that the grace he extends be capable of perversion. Certainty eludes us. Regardless, the Bible is clear that God's grace can be twisted.

Grace can be received in vain. There is another reason to challenge grace's complete and entire benevolence. God's grace can be extended and yet fail to be received:

> Working together with him, then, we appeal to you *not to receive the grace of God in vain.* For he says, "In a favorable time I listened to you, and in a day of salvation I have helped you." Behold, now is the favorable time; behold, now is the day of salvation. (2 Cor. 6:1–2)

Apparently, there are some who can receive the grace of God in an empty fashion (cf. 1 Cor. 15:10). Ultimately certain individuals reject God's specific saving grace, the gospel. They do not heed the clarion call to participate in God's salvation in Jesus the king. The specific Christ-grace is not infinitely fruitful and hence not universally benevolent in that way. Not only is non-receipt of grace a threat to the wicked, Paul and others say that those who once received the Christ-gift can fall away from it:

> You are severed from Christ, you who would be justified by the law; you have *fallen away from grace.* (Gal. 5:4)

> For if we go on sinning deliberately *after receiving the knowledge of the truth*, there no longer remains a sacrifice for sins, but a fearful expectation of judgment, and a fury of fire that will consume the adversaries. Anyone who has set aside the law of Moses dies without mercy on the evidence of two or three witnesses. How much worse punishment, do you think, will be deserved by the one who has trampled underfoot the Son of God, and has profaned the blood of the covenant by which he was sanctified, and has *outraged the Spirit of grace*? For we know him who said, "Vengeance is mine; I will repay." (Heb. 10:26–30)

Even those who have received grace can find that it is not productive. Whether this actually involves loss of salvation is a matter of dispute and beyond this book's scope.

The Bible is clear that the specific saving grace God chose to give—the gospel—is not maximally benevolent in every way. Interpreters who have tried to avoid this conclusion end up in the wrong place. To preserve the absolute benevolence of God's grace, they suggest that the God of the Old Testament is entirely different from the God of the New (e.g., Marcion). Or that God is Christ-like (true!) and therefore does not (or will not) actively punish the wicked (untrue!).[14]

How much, then, does the Bible support the *desire to benefit* of God's grace? It is best to say this: God's plan in the Christ is as maximally benevolent as it could have been given the constraints of God's unchanging nature and how this informs his desire to save his creatures through the gospel. But grace can be received in vain or perverted. So the benevolence of God's grace does *not* entail universal salvation, failure to punish the wicked, or grace's incorruptibility. Christians should agree that even though God's grace is unbelievably kind, it is not maximized in these ways.

Timing

Your son will eventually head to college. You want to buy him a car. You could buy it far in advance—right now even. But the car will rust and depreciate in the meantime. Maybe you should surprise him and buy it the very day he leaves? But waiting is risky, because he may buy a lesser car before that. What's the best timing? Before he is even born? Now? In five years? We all might answer differently while agreeing that if a gift is going to be great *the timing matters*. Timing is our fourth dimension of grace.

When Did Grace Begin?

When did grace first appear? If we treat grace as a general concept in a salvation system, we can answer that it has always been present. For God as creator and provider has necessarily acted in generous ways toward us again and again for us to exist and to be sustained (1 Cor. 4:7; James 1:17). All Christians agree that God's *general grace* extends to everyone in this fashion. At the very least, personal faith (*pistis*) must be construed as a gift within the bounds of God's providential grace. Let's be clear: faith (or allegiance) is certainly a gift from God. But this is not what most theologians intend when discussing eternal salvation. A special *saving grace* is in view.

Saving grace's timing for the individual is disputed. The majority of Christians—Catholics, Orthodox, and most Protestants—agree that it is individualized for the first time when a specific person expresses "faith" in Jesus or is baptized. Meanwhile a minority of Protestants think that grace demands that God's agency must always precede or take primacy over each individual's agency in every step of personal salvation. So even though God acted in history to bring about the gospel, God graciously chose individuals in eternity past and must act in grace to regenerate each individual who is predestined to be "saved" before that person can express faith.

For our purposes, let's allow that either view might be correct. This will permit us to better develop the core gospel-allegiance model, because if we were to choose one side over the other, the result would be less firm. At the same time, given that some believe God's prior saving grace for the individual is self-evidently biblical, it is prudent to show why it is not clear-cut.

Individual versus Collective Grace

God's prior choice to save or condemn specific individuals eternally is a matter of speculation. It may or may not be true. The primary reason for uncertainty is the Bible's use of group language.

A favorite prooftext for God's election of specific individuals before creation is Ephesians 1:4–5: "God chose us in the Messiah before the foundation of the world, that we should be holy and blameless before him, having predestined us for adoption unto himself through Jesus the Messiah" (AT). John Piper and R. C. Sproul, for example, both cite it in support of individual predestination.[15] The problem is that this text and others like it do not prove that *individuals* were chosen for eternal life before time began. It proves that God chose *the church collectively in the king* before time began. But this choosing does not necessarily pertain to individuals. For Paul is speaking about the church, not individuals.

Imagine that you receive the following letter from your pastor, addressed to your entire church:

> From Pastor Joe. To the church in Quincy. Greetings. May God's name be blessed. *We* have received a million-dollar gift, including a down payment. So *we* know the rest is guaranteed. How are *you* going to spend it? I want *you* to pray about it!

Since the letter is addressed to a *group*, its language can be applied to particular individuals within the group only with extreme caution. Regarding the "you," Pastor Joe wants each person to pray about this matter individually, but each person does not get to spend the money. If I were to misread this letter by individuating all of it, I might incorrectly think that I personally can use the money to buy myself a new car. But that is not the intent. The money belongs to you *collectively*, the church in Quincy. It does not belong to me or you *individually*.

Moreover, we cannot assume that the specific individuals who constitute the church in Quincy will remain static over time. If I am presently a member but quit attending, then I will not receive the benefits of the money. I will no longer be part of the group addressed by the letter. The gift to the church as a whole is secure, as the deposit guaranteeing what is to come for the group has already been paid out. But the identity of the *us* and *you* that makes up the church might change.

Paul's letter to the Ephesians, like Pastor Joe's letter, is addressed to a group. If one believes that Paul or others intended to individuate group language, that must be argued. There are mechanisms in Greek that Paul uses when he wants to stress individuation—like "each one [singular] of you [plural]" (e.g., 1 Cor. 1:12; 1 Thess.

2:12; 4:4). But Paul opts not to use this language in Ephesians 1:1–14. Nor is individuation overtly in view in other passages that are popularly used to support individual predestination for salvation, such as Romans 8:29–31 and 2 Timothy 1:9.

In fact, there is not a single passage in the Bible that explicitly affirms that specific individuals (apart from God's Son) have been chosen *before creation* for either eternal life or eternal damnation. There are a few passages that affirm that God appoints individuals for salvation at an *unspecified time* (John 6:44, 65; cf. Acts 13:48)—this could be prior to or simultaneous with the individual's "faith" decision—but none of the passages extend that choosing to before time began. God's agency in personal salvation certainly must be acknowledged as valid on the basis of several verses (e.g., God "cleansed their hearts by faith," Acts 15:9). But much more frequently Scripture describes human agency in initiating the saving *pistis* action (e.g., John 1:12; 3:16; Acts 4:4; 8:12–13; Rom. 1:16; Eph. 1:13). So active human agency regarding faith must be emphasized too. All affirmations of the primacy of God's agency in *individual* salvation—for example, "no one can come to me unless the Father who sent me draws him" (John 6:44)—must be harmonized with passages that affirm that postascension Jesus now draws *all* to himself (John 12:32). He died for *all* (John 1:29; Rom. 6:10; 2 Cor. 5:14–15; 1 Tim. 2:6; Heb. 2:9; 1 John 2:2). When we synthesize what the Bible teaches about personal salvation, we must respect the whole biblical witness regarding the timing and coordination of God's agency with respect to personal human agency.

When Scripture speaks elsewhere of singular individuals, the choosing pertains to God's call for that person to play a special role within God's plan—Pharaoh (Rom. 9:17), Judas (John 13:18), Paul (Gal. 1:15). This vocational choosing is not described as an *eternal* choosing, although sometimes it does relate to God's overarching plan and that individual's salvation or loss (e.g., for Judas, see John 17:12; Acts 1:25). Not only is vocation rather than eternal fate emphasized when God chooses individuals; sometimes a chosen individual explicitly represents a group, making claims about personal predestination even more hazardous (e.g., Jacob and Esau in Rom. 9:10–13).[16]

The best biblical theologies of salvation recognize that in eternity past God chose the Son, the Messiah, for salvation—as well as all who are found to be in him. This choice is irrevocable, and the down payment of the Holy Spirit has already been given to the church as a corporate body (Rom. 8:16; 2 Cor. 1:22; 5:5; Eph. 1:13–14), a collective body in which individuals participate (1 Cor. 12:27). And yet the boundaries of the group may or may not be porous.

In sum, the Bible does not explicitly teach that the advance timing of God's grace includes God's predestining choice to either save or damn specific individuals. Some passages indicate God's sovereignty over personal salvation, but it is more characteristic of the Bible to stress the human need to give *pistis* to the Christ-king (e.g., John 20:31; Acts 11:17; 16:31; Rom. 10:9–10). In our preaching and teaching we too should mirror the Bible's emphasis on the necessity of giving allegiance to Jesus the king. Yet the question of grace's timing for personal salvation is best left aside in an initial articulation of the gospel-allegiance model.

At the Christ Event Time

A more grounded answer regarding the timing of God's saving grace would be that it appeared for humanity collectively when the gospel events happened historically. When Paul speaks about the timing of grace, he has the gospel in view: "For *the grace of God has appeared*, bringing salvation for all people, training us to renounce ungodliness and worldly passions, and to live self-controlled, upright, and godly lives in the present age" (Titus 2:11–12). Paul is not speaking of grace's appearance as an abstract principle, but of the arrival of the Christ events that constitute the gospel.

The timing of the saving grace of God is bound up with the gospel. Saving allegiance was finally revealed only with the coming of the king (Gal. 3:22–27). Paul speaks about the timing of the

Christ events as follows: "But *when the fullness of time had come*, God sent forth his Son, having come into being by woman, having come into being under the law, to redeem those who were under the law, so that we might receive adoption as sons" (Gal. 4:4–5 AT; cf. 1 Tim. 2:5–6). God supplied the gospel when he deemed the time ripe. Jesus says much the same: "The time is fulfilled, and the kingdom of God is at hand; repent and believe in the gospel" (Mark 1:15). The grace revealed in the gospel is the power of God for salvation right now and in the future.

Above all, the Bible says that God gave the grace of the gospel to us at the optimal time with respect to our need. The Messiah died for us, the ungodly, "when we were still weak" (Rom. 5:6). We humans as a whole were "dead in our trespasses," undeserving, and powerless for salvation (Eph. 2:5). Saving grace (the gospel) was historically actualized when we were in need as a universal human group.

In sum, God's saving grace was granted to the church as a group in the Messiah before time, even before creation. God worked out this salvation history through his calling of Abraham and his seed. Grace appeared when we were in need as the events that constitute the gospel transpired. Models for God's sovereignty, especially with regard to individual salvation, must account for his love and freedom. Some may prefer to set God's saving grace for individuals in the eternal past, but because of group language this goes beyond what Scripture teaches with certainty.

Effectiveness

Since you're always cold, I give you a wool sweater for Christmas. But you are allergic. Or, let's say that I present to you a brand-new road bike for your commute. Yet you work on a boat in Alaska. Or, because you appreciate music, I purchase you a rare vinyl record. But you don't own a record player. All these gifts are nice, but none are *effective*. None achieve their intended purpose.

Effectiveness is different from the other angles of grace that we've explored. We are not assessing the *merit* of the gift or its *size*. Nor does this pertain to the *desire to benefit* or the *timing* of the gift. Gifts are usually given for a specific purpose. The effectiveness of grace concerns its ability to achieve its intended goals.

Is God's grace effective? Reflexively, those who know Jesus shout, "Yes!" We, and others whom we know and love, have personally been changed, so our hearts overflow with thanksgiving. "I was blind but now I see." We have such a rich experiential knowledge of God's saving grace that any conclusion to the contrary is impossible.

Scholars associated with the so-called apocalyptic school of Paul's theology speak effusively of grace as "*unconditional* actions by God that deliver salvation" or even of "militant grace"—grace so limitlessly effective that it does not even require human response.[17] Though it is prudent to affirm that God's grace is tremendously effective, we should have doubts when it is suggested that saving grace does not even require a human response for it to work. Grace's effectiveness has limits.

Individually Effective

I do not intend to question the efficacy of God's grace to transform the individual who remains in the Messiah. God does not leave individuals helpless in sin. We have died to sin if we are in the Messiah (Rom. 6:6–7). We are no longer ruled by it. God and the king, and their righteousness, rule instead (Rom. 6:11–14, 17–20). Indeed, *we are ruled by grace* (Rom. 5:21)! God's saving grace, the good news of Jesus the king, breaks sin's domination, allowing us to live new lives. Grace is perfectly effective for all those who abide in the Christ since we will be conformed to his image at the consummation of the ages (Rom. 8:29; 2 Cor. 3:18). But this is not the primary purpose of saving grace per se in Scripture. For the Bible emphasizes *group* more than *individual* salvation.

We can sharpen our way of speaking about grace's effectiveness by thinking about the boundaries that Scripture places around it. Consider that God's grace, though truly amazing, has not yet totally transformed us. We all still sin (1 John 1:8). Moreover, not everyone has been or will be changed by God's grace, so it is not universally effective for all humanity. And contrary to some incautious expressions that we hear today, the Bible indicates that for God's saving grace to be effective, humans must respond to it with repentance, faith/allegiance (*pistis*), and baptism.

Purpose Determines Grace's Effectiveness

How can we assess the true effectiveness of God's saving grace? We know in general that grace exists for the sake of salvation.[18] Just as with a sweater or a road bike, we cannot evaluate whether the specific gospel-grace is a good gift apart from considering its purpose in light of the recipient's need. If we want to learn how the Bible treats the effectiveness of grace, we need to inspect relevant purpose statements.

What is saving grace's principal purpose? After detailing the gospel, Paul says, "We received *grace* and apostleship *for the obedience of pistis in all the nations*" (Rom. 1:5 AT). Paul and the other apostles received *grace* for a specific reason. The purpose of saving grace is allegiance to Jesus the king.

Because grace's purpose is so closely associated with and defined by the specific Christ events of the gospel, we must measure its effectiveness according to that criterion. The question "How effective is God's saving grace?" becomes "How effective has the gospel been at bringing about allegiance to Jesus the king in every nation?" Thus, the most precise measure of saving grace's effectiveness is allegiance to Jesus the king in all the nations (cf. Rom. 16:26). Paul speaks similarly about grace and the gospel elsewhere:

> Of this *gospel* I was made a minister according to *the gift of God's grace*, which was given me by the working of his power. To me, though I am the very least of all the saints, this *grace* was given, *to preach to the Gentiles* the unsearchable riches of Christ, and *to*

> *bring to light for everyone* what is the plan of the mystery hidden for ages in God. (Eph. 3:7–9)

Again, the purpose of grace is to bring the nations under the banner of the king, to engender allegiance to the king in all the nations. This reveals the mistake of those who might make too much of the effectiveness of God's saving grace. Paul did not see God's specific saving grace as perfectly effective or irresistible, for his compatriots, his Jewish comrades, had by and large rejected the gospel when he proclaimed it (Acts 13:46; 18:5–6; 28:28). Although the word of God had not failed (Rom. 9:6), it had only succeeded in creating a remnant chosen by grace (Rom. 11:5–6). In the mysterious economy of God's mercy, all "Israel" will ultimately be saved in the Messiah (Rom. 11:26), but this is not all humanity. Even though saving grace, the gospel, has been extended to all humanity, it has not effectively succeeded in saving all humanity. Thus it is not maximally effective. Many past and present have rejected God's grace (Gal. 5:4; Heb. 10:29; 12:15; Jude 4).

From Poor to Wealthy Co-Rulers

Another statement about God's grace shows the degree to which it is defined by the gospel. In it we discover that grace is also purposed toward our co-reign alongside Jesus the king:

> For you know the grace of our Lord Jesus Christ, that though he was rich, yet for your sake he became poor, so that you by his poverty might become rich. (2 Cor. 8:9)

This poignant description of grace is also a description of the gospel, since it indirectly summarizes the specific Christ events that make up the full gospel.

God gave us gospel-grace so that by the king's willing acceptance of poverty, *we might become rich*. How will we who are in the Messiah become rich? Jesus was first rich when he was in glory alongside the Father. In his incarnation and death he became poor.

But he became rich once again when he returned to glory to reign (cf. Phil. 2:6–11). Context suggests that *we too will become rich* when we reign in glory alongside Jesus in the presence of God the Father. We already have the down payment by our participation in the Messiah. Here grace is purposed toward bringing about our kingly reign alongside Jesus in glory.

Paul elsewhere confirms that our co-reign with the Messiah is a key purpose of grace:

> [God] made us alive together with Christ—by grace you have been saved—and raised us up with him and *seated us with him in the heavenly places in Christ Jesus*, so that in the coming ages he might show the immeasurable riches of his grace in kindness toward us in Christ Jesus. (Eph. 2:5–7)

We are seated in the heavenly realms in the king—that is, in the very position from which he rules. Saving grace is purposed not only toward the allegiance of the nations but also toward the co-reign of the allegiant ones alongside their king in the resurrection age.

In sum, the effectiveness of saving grace must be assessed in light of the gospel's purpose. We should be quick to celebrate the gospel's power to ultimately transform all individuals who remain united to the king. But saving grace's effectiveness is primarily a corporate category in the Bible. Since some have not given allegiance to Jesus the king, saving grace's effectiveness is not maximized in the Bible. Wherever allegiance to Jesus allows the Spirit to dwell in the midst of God's people, there God's saving grace is maximally effective—and nowhere else.

Return-Gifting

The last aspect of grace, return-gifting, is the most important because it is the most misunderstood and has introduced the largest distortions in how theologians systematize salvation. In short, the receiver of a gift must reciprocate by giving a return gift in order for the original gift to be received.

A pure gift is a gift given freely, with no strings attached and no expectation or obligation to reciprocate in order to accept the gift. In our modern world we tend to idealize the pure gift as the best kind. Let's say a woman gives her boyfriend running shoes that he has been craving. We would think it unseemly if she were to condition her gift on his reciprocation. That is, if she were to think or indicate, "I'll only let him keep the shoes if he returns the favor by buying me the tennis racquet I want." As moderns we think it ill-fitting to give a gift if we are going to require a gift in return.

But nobody in the ancient world, including the biblical authors, felt that gifts should be pure or freely given so that reciprocation was unnecessary. Our contemporary values suggest that an ideal gift is noncircular, but this does not correspond to ancient values. They believed the opposite! A grace or a gift had to be reciprocated through a return gift. If not reciprocated, the receiver had rejected the gift.

John Barclay argues that the idea of a "pure gift" is a relatively recent invention that finds no root in the Bible or the ancient world. The pure gift, according to Barclay, became a prominent model in Western civilization only in the sixteenth century under the influence of new notions about what sovereign gift-giving should involve.[19] The pure gift became the ideal when certain kings felt that their absolute sovereignty demanded they give gifts without any concern for reciprocation. Not so in the Bible. *An initial gift required a return gift in order for that initial gift to be socially received.*

The return gift was not ordinarily an even exchange. For example, if I were a steward in the city of Corinth, such as the Christian named Erastus (Rom. 16:23; cf. Acts 19:22; 2 Tim. 4:20), I might grace the city by paving a portion of it. In return for my benefaction, I might expect the city of Corinth to erect a monument publicly thanking me. Just such an ancient inscription was found in 1929 in Corinth: "Erastus in return for his aedileship [elected office] paved it at his own expense." If the Corinthians had refused to erect this monument, Erastus as the benefactor could have withheld the gift or subsequently ripped out the pavement. This would have been deemed normal prudence in the ancient world. Failure to reciprocate meant the grace had been spurned. In the ancient world, if a gift is given, some sort of return gift *must* be given. If not, it sends a social signal that the initial gift has been rejected.

Grace required a reciprocating response. It is nearly impossible to overestimate the importance of this for understanding the Bible's view of salvation. For God's specific grace (the gospel) to be accepted, a return gift was necessary. What is this return gift? The Bible's consistent answer is *pistis*, embodied loyalty to Jesus the king. This is why the New Testament can without contradiction recognize *pistis* as the only acceptable saving response to Jesus the king (e.g., Rom. 1:17; 3:21–26; 4:5; 5:1; Gal. 2:16; 3:26) and at the same time speak of the necessity of obedience and performing works that accord with God's commands for eternal life (e.g., John 3:36; Rom. 2:6–16; 2 Cor. 5:10; Gal. 5:21; 2 Thess. 1:8; Heb. 5:9; 1 Pet. 4:17).

In antiquity, grace could be unmerited and still require bodily reciprocation. Merit and reciprocation are separate dimensions of grace, emphasized in different degrees by various ancient authors. When we fail to differentiate these, pretending that unmerited grace cannot be considered grace at all if it requires behavioral reciprocation (including good deeds of allegiance; see chap. 6), we have failed to understand grace as the Bible presents it.

This is precisely what has happened in the free-grace movement. Consider Zane Hodges: "Nothing can be by grace and by works at the same time. They are mutually exclusive. . . . If God accepts us by grace it cannot have anything to do with works of any kind."[20] Hodges has treated grace as if it were a pure gift, but this is not how grace was understood in the Bible or in the ancient world.

The free-grace movement is plagued by numerous errors. It promotes *false grace* because it fails to see that Paul, like his contemporaries, believed that grace required embodied reciprocation. It deploys a *false gospel* because it reduces its fullness down to Jesus's death for sins. It encourages a *false faith* because it voids faith of its allegiance demand. And, as we will see in the next chapter, it wrongly treats faith as if it were primarily a mental or psychological posture untainted by bodily actions.

As Paul reminds us, the gospel gift, the message of the cross, is folly (1 Cor. 1:18), because that is the only medicine that can effect the cure. Grace needs to be shocking if it is going to arouse us from our willful stupor. "Really?" we say, "God loves me so much that he is willing to do *that*?" Like Philip Yancey upon hearing of his friend Tom's conversion, when we fully grasp the gospel, we can only laugh as we cry tears of grateful joy.

Saving grace cannot be defined apart from the specific events of the gospel. It is unmerited and large in size. It is benevolent but not infinitely so, for it can be spurned and corrupted, and it does not result in universal salvation. It was given to the church as a whole—though not necessarily to specific individuals—in the Son before creation itself. Saving grace is totally effective for transforming individuals who remain united to the king. Yet given that grace's macropurpose is allegiance to Jesus the king in all the nations, it has not been perfectly effective in bringing this about.

Finally, grace is freely given but its special saving benefits are received only when the condition that attends the gift are met. Grace demands reciprocation. The premier saving grace (gift) is the gospel. The return gift showing that the gospel has been accepted is allegiance (*pistis*) to the king. The next chapter seeks to show that the return gift of "faith" is embodied, outward facing, and unique.

5

Faith Is Body Out

Baptism reminds us that faith and bodily activity cannot be separated. Gospel allegiance helps us better understand why. My friend John recently baptized his daughter. I have been talking with John about gospel allegiance for several years. His previous understanding of salvation was very simple: "You just have to trust Jesus. Jesus takes the sin for you. Once he does that, you're clean." He needed new information. Books by N. T. Wright helped him appreciate the royal gospel. I gave him my earlier book *Salvation by Allegiance Alone* to help him rethink faith as allegiance. But beyond information, he had a lot of emotional and spiritual processing to do.

That long journey made this baptism special for John. Having worked through this, he could now help his daughter encounter baptism as a gospel-allegiance ceremony. "You need to understand that you are pledging allegiance to Jesus. This is a permanent thing you're pledging to." But my friend's baptismal discussion with his daughter is not just about correct soteriology. It is about everyday behavior.

Baptism is ordinarily the first movement of bodily submission to Jesus's lordship, the first step in what must become a habit of embodied discipleship. If John had simply reiterated the gospel that he learned as a child to his daughter, then not only would it not be the full gospel, but Jesus's kingship would not make demands on her daily practices. If our gospel is too small—if it is reduced down to a pin-prick atonement exchange—then we are bereft of its power for discipleship. Or worse. We might be fooled into believing that our discipleship has no bearing on our final salvation.

Now her baptism stakes a claim on her future choices. "When my daughter asks why she has to put up with her stinky brother that bothers her so much, I say, 'This is what you signed on for when you gave allegiance to Jesus, right?'" John can summon his daughter back to discipleship by reminding her that her baptism embodied allegiance—and that being a Christian requires learning to enact it again and again. "Faith" in Jesus includes bodily loyalty to him in baptism and thereafter.

Faith and Works Today

All major Christian denominations and groups—Lutherans, Baptists, Presbyterians, Wesleyans, Mennonites, Catholics, and Orthodox (all except free-gracers)—agree that good works are necessary for final salvation. Both Protestants and Catholics believe this, though they have various ideas about how. The next two chapters will show how faith and works fit together to make one coherent system of Christian salvation within the gospel-allegiance model. Chapter 2 gave evidence for saving faith as allegiance. This chapter builds on that by showing that faith is outward facing, inescapably embodied, and uniquely saving. This will lead to a discussion in the next chapter on how works are fundamentally (not just congruently) saving. Since the gospel-allegiance model describes the relationship between faith (*pistis*) and works differently from other Protestant models, we begin by comparisons with today's standard pastoral resources.

Free Grace

Zane Hodges, writing from a free-grace perspective, argues that "submission to the lordship of Christ is not in any sense a condition for eternal life."[1] He thinks faith is purely an inward conviction about the gospel's truth so that works have absolutely no relationship to salvation: "What faith really is, in biblical language, is receiving the testimony of God. It is the *inward conviction* that what God says to us in the gospel is true. That—and that alone—is saving faith."[2] Notice the focus on "inward conviction" in defining faith. We will see it again. The free-grace position rests on definitions of the gospel, grace, and faith that cannot be defended from Scripture.

Lordship Salvation

Contrary to Hodges, John MacArthur believes that true saving faith must include a commitment to Jesus's lordship. I could not agree more. Yet perhaps there is room to add nuance regarding how MacArthur speaks about works in salvation:

> True salvation cannot be earned by works. . . . Every false religion ever devised by mankind or by Satan is a religion of human merit. . . . They focus on what people must do to attain righteousness or please the deity. Biblical Christianity alone is the religion of divine accomplishment. Other religions say, "Do this." Christianity says, "It is done."[3]

MacArthur, correctly, does not think that works play any positive role in earning salvation—salvation has been won entirely by Jesus for us. But more questionably, MacArthur takes justification to be the moment of personal entrance into salvation on the basis of God's irreversible declaration of innocence.[4] And yet, for him (and I would agree), faith still requires submission to Jesus's lordship. So how does he reconcile faith and works?

> Does this mix faith and works? . . . Not at all. . . . Faith is an *internal* reality with *external* consequences. When we say that faith encompasses obedience, we are speaking of the God-given attitude of obedience, not trying to make works a part of the definition of faith. . . . Faith itself is complete before one work of obedience ever issues forth. But make no mistake—real faith will always produce righteous works. Faith is the root; works are the fruit.[5]

MacArthur thinks that, like oil and water, faith and works cannot mix with respect to the foundations of salvation. Despite his disagreement with Hodges, MacArthur too finds faith to be an *internal attitude* that is complete in and of itself before it ever subsequently leads to any external good works. As MacArthur puts it, "Faith and unbelief are states of the heart. But they necessarily impact behavior."[6] In other words, faith is an inward mental or emotive posture that must come first, and external good works will unquestionably follow.

The Standard View

MacArthur's basic position reflects the standard view among Protestants. It is defended by numerous others—including John Piper, R. C. Sproul, Matt Chandler, and Thomas Schreiner.[7] All of these treat faith as predominately an inward confidence in God's promises in Christ, especially confidence that a person can be justified by faith. Works, as external actions, are excluded as a basis for salvation. But good external deeds will invariably follow if the inward faith is genuine. These good works are considered not part of justification, but sanctification. This articulation, as we shall see, expresses the classic Protestant position first limned by Calvin as he built on Luther's foundational insights. This is why not just Catholics but nearly all Protestants have always agreed that good works are required for salvation.

Gospel Allegiance

The gospel-allegiance model offers a slightly different conclusion about how works relate to faith (*pistis*). During the course of church history, understandings of faith shifted. Conceptualizations of faith began as exterior, bodily, and active but moved to interior, affective, and passive. Catholics and Protestants alike were impacted. Because this shift was largely unnoticed, the church has subsequently struggled to delineate the correct biblical relationship between faith and works. As we become aware of the shift and the gospel's royal focus, a new synthesis is possible within a gospel-allegiance framework.

Protestants are right that we are saved by faith alone. Yet the classic Protestant position must be further refined, for saving good works do not merely follow upon *pistis* in Jesus. They are part of *pistis* as embodied allegiance to Jesus the king. This is true because saving faith is not predominately an inward conviction. Nor is it first a mental operation with the flesh only following thereafter. *Pistis* happens in the flesh from the beginning. As such, good works are never saving when independent of *pistis* to Jesus the king, but only when they are an embodiment of it.

Faith as Outward Facing

When referring to human activity, faith is generally relational and outward facing rather than psychological or emotional. That is the principal conclusion of the most comprehensive, authoritative study ever conducted of faith in the New Testament era. Teresa Morgan in her book *Roman Faith and Christian Faith* surveys myriad uses of *pistis* (and its Latin counterpart *fides*) in antiquity, focusing especially on the New Testament and other relevant documents.

In the New Testament era, a person would enact faith (*pistis*) toward someone or something else by *outward doing*. *Pistis* predominately intends external performance rather than inner attitudes or feelings. This is not to say it is entirely devoid of interiority or mental content, but the emphasis is on outward performance. Here are some examples from ancient documents: A lawyer practices *pistis* (loyalty) toward a powerless client even when it is socially risky.[8] A person who might be doubted gives *pistis* (evidence or security) as proof of their present or future reliability.[9] You act to show *pistis* (fidelity) to your oath.[10] A subject people shows their *pistis* (loyalty) to their overlords by supporting rather than undermining the regime.[11] An evil leader practices bad *pistis* (faith) toward others by violating his treaty.[12] An administrator is commended for displaying *pistis* (fidelity) to his king in the daily affairs of statecraft.[13] Soldiers stand by their king in battle, showing him *pistis* (allegiance).[14] All of these examples show that the actions that attend *pistis* are often outward facing and relational.

Pistis in the New Testament era is not a mere "function of the heart or mind."[15] Writers in this time period do not describe faith as an emotion-laden feeling, attitude, or a psychological stance. Instead they "focus constantly on its relationality." Moreover, the ancients and the biblical authors, when grouping together or classifying emotions and affections, do not include *pistis* in such lists. They simply did not primarily regard *pistis* as inward-facing personal trust or confidence. And yet emotions or affections often attend *pistis*, so it is impossible to entirely disentangle inward attitude and external behavior. It is safest to say that *pistis* is related to inward feelings and emotions, but is not itself one. In short, as Morgan concludes, "sources of this period have very little interest in the interiority of *pistis/fides*."[16]

Even the instances of *pistis* as mental activity focus on correct relational alignment with external facts or truths.[17] For example, Martha says to Jesus, "I *believe* [*pepisteuka*] that you are the Christ, the Son of God, who is coming into the world" (John 11:27). Martha believes a proposition about an external reality. She affirms that Jesus is the Christ. Even this mental activity cannot be done without it originating and being carried out in a physical body.

Other possible counterexamples might spring to mind. For instance, doesn't Paul say, "With *the heart* one believes [*pisteuetai*] and is justified" (Rom. 10:10)? Yes. And here heart (*kardia*) means the seat of the intellect, often including both affections and the will. Yet context does not suggest that Paul has a *feeling of inward confidence* in God's promises in view, but rather the believing is directed factually toward an outward gospel event, Jesus's resurrection (see 10:9)—the action that precipitated his enthronement as king.

In sum, there is considerable evidence that *pistis* was not primarily regarded as an internally focused mental, psychological, or emotional posture in the Greco-Roman world or the New Testament. Moreover, the claim that faith is purely receptive or passive is a philosophical and systematic position about the Bible rather than a straightforward biblical teaching. *Faith was relational and externalized*. Faith faced outward as *displayed* trust or loyalty toward the other (or toward external objects) more than inward as a *feeling* of confident reliance or trust.

The Faith of Abraham

Abraham-related questions are frequently asked by those who are closely scrutinizing the gospel-allegiance model. Rightly so.[18] For Paul, Abraham's faith (*pistis*) is best termed "loyal trust." Anticipating my conclusion, the gospel of Jesus the king, including its demand for allegiance in all the nations, was already present in the promise.

Abraham is Paul's parade example of *pistis*. Yet we must recognize that Abraham's *pistis* is defined not abstractly (confidence in God's promises in general) but by the gospel. Saving *pistis* is not a private interior confidence that either faith itself is effective or that Christ is present in all God's promises. Saving *pistis* is external, relational, and specific to the royal gospel. Abraham's faith aims *outwardly* at the allegiance-demanding gospel and *relationally* at the God who promised it via a covenant.

Abraham's trust was directed toward the gospel of Jesus the king to the degree it had been announced in advance to Abraham. The key verse reads, "The Scripture foresaw that God would justify the Gentiles by *pistis* and announced the gospel in advance to Abraham, 'All nations will be blessed through you'" (Gal. 3:8). Abraham received the gospel, here, that "all nations will be blessed through you."

For Paul, what is this gospel of the blessing of all nations? It is that the nations are in the process of coming under the banner of Abraham's offspring, King Jesus, as they yield allegiance to him and are integrated into the Holy Spirit's community (Gal. 3:14). That is, in Galatians 3:11 (much as in Rom. 1:17) we discover that "the righteous will live by allegiance" (cf. Hab. 2:4)—and that this refers to the king's fidelity in redeeming his people (Gal. 3:13) so that they can practice allegiance via the promised Spirit (Gal. 3:14). The blessing promised to Abraham relates directly to the gospel's purpose: to bring about the "obedience of *pistis*" of the nations (Rom. 1:5; 16:26; cf. 15:15–18).

Abraham was justified not by trusting in God's promise of justification by faith in Christ, as if that were the gospel's content or its center, but by trusting the gospel that all nations would be blessed through his own offspring. Abraham's trust is part of his *ongoing* loyalty or allegiance to the God of the gospel. As James reminds us, "Was not Abraham our father justified by works when he offered up his son Isaac on the altar? You see that faith [*pistis*] was active along with his works, and faith [*pistis*] was completed by his works" (2:21–22). The righteousness of Abraham was credited not just on the basis of his initial *pistis* toward the promised royal gospel, but on the basis of its endurance (James 2:23). Abraham shows imperfect but real allegiant trust in God throughout his life journey. Saving *pistis* is not a once-for-all-time act.

Paul details a dramatic moment of trusting loyalty in Romans 4:16–25. The raising up of Isaac as Abraham's seed anticipates Jesus's resurrection and enthronement (vv. 19–25). Abraham trusted that God could bring life (i.e., Isaac, corresponding to Jesus and to the resurrection) from death (Sarah's lifeless womb, corresponding to the virgin's womb and to the tomb) through a singular offspring (Rom. 4:17–18; cf. Gal. 3:16). Abraham had to trust bodily the specific gospel promise that through this seed the blessing to the nations could be delivered. What could be more body-centered than sex?

The text says that his *pistis* was externalized: "He was empowered by *pistis*, *giving glory to God*, being fully persuaded that what God had promised he was also able to do" (Rom. 4:20 AT). Abraham's trust was externalized since it was expressed bodily as glory-giving loyalty and through his *immediate* and *repeated* obedience to God's instructions (e.g., Gen. 12:1–4; 15:1–10; 22:1–12). The blessings to the nations through the seed transpired in and through the royal Christ, since the Holy Spirit has now been given (cf. Gal. 3:14). We cannot separate mental trust from bodily allegiance, nor can we insist that the former is necessarily prior to or the cause of the latter.

Did Abraham demonstrate saving allegiance to King Jesus? Yes and no. Yes, inasmuch as he was allegiant to the God (ultimately triune: Father, Son, and Spirit) who promised to bless the world through the death and resurrection of a future seed, Jesus the king. No, inasmuch as the Second Person of the Trinity had not yet become the *human* king, fulfilling God's intention for creation to be ruled by unmarred humanity. Nor had he yet ascended to the right hand of God. Moreover, fully saving *pistis* was not revealed in the Old Testament era, as that was only to come in the Messiah (Gal. 3:23–25). When it came, the Messiah's death for sins would then cover previously committed sins (Rom. 3:25).

In sum, Abraham's saving *pistis* corresponds with our *pistis* as present-day Christians. The same allegiance-demanding gospel of Jesus the king is ultimately in view with regard to faith and the crediting of righteousness. Abraham gave allegiance to God by an enduring trust in God's specific promises that pertained to Jesus the king. Abraham embodied this trusting loyalty to God (at his initial calling and throughout his lifetime). The content of these promises anticipated not just the atonement but the gospel in its entirety—the Messiah's death for sins, his resurrection, his vindication as king, the sending of the Spirit, *and his allegiance-demanding rule over the nations*. This is why saving faith is not just trusting the promise that Jesus's merit counts as righteousness for us. Such a construal of faith does not take seriously the overall shape of the gospel. "Jesus is the king" is the gospel's framework and climax, so the applied meaning of *pistis* in response to the gospel does not deny trust but foregrounds bodily allegiance to a king.

Abraham's *pistis* resulted in righteousness being credited to him because it was *externalized bodily* and faced *outward relationally* toward the God of the gospel. The same is true for us (for this logic, see esp. Rom. 4:23–25). Abraham's *pistis* (trust) involved loyalty to the triune God because the gospel of Jesus the king is purposed toward allegiance in all the nations, and this gospel was already present in the promise.

Outward Became Inward

I hope two points have now been established. First, most today see faith as an inward mental sense of reliance on God's promises in Christ. Second, faith in the New Testament was primarily outward facing and relational. This means that Western theology has been dominated by questionable understandings of faith for a long season.

Exactly how faith moved from outward to inward is beyond the scope of this book. But if we trace the overall shape of the shift, we will be in a better position to see why gospel allegiance may help blaze a trail forward.

The movement from outward to inward rapidly accelerated with Saint Augustine (354–430). He famously treated faith as having two parts: "the faith which is to be believed" (that is, the content of Christian doctrine to be intellectually affirmed) and "the faith by which it is to be believed" (that is, the interior movement of trusting agreement). Morgan shows that neither of Augustine's definitions accurately handles the meaning of *pistis* in the New Testament and related literature. This is not to say that Augustine's twofold understanding of faith has no connection to the biblical idea. But both are off center.[19]

Augustine's infinitely influential views on faith informed the medieval Catholic synthesis, as well as the Protestant Reformers. Faith became more introspective, psychological, emotive, and passive (or receptive) than is encouraged by the biblical witness. Faith came to be less about external allegiance to Jesus the king and more about what God does in us to cause intellectual belief in correct doctrine as shaped by love (medieval Catholicism) or cause inward trust in his promises (Protestantism).

In the sixteenth century, Martin Luther's most extensive definition of faith describes it as God's gift, as belief in the correct body of doctrine, and as invariably resulting in good works. Since it involves seizing upon God's certain promises it does face outward, in part. Yet Luther stresses that it is characterized by *personal confidence* or certitude and specific *internal emotions*:

> Faith is a living and unshakeable confidence, a belief in grace so assured that a man would die a thousand deaths for its sake. This kind of confidence in God's grace, this sort of knowledge in it, makes us joyful, high-spirited, and eager in our relations with God and with all mankind.[20]

Luther's treatment, akin to Augustine's, primarily divides faith into *doctrine to be believed* and *internal feelings of trusting confidence*.

Like Luther, John Calvin grounds faith in God's external promises but also treats it as if it is primarily an inward conviction (passively received) rather than actively embodied in outward-facing relationships:

> Now we shall possess a right definition of faith if we call it a firm and certain knowledge of God's benevolence toward us, founded upon the truth of the freely given promise in Christ, both revealed to our minds and sealed upon our hearts through the Holy Spirit.[21]

For Calvin, faith is "not content with a doubtful and changeable opinion," but "requires full and fixed certainty"—even though fear, temptation, and doubts will assail. For faith to be genuine, God's promises of mercy must not remain "outside ourselves" but must be "inwardly embraced" with confident assurance.[22]

Calvin finds scholastic distinctions worthless between *implicit faith* (faith without knowledge, e.g., allegedly by infants at baptism), *unformed faith* (faith as mere intellectual assent), and *formed faith* (intellectual assent shaped by hope and love). This is primarily because the first two are not regarded as biblical faith at all, and the third compromises faith's uniqueness. Saving faith involves true albeit imperfect knowledge in response to God's proclaimed word, but always goes beyond intellectual assent. The assent portion of faith is "more of the heart than of the brain, and more of the disposition than the understanding," so that true faith can never be separated from a "devout disposition." Calvin thinks this is what Paul is trying to convey by the phrase "the obedience of faith" in Romans 1:5. Calvin correctly notes that in the Bible *pistis* has many definitions. But for him saving faith, as the Spirit permits, is primarily an internal conviction that God's promise of mercy in the atonement through Jesus's priestly mediation is indeed trustworthy.[23]

As the Reformation progressed, definitions of faith were systematized. Luther's associate Philip Melanchthon (1497–1560) divided faith into three parts: (1) *notitia*—the content of the faith or body of correct doctrines; (2) *assensus*—intellectual agreement that the content, the *notitia*, is in fact God's truth; and (3) *fiducia*—a disposition of trust or reliance on God's promises rooted in the will or affections. Even though inclusive of the other parts, *fiducia* alone was worthy of the name "faith" in the saving sense. Francis Turretin (1623–1687) accepted these three subdivisions, but added four additional parts: (4) *act of refuge*—where we desire union with Christ; (5) *act of reception and union*—the desire for union is realized and applied; (6) *reflex act*—through introspection we realize that we personally have indeed been united to

Christ; (7) *act of confidence and consolation*—the joy and assurance of salvation that follows.[24]

The flight of faith toward inward subjective feelings of trusting confidence would only accelerate thereafter. Friedrich Schleiermacher (1768–1834) is often regarded as the first modern theologian. Largely because of his wrongheaded ideas about *pistis*, he believed the essence of Christianity was a *feeling* of absolute dependence. Søren Kierkegaard (1813–1855) would find the heart of Christianity to be an existential trust in God not because of evidence but precisely because of its irrational absurdity. Rudolf Bultmann (1884–1976), a leading New Testament scholar, sought to purge the New Testament of its allegedly mythic elements. He believed that the New Testament had no real reliable historical basis, but this did not matter for faith. All that matters is a personal response of trust in the face of the law's demands. Schleiermacher, Kierkegaard, and Bultmann would have been much nearer the mark had they found the essence of faith to be embodied loyalty to a king rather than feelings of dependence or inward trust.

This brief recounting sketches how over time faith became less about outward allegiance to Jesus the king and more about inward feelings of personal confidence in God's promises. This tendency was exacerbated when the heart of the gospel was wrongly understood to be justification by faith rather than Jesus is the saving king.

For when faith became internal to the gospel, one needed to have inward faith not just in the sufficiency of Christ's work but also in the sufficiency of faith itself. One needed to have faith in faith. When this happened, the cross, as essential as it truly is to the gospel, eclipsed something equally critical—the gospel's royal framework and allegiance demands. *Throughout the history of Western theology, faith increasingly became inward personal confidence in the effectiveness of the exchange transaction on the cross rather than outward allegiance to Jesus the saving king.* Without denying its interiority, saving faith must be externalized as allegiance to Jesus the forgiving king for it to save.

Faith as Embodied

The flight of faith from the outward to the inward was helped along by related ideas. Faith, as it moved from outward to inward, became something that happens in your mind or will or spirit, rather than in your body. Yet this is not how faith was generally understood in the New Testament world. Faith was embodied.

Faith (*pistis*) was not conceptualized in antiquity as a purely nonphysical mind or spirit activity disconnected from the body. Recent studies by scholars such as David Downs, Gary Anderson, and Joshua Jipp have shown that good deeds, such as giving alms and practicing hospitality, were viewed as having a positive saving function in the New Testament.[25] I would suggest that this is not because works were viewed as independently saving, but because such actions were understood to be embodied acts of *pistis*. If today we think about faith as only mental (with Hodges), or as first mental and only subsequently physical (with MacArthur and many others), it is because of the peculiar history of ideas in Western civilization rather than because of the Bible's own witness. The New Testament does not consistently support substance dualism (the belief that the body and the mind, or the flesh and the spirit, are distinctly separate from one another) in the fashion championed by Plato and much later by René Descartes.

When flesh and spirit are regarded as differing substances in the Bible, the intention is not to contrast the physical with the nonphysical. Like his contemporaries the Stoics, Paul probably believed spirit/Spirit to be an invisible diffuse *material* substance of heavenly origin, and so it had a physicality just as flesh does. For Paul, the distinction is that the Spirit above all characterizes God's realm and the new age of the Messiah that God is unveiling, but the flesh characterizes the mundane old order. This is why Paul thinks that those who live according to the flesh will die, but those who live according to the Spirit will find eternal life:

> Those who are in the flesh cannot please God. You, however, are not in the flesh but in the Spirit, if in fact the Spirit of God dwells in you. (Rom. 8:8–9)

This does not mean that only those who have left behind their actual fleshly, physical bodies can please God. If that were true, no Christian—not even Jesus himself—could please God. (If someone offers you Gnosticism or Docetism, even if they look nice, just say no. Teach this to your kids.) Jesus and all those who have accepted him have real flesh-and-bone bodies and still can please God. "For if you live according to the flesh you will die, but if by the Spirit you put to death the deeds of the body, you will live" (Rom. 8:13). The contrast is not between physical and nonphysical. Rather it is between the old order and the new. The flesh and its sinful appetites are associated with death and the old order, the Spirit with life and the new order.

Spiritual Yet Physical Bodies

Paul does not consider body and spirit to be opposite and mutually exclusive in their physicality. For example, when Paul juxtaposes our present natural body (*sōma*) with our future spiritual body after the resurrection, both are material and physical:

> It is sown a natural body [*sōma psychikon*]; it is raised a spiritual body [*sōma pneumatikon*]. If there is a natural body, there is also a spiritual body. (1 Cor. 15:44)

Both our present earthly bodies and our future resurrection bodies are physical and material. Our present physical body is *natural* or *soul-ish* (related to *psyche*). And when we are raised from the dead in the new age in the Messiah, our new *physical* bodies will be *spiritual* (related to *pneuma*). We know that this spiritual body is nevertheless physical because resurrection of the same material corpse is in view. Thus, in the resurrection age, the leading description of our *physical, material body* is that it will be *spiritual* (or better, Spirit-ish). Paul believes that the Spirit has qualities that impinge on the physical body. Paul does not see the physical and the spiritual as separate, opposite substances that remain aloof from one another.

It may be popular today to think that the Bible envisions a non-material spirit world that is in contrast with the physical, bodily world. But this is a simplistic reading of the Bible. And it has direct bearing on the faith-works question. For we cannot argue that faith is a spiritual or mental thing separate from bodily doing. Faith is embodied and enacted from start to finish.

Colonization of the Flesh

Faith is embodied because our bodies are open to the environment and can be colonized. A colony is established when a small number of foreign agents inhabit a territory or body. A successful colony grows so that eventually the territory is fully occupied by the foreign agents. Over time the foreign agents become natives as they are acclimated to their new world.

Paul viewed the human body as open to colonization. For Paul and his contemporaries, human bodies are "permeable, unbounded, and of a piece with their environment."[26] This accords well with many contemporary scientific and philosophical views of the body. Who we are as selves is constructed with respect to other selves and to outside forces that can be internalized.

This is why Paul speaks of sin as a personified, colonizing agent. In speaking about the human under sin, apart from the Christ, he says, "*I* no longer am doing it, but *Sin dwelling in me*—that is . . . *in my flesh*" (Rom. 7:17–18 AT). For this human, Sin has permeated the flesh and is active. The human *I* is porous to the environment in such a way that it can be materially colonized by an external power, Sin. This permeability of the *I* to Sin is environmentally present everywhere in the old order via the *stoicheia*, the organizing elements that permeate the entire cosmos (Gal. 4:3, 9; Col. 2:8)—and hence also *the flesh* of human bodies. This external power inhabits the flesh of the self, forcing it to act against what the whole self might otherwise desire. This is what happens apart from the king's assistance.

Salvation involves a recolonization through union with the Messiah. When this happens the *I* is permeated by a new master, the Christ: "I have been crucified with the Messiah. It is no longer *I* who lives, but *the Messiah who lives in me*. And the life I now live *in the flesh* I live by *pistis*" (Gal. 2:20 AT). Jesus the king has recolonized the *I*, including the self's flesh, overwhelming Sin's colonization. This colonization by Jesus the king is not a mental, nonbodily faith. On the contrary, Paul specifically says that *pistis is lived out "in the flesh."* Regardless of where in the body *pistis* is felt to originate (e.g., in the heart, head, or stomach), for Paul, this *pistis* is certainly an embodied happening, a fleshly activity.

Passages such as Romans 8:9 involve a similar recolonization but feature the Holy Spirit. In Galatians 2:20 the king takes control of the human flesh, but in Romans 8:8–9 it is the Spirit: "Those who are *in the flesh* cannot please God. You, however, *are not in the flesh* but in the Spirit, if in fact the Spirit of God dwells in you." If the Spirit of God dwells in you, then the Spirit has taken over your fleshly body to such a degree that Paul can say that you are no longer in the flesh at all!

In the Spirit we are no longer being jerked around by the hostile power of Sin that colonized the flesh under the old order. The Spirit uses its new-creation power to recolonize the human flesh thoroughly, delivering it from its previous enslavement to sin, the law, malevolent spiritual powers, and the fundamental structures of the old order. In the Messiah via the Spirit the entire allegiant community has been colonized, each self, all the way down to each person's living-by-*pistis* flesh.

Faith Is Bodily

These texts show that for Paul, if a person is to exercise faith at all, this cannot be done apart from his or her human flesh. We are not faith-alone spiritual ghosts inside a separate works-doing body machine. *A person can only exercise faith while making use of the body, doing something, working.* James says that a non-enacted understanding of faith is not faith at all but a dead thing: "Faith by itself, if it does not have works, is dead" (James 2:17). Moreover, James adds, "I will show you my faith *by my works*" (2:18).

This helps us see why "allegiance" is sometimes more fitting than "faith" when translating *pistis* in today's world. In the Bible *pistis* is not a mental event separated from the physical body. When a person is living by *pistis* in the Messiah, *the flesh* is colonized by the Messiah and the Holy Spirit. *Pistis* ("faith" or "allegiance") happens in and through the physical body from start to finish.

The Christ Embodies Faithfulness

That faith is embodied is confirmed by the Bible's description of Jesus the king's own faith. In several important salvation passages, when Paul uses the phrase "faith of Christ," it is more likely that Paul is speaking about *the faithfulness of the Messiah* than about *our faith in him*. In such passages the Greek text actually says "*pistis of* Christ," but this had come to be translated traditionally as "faith *in* Christ." (Technically, a decision about the correct translation hinges on whether the genitive noun functions as the subject or object of the implied verb in *pistis*.) A thoroughgoing case in favor of "*pistis of* Christ" as the *Christ's faithfulness* rather than *faith in Christ* was made by biblical scholar Richard Hays in the 1980s. Since then it has been extensively researched and tested by other scholars. Not everyone agrees with Hays, but a great number have been persuaded.[27]

Whether Hays is right certainly does not make or break the gospel-allegiance proposal. It is compatible regardless. Nevertheless, it is a fascinating question for those interested in how salvation works. For these "faith of Christ" phrases are invariably found in key passages about justification.

The Faith of the King

Let's see why many have found Hays's overall proposal attractive by looking at a couple examples. Paul speaks about the faith of the Christ in Philippians 3:9, a particularly interesting passage because Paul is speaking about an individual's (his own!) quest for righteousness before God:

> . . . not having my own righteousness that is from the law, but the righteousness through the *pistis* of the Christ [*dia pisteōs Christou*], the righteousness *from God* [*ek theou*] based on *pistis* [*epi tē pistei*]. (Phil. 3:9 AT)

In my judgment, Paul is not saying that he found right standing from God by putting his *faith in Jesus's sacrifice*; rather, he obtained a right standing from God when *the Messiah acted faithfully*, or allegiantly. That is, *faith in Christ* is a less likely translation here than *the faithfulness of the Christ*—or, as I prefer, *the allegiance of the Christ*. Why?

Paul gives two phrases in a row, and the second is designed to explain the first. We can use the second phrase, which is more clear, to help elucidate the first phrase, which is less clear. The unclear first phrase is "the righteousness through the *pistis* of the Christ." The explanatory second phrase is "the righteousness *from God* based on *pistis*."

We work from the second to the first. Since divine action ("righteousness *from God*") is stressed in the second phrase, divine action is likely also in view in the first. In other words, Paul is saying that the *Christ acted* in a *loyal* fashion to secure our righteousness, and then he explains that this *pistis* action by the Christ was also *from God* (*ek theou*) because it was God's righteousness-establishing activity. Divine action on our behalf is emphasized in both phrases. So it is probable that Paul here speaks of the allegiant activity of the king in securing our righteousness, not of our faith in Jesus.

I am *not* saying that we do not need to have faith in Jesus as the saving king, or that we do not need to trust him. We absolutely do.

The full gospel speaks of the king's death for our sins, and so an allegiant response to Jesus includes trust in the effectiveness of his sacrifice. There are numerous passages that speak clearly of our need to "have faith in" or "give *pistis* to" the Christ holistically. For example, *pistis* or *pisteuō* is aimed toward the Lord Jesus in Ephesians 1:15 ("the *pistis* in the Lord Jesus that accords with you"); Philippians 1:29 ("to give *pistis* unto him"); Colossians 2:5 ("your *pistis* unto the Christ"); Philemon 5 ("the *pistis* which you have toward the Lord Jesus"); and 1 Timothy 3:13 ("*pistis* which is in the Christ Jesus"; cf. 2 Tim. 1:13; 3:15).[28]

Moreover, there are several interesting passages that combine statements of the Christ's own allegiance with indications that we need to give allegiance to the Christ:

> . . . the righteousness of God through the *allegiance* of Jesus the Christ *for all who give allegiance*. For there is no distinction: for all have sinned and fall short of the glory of God, and are justified by his grace as a gift, through the redemption that is in the Christ, Jesus, whom God put forward as a propitiation by his blood, through his *allegiance*. (Rom. 3:22–25 AT)

This passage must speak first of *the allegiance or faithfulness of the king*, and second of *our allegiance to him*—otherwise Paul is repeating himself in a confusing way. It is unlikely that Paul intends, "through faith in Jesus the Christ for all who have faith [in him]" (v. 22), as it would be redundant to speak of our faith in Jesus twice in this way. But it is not repetitious to say "through the allegiance of Jesus the Christ for all who give allegiance [to him]" (v. 22), since different actors—Jesus and us—are performing the allegiance. So in speaking of how we are declared innocent before God, Paul first describes the king's allegiance and second our allegiance to the king.

We find the same interplay between the king's allegiance and our own in a passage we treated in the last section:

> We ourselves are Jews by birth and not Gentile sinners; yet we know that a person is not justified by works of the law but through

> the *allegiance* of Jesus the Christ, so we also have given *allegiance* unto the Christ, Jesus, in order to be justified by the *allegiance* of the Christ and not by works of the law, because by works of the law no one will be justified. (Gal. 2:15–16 AT)

This passage speaks both of Jesus's *pistis* (allegiance or faithfulness) and of our required allegiance unto the king, Jesus. If we don't give allegiance to him, it is implied that Jesus's allegiance for our sakes has not been effective for securing our justification.

The King Expresses Trusting Allegiance

A related but different example shows how Jesus the king himself practiced gospel allegiance. In 2 Corinthians 4:7–15, Paul details the strange business of being a minister of the new covenant. Even though Christians are fragile jars of clay, they house an inexhaustible divine power. Human weakness makes the resurrection life of the Messiah more transparent in ministers of the gospel.

As evidence Paul cites words from a psalm, concluding that the core gospel events are purposed toward the enormous *size* of grace, one of the six aspects of grace examined in chapter 4. This is combined with a stress on the king's own trusting allegiance:

> Moreover, since we have the same spirit of trust in accordance with which it stands written, "*I trusted, therefore I spoke*" [Ps. 116:10], so also we *trust* and therefore are *speaking*, knowing that the one who raised the Lord Jesus also will raise us with Jesus and he will present us together with you. For all this is for your sake, in order that as *grace expands to more and more people*, thanksgiving will increase, to the glory of God. (2 Cor. 4:13–15 AT)

The Messiah himself practiced gospel allegiance in bringing about this largess of grace. Paul indicates that he and his coworkers should have the same disposition of trust and loyalty (*pistis*) as the psalmist who said, "I trusted, therefore I spoke" (*episteusa, dio elalēsa*). But who ultimately is the speaker of these words?

The traditional position is that Paul wants his readers to imitate the faith of the generic psalmist, or David—translating *pistis* as "faith" and the verb *pisteuō* as "I believed." In this view, the psalmist and Paul are both encouraging a nonspecific faith in God—faith for faith's sake.

But many contemporary scholars, myself included, think the evidence proves otherwise.[29] We are convinced that Paul identified *the Messiah* as the speaker of the words, "I trusted, therefore I spoke." Thus, Paul does not give a general exhortation to "believe" God or "have faith," but instead issues an exact call to *imitate the Messiah* in his trusting allegiance to God while suffering. For many readers this will be a new way of thinking about the meaning of 2 Corinthians 4:13–15.

Paul understands the psalmist (David) to be speaking in the person of the Messiah in Psalm 116. *Prosopological exegesis* is the technical term for this phenomenon of a prophet speaking from the vantage point of another person and its subsequent interpretation. It occurs frequently in the New Testament. Here the Messiah is speaking to God the Father after he has been seated in glory at his right hand. The enthroned Christ tells the Father about his *past moment* of crisis and trust during the crucifixion.

More precisely, for Paul, "I trusted, therefore I spoke" (Ps. 116:10) refers to an earlier event narrated in the psalm—the Messiah's death. "Anguishes of death surrounded me; the dangers of Hades found me; I found affliction and pain" (v. 3 AT).[30] During this crisis unto death, the Messiah responded by *loyally trusting*. Then he *spoke*. That is, he cried out for rescue: "And I called upon the name of the Lord, 'O Lord, rescue my soul'" (v. 4 AT). God responded to this plea by raising him from the dead, delivering him to "the land of the living" (v. 9).

For Paul, when David said, "I trusted, therefore I spoke," he was speaking as a prophet in the person of the Messiah. Compare this to a similar move in Hebrews 2:12–13 and also the specific allusions to Psalm 116:1–9 in Hebrews 5:7. Paul also understands the Messiah to be the speaker of certain psalms in Romans 15:3 (Ps. 69:9) and 15:9 (Ps. 18:49), among other texts. The Messiah suffers death on the cross, perseveres in *loyal trust* through the crisis, and calls out to God for deliverance. Then God declares the Messiah *righteous* and restores him to the land of the *living*.

Sound familiar? It fits the pattern we discussed in chapter 2: "The *righteous* one will *live* by *allegiance*" (Rom. 1:17, citing Hab. 2:4). The one who shows *allegiance* is vindicated as *righteous* and *lives*. For Paul, Jesus the Messiah practiced allegiance to God, cried out, was rescued, and now lives—and this was all announced in advance in Habakkuk 2:4, Psalm 116, and other texts. We can expect that we too will be vindicated and live when we give our allegiance to Jesus the king. This is true because the righteousness of God is revealed "*by* allegiance, *for* allegiance" (Rom. 1:17)—that is, *by* the allegiance of King Jesus in his self-donation, and *for* the purpose of our allegiance to him as King of kings. This is the *good news*, the *specific grace*, that is expanding to more and more people each day (see chap. 4).

In short, "faith *of* Christ" passages in the Bible's original language have been traditionally translated as "faith *in* Christ." But some are better understood as announcing the "faithfulness of the Christ"—that is, the king's fidelity or allegiance in carrying out the saving events of the gospel. Scripture speaks not only of faith in the king but also of his faith toward God and toward us. Jesus acted in a faithful way (he showed *pistis*) by dying on the cross, and so God responded by justifying him—that is, vindicating him and declaring him innocent.

We give *pistis* (allegiance) to Jesus as the king, and in doing so we show loyalty to him and to God. Allegiance means we are seeking to enter into the Messiah's pattern of death for the sake of others so that we find life through union with him. Allegiance to Jesus the saving king includes trust in his atoning death but goes beyond it to include embodied acts of loyalty as we live a life of discipleship in imitation of him.

Faith Is Unique

Our discussion of faith would be incomplete without asking whether it is uniquely saving. The best entry point is Paul's exhortation to freedom in Galatians 5:1–6, since in this portion of the letter he most clearly states that *pistis* uniquely avails.

Stay Free in the King

Paul reminds the Galatians that the Christ freed them in order that they might remain free (5:1). He builds his case for freedom by asserting that circumcision would disallow the end-times benefits associated with participation in the Messiah. It would re-enslave them, making them debtors to the whole law:

> Look! I, Paul, tell you that if you allow yourselves to be circumcised, then the Christ will not profit you. Again, I testify to each man who lets himself be circumcised that he is a debtor, obliged to do the whole law. All you who are attempting to be justified in the law have been cut off from the Christ! You have fallen away from grace. (Gal. 5:2–4 AT)

Paul warns about the disastrous consequences of reinstituting circumcision as a work of the law. Then he explains his rationale:

> For we, on the basis of the Spirit, through faith, wait eagerly for the hope—namely, righteousness. For in the Christ, Jesus, neither circumcision nor uncircumcision avails [*ischuei*], rather, faith [*pistis*] itself working [*energoumenē*] through love. (Gal. 5:5–6 AT)

It is so dangerous to reinstitute life under the law because *the Holy Spirit is the basis for the hope of final vindication*—for righteousness on the day of judgment. Paul sees this hope as secured already for all who remain in the king. Furthermore, allegiance (*pistis*) is exclusively the means by which this hope has been secured. Paul, by way of summary, explains that circumcision is totally irrelevant to justification. The only thing that matters is allegiance working through love by means of the Holy Spirit. Let's unpack a few details to sharpen Paul's understanding of allegiance's uniqueness.

Rules Fail, Allegiance Avails

In Galatians 5:6 Paul provides two reasons why the Galatian Christians should remain free by continuing to resist circumcision. First, circumcision no longer has any meaning or any consequence. The verb *ischuei* generally means "to have power, to be competent, to be able," but in legal texts it carries the nuance of "have meaning, be valid, being in force." In short, circumcision no longer *avails*.

Second, circumcision should not be adopted because the only thing that has meaning or validity in God's eyes is "faith [*pistis*] working [*energoumenē*] through love." This is a potent affirmation of *pistis* as uniquely and exclusively saving.

The word "working" (*energoumenē*) has been much discussed. In Greek it is almost certainly middle, not passive, in voice.[31] This means that Paul emphasizes *not* that "faith *is being worked* through love," which might place love on equal footing alongside *pistis* in availing in God's eyes. Love could then be seen as the primary agent causing the faith. Rather, Paul gives the primacy to faith *itself* working through love, which makes it the primary agent rather than love. In other words, faith uniquely avails for our innocence, but *pistis* is embodied through love when *pistis* expresses itself.

If Paul understands *pistis* as predominately allegiance to the king, it makes perfect sense to say that "allegiance works itself out through love." Love is not primarily a tender feeling. Paul spends a whole chapter describing it (1 Cor. 13). It is certainly not romantic in our modern sense. It is perhaps best described as practical, non-self-oriented giving to others. Thus allegiance works itself out in non-self-oriented embodied practices directed toward others.

Given that *pistis* uniquely avails as it works through love, what characterizes it? How is it facilitated? In light of the fact that the Galatians received *the Spirit* through the message of *pistis*, there is a strong link between *pistis* and life in the Spirit (Gal. 3:1–5). And a firm connection with love too, since this is the very first fruit of the Spirit listed by Paul (5:22). The Spirit's coming is part of the gospel as the blessing promised to Abraham (3:8, 14) and is the definitive marker of adoption into God's family (4:6). Life must be lived both by *pistis* and by the Spirit if it is to be a free life in the king (5:1–6, 16–18) and result in eternal life (6:8).

The Spirit-led life (as opposed to one governed by works of the law) is the *only* mode by which allegiance is able to express itself through love. This makes excellent sense of the development of Paul's argument in Galatians, which is moving toward a climactic exhortation to live a life of love through the Spirit to fulfill the intent of the law of Moses (5:13–26; cf. Rom. 8:1–17).

Paul is saying that circumcision has no power and no validity; it is a meaningless non-issue in God's eyes because it cannot be universally required for allegiance. Only Spirit-led allegiance can fulfill the true intent of the law of Moses. That is, circumcision and other works of the law are non-issues until one seeks to be justified by them rather than by *pistis* alone. If that happens, Paul says that person has been "cut off from the Christ" and has "fallen away from grace" (Gal. 5:4). Serious words indeed!

Paul later in Galatians insists that right behavior is required for eternal life (6:8). And in our next chapter we'll see that Paul and the rest of the New Testament authors say the same thing time and time again. But how can it be that Paul seems to regard good behavior (deeds) as having saving value after all? In the next chapter we will need to think carefully about the difference between good works in general and works of the law like circumcision—especially as we nuance Protestant-Catholic differences in light of Scripture.

This chapter opened by recounting my friend John's baptism of his daughter. Loyalty to Jesus must change how she uses her body. She must treat her brother kindly. John's daughter can rest secure knowing Jesus's perfect allegiance is primary. He is the forgiving king. But she cannot totally abandon bodily fidelity to Jesus and expect final salvation to result.

This is true because saving faith is not primarily interior mental confidence that Jesus died for our sins. Rather, saving allegiance (*pistis*) faces outward relationally in response to Jesus's kingship, is inescapably embodied, and is also the basis of the Messiah's own salvation. The Christ displayed *pistis* toward God in choosing the path of the cross for us. In recognition of his *pistis*, he was rescued from death and seated at God's own right hand. We can expect the same too when we are united by allegiance to him, embodying his way of life. Allegiance uniquely avails with God.

Gospel allegiance's embodiment in baptism is not just instructive for individuals. When John and his daughter stood before their church, everyone was reminded that his daughter was not merely joining a community united by belief in Jesus's death for sins, but one united by bodily allegiance. The congregants are now in a better position to live out their own baptismal commitments to Jesus's lordship. When we get the gospel right, our present life *together* enters into the eternal quality of life through discipleship.

6

How Works Are Saving

"A private hell for a couple of years." That is how Doug describes it. In speaking to others, I know his experience is not unique.

My friend Doug's first memories of faith, works, and salvation connect to the Vacation Bible School he attended at age six. Salvation was presented using booklets: a green page for Eden, black for the fall, red for Jesus's death, white for salvation, and gold for future glory. While the other kids were enjoying cookies and punch, Doug wore circles around a magnolia tree: "I knew I had done wrong things. Hell sounded really, really bad to me."

Doug's father had abandoned his family around this time. "God as a Father who loved me was really powerful to me. I wanted that." So Doug prayed the sinner's prayer and invited Jesus into his heart.

After high school he worked at a Baptist summer camp. Soon his fellow counselors, all of whom had definitely affirmed that they were "saved" prior to camp, began saying, "I just got saved last night" and "I thought I had trusted Christ when I was young, but I had just been pretending." Already wobbly, Doug began to seriously doubt his salvation.

He attended Bible college and then seminary, but his doubts only intensified when these reconversions continued happening. A script ran through his head throughout these years, creating his private hell:

> I didn't remember my six-year-old experience. So I was willing to get resaved like all these others. But then the thought was, if I just got "saved" then I am not the spiritually mature Christian everyone thought that I was. I was a youth pastor part-time, I was preaching occasionally. . . . I was worried that I would lose all these things.
>
> So then I would say to myself, "This is just crazy, I don't need to get resaved—What is going on here?—I'm working for the Lord, I love him." But then verses would pop into my head like, "If you deny me before men I'll deny you before my father." I took the fact that I didn't want to give up all these spiritual trappings to be the pride that proved that I really hadn't been saved.

Doug's deeds of loyal Christian service only heightened his suspicion that he must actually be trusting in his works rather than Jesus. Every good deed that he did mocked him. Doug found it impossible to purge subjective uncertainties about his faith. The vicious cycle of the script continued to devour him.

Doug's private hell is not unique because it reflects a tension in classic Protestant theology. It is hoped that gospel allegiance can relieve it. In the previous chapter we saw why faith (*pistis*) is not just interior trust but is embodied and externalized. It is uniquely saving. Circumcision cannot contribute to our innocence. Yet good behavior is still demanded for salvation. Nearly everyone—Protestants, Catholics, and Orthodox alike—agrees that good works are required for salvation. The question is how.

Works as the Problem

Classic Protestant theology has a confusing love-hate relationship with good deeds. For Luther the gospel itself condemns our works in favor of faith in Christ's accomplished saving work on our behalf:

> The gospel demands no works to make us holy and to redeem us. Indeed, it condemns such works, and demands only faith in Christ, because He has overcome sin, death, and hell for us. Thus it is not by our works, but by His work, His passion and death, that He makes us righteous, and gives us life and salvation.[1]

In this view, good works are the great enemy of the gospel because they might cause us to trust in our own righteousness rather than Christ's. Luther expresses this anxiety:

> Very many have been deceived . . . and have proceeded to write and teach concerning good works and how they justify without even mentioning faith. They go their way, always being deceived and deceiving . . . wearying themselves with many works and still never attaining to true righteousness.[2]

For Luther and his heirs, good works are a threat because they are deceptive. It is so tempting and easy to trust in our own achievements, our own righteousness, rather than God's. Luther sees this confidence in our own works as the fundamental human error, institutionalized in his own day in Judaism and Catholicism. Luther blatantly labels "false trust in works" as "idolatry."[3]

Subsequently, Protestants have taken their cue from Luther in articulating a fear of works in salvation. Protestants are eager to avoid *salvation by legalism*: the error of thinking one can earn salvation by remaining sufficiently obedient to God's law or to some other moral standard. They also seek to avoid its mirror image, *salvation by works righteousness*: the error of believing one can earn salvation by doing enough good deeds (e.g., more good than bad) and so avoid condemnation.

Whether legalism and works righteousness are actually the target of criticism in the Bible is important and disputed (see under "The New Perspective on Paul" below). But to the degree that they are, the Bible makes it clear that both are errors. As for salvation by legalism, Paul affirms that we cannot obey God's law perfectly:

> I do not nullify the grace of God, for *if righteousness were through the law*, then Christ died for no purpose. (Gal. 2:21)

> I testify again to every man who accepts circumcision that he is obligated to keep the *whole* law. You are severed from Christ, *you who would be justified by the law*; you have fallen away from grace. (Gal. 5:3–4)

> For *by works of the law no human being will be justified* in his sight. (Rom. 3:20; cf. Gal. 2:16)

> For *all who rely on works of the law are under a curse*; for it is written, "Cursed be everyone who does not abide by *all things* written in the Book of the Law, and do them." (Gal. 3:10)

Paul stresses that the *entire law* must be performed if the curse is to be avoided. It is impossible to be saved by legalism, keeping enough of God's rules.

Nor can we heap up a large enough pile of good deeds to overcome our sin problem, as salvation by works righteousness demands:

> As it is written: "*None is righteous, no, not one*; no one understands; no one seeks for God. All have turned aside; together they have become worthless; *no one does good, not even one*." (Rom. 3:10–12)

> It is by grace you have been saved through faith . . . *not by works*, so that no one can boast. (Eph. 2:8–9 AT)

> He saved us, *not by works done by us in righteousness*, but according to his own mercy. (Titus 3:5 AT)

Works righteousness fails too. We certainly cannot earn salvation by doing good works. Protestant fears about allowing legalism or works righteousness to determine salvation have at least some validity. Both are contrary to Scripture. But *how* these were threats when Paul and other New Testament authors wrote needs clarification. Works as salvation's enemy is not the whole story. Far from it.

Works Are Not the Problem

Suspicious dislike of works may be the dominant current in classic Protestantism, but a strong undertow is present too. Even while championing faith alone, Luther expresses an ardent love for works, urging their necessity. "We therefore maintain that faith justifies us apart from any works, although *we must not draw the conclusion that we have no need to do any good works*. Nay, rather, works of the right kind must not be neglected, works of which the mere ceremonialists know nothing."[4] Luther judged that good works were in no way saving—but *after* a person had been declared righteous (justified) by faith, good works were an *inevitable* outflow. He did not think such good works pertained to ceremonial rites, as in Catholicism, but to Spirit-inspired deeds and virtues. "O, when it comes to faith, what a living, creative, active, powerful thing it is. *It cannot do other than good at all times*. It never waits to ask whether there is some good work to do. Rather, before the question is raised, it has done the deed and keeps on doing it."[5] For Luther, good works in no way contribute to being declared innocent or righteous before God, but inevitably accompany faith.

John Calvin was equally appalled by the suggestion that good works are optional. He says that only a shamelessly impious person would dare to slander Protestants by accusing them of "abolishing good works." (One need not wonder, then, what Calvin would say to free-gracers!) Calvin defends the necessity of good works by saying, "We are justified not without works yet not through works."[6]

An uneasiness about good works lingers, however. Calvin urges that God alone must get credit for these good works, since for Calvin, God's agency remains primary in achieving them. "The first part of a good work is will; the other, a strong effort to accomplish it; the author of both is God. Therefore we are robbing the Lord if we claim for ourselves anything either in the will or in the accomplishment."[7] Classic Protestantism warns against the danger of trusting in good works—especially legalism, works righteousness, and stealing honor from God—while at the same time contending that good works will invariably and spontaneously emerge in the wake of true faith.

More Reasons Works Are Not the Problem

Now the plot thickens. Even though the Bible warns repeatedly that we are not declared innocent by God by our works (see section "Works as the Problem" above), it also repeatedly affirms that a certain standard of good behavior is necessary for salvation.

Evil Deeds Result in Condemnation

Paul says that certain works or deeds, if they continue unchecked (apart from repentance), will exclude us from the kingdom of God and cause our destruction:

> Now the *works* of the flesh are evident: sexual immorality, impurity, sensuality, idolatry, sorcery, enmity, strife, jealousy, fits of anger, rivalries, dissensions, divisions, envy, drunkenness, orgies, and things like these. I warn you, as I warned you before, that *those who do such things will not inherit the kingdom of God.* (Gal. 5:19–21)

Those who perform certain evil *works* will not "inherit the kingdom of God." Eternal life, not just reward, is in view with regard to these evil deeds, as Paul later clarifies that these sinful activities result in the opposite of eternal life: "Do not be deceived; God is not mocked. For the one who sows to his own flesh will from the flesh reap *destruction* [*phthoran*], but the one who sows to the Spirit will from the Spirit reap *eternal life*" (Gal. 6:7–8 AT).[8] Since the destruction is contrasted with eternal life, we are talking about not a person's rewards but eternal destiny.

Paul says much the same thing in other places, repeatedly telling his churches (speaking to those he regards as already "justified" in the Christ) that those who persist in unmodified unrighteous behavior will be excluded from eternal life:

> But what fruit were you getting at that time from the things of which you are now ashamed? For *the end of those things is death.* (Rom. 6:21)

> For if you live according to the flesh *you will die.* (Rom. 8:13)

> For you may be sure of this, that everyone who is sexually immoral or impure, or who is covetous (that is, an idolater), *has no inheritance in the kingdom* of Christ and God. (Eph. 5:5)

It is not just Paul who says that certain bodily works or deeds are incompatible with final salvation (see also 1 Cor. 6:9–11; Col. 3:5–6; 2 Thess. 1:5–10). Other New Testament authors say the same (Matt. 7:21–23; Heb. 6:4–6; 10:26–27; James 5:19–20; 2 Pet. 2:20–21; 1 John 3:6–9; Rev. 21:27; 22:15). This is the consistent New Testament view.

Good Works Are Saving

Paul repeatedly says *good works will determine final salvation* on the day of judgment. We cannot ignore these texts:

> But because of your hard and impenitent heart you are storing up wrath for yourself on the day of wrath when God's righteous judgment will be revealed. God will render to each one *according to his* [*or her*] *works*: to those who by steadfastness in *well-doing*

> seek for glory and honor and incorruptibility, *eternal life*; but for those who are self-seeking and do not *obey* the truth, but *obey* unrighteousness, wrath and fury. (Rom. 2:5–8 AT)

This passage is extremely important. Reread it! The apostle Paul is frank: on the day of judgment *the quality of our works* will determine whether or not we receive *eternal life*.

Not merely rewards but eternal life itself is in view. On that day God is going to *render* (Greek: *apodidōmi*, meaning to "pay" or "repay") to each person according to his or her *works* or *deeds* (Greek: *erga*). In other words, God is going to pay out what our *performance* indicates that we deserve. God will look at what each person has done—the caliber of *well-doing* and of *obeying the truth*. Failure to obey the truth is not simply disbelieving in Jesus's death for sins, for "not obeying the truth" is further described as *obeying unrighteousness*—that is, acting in unrighteous ways—doing sinful deeds.

Actual works or deeds are said to be the foundation of the judgment for eternal life in Romans 2:5–8. God will inspect not how we wish we would have performed or how we intended to perform or how Christ performed on our behalf, but each person's *actual behavioral performance*. And Paul is speaking to his fellow Christians (not non-Christians) when he affirms that God will look at each one's actual deeds.

Paul does not leave any doubt that the *quality* of our good deeds will at least partially determine salvation, for he contrasts those who perform high-quality good deeds ("those who by steadfastness in *well-doing* seek for glory and honor and incorruptibility") with those who perform low quality ("those who are self-seeking and do not *obey* the truth, but *obey* unrighteousness"). Those who perform well will receive *eternal life* and those who do not will get wrath and fury on the day of judgment. We are not permitted to say that this judgment according to works is merely about heavenly rewards rather than about eternal life itself.

Attempts to Avoid Works within Justification

Nearly all Christians agree that works are required for salvation. This includes all the major Protestant denominations as well as Catholics and Orthodox alike. (Sometimes Protestants are confused about this, misunderstanding their own heritage.) Nevertheless, Paul's words have caused anxiety for certain camps within Protestantism—and there have been various attempts to dodge what Paul says about the function of works within justification—for Paul's words are felt to threaten the faith-alone system. I think we can integrate good works into justification by faith alone if we see saving *faith* as predominately *allegiance*.

Hypothetical Speaking?

One attempt to avoid works as fundamentally saving is to suggest that Paul was just speaking *hypothetically* in Romans 2:5–8 in order to encourage the helpless sinner to flee to Jesus. Paul says that God will repay each according to his or her own works. But if God were actually to do this, all would be condemned because all our deeds are imperfect. Therefore, God will not do this. It's only hypothetical.

Those favoring a hypothetical solution appeal to the overall argument of Romans 1:18–3:20. Paul's overarching purpose in this section is to contend that none are righteous (see esp. Rom. 3:9, 20). They claim Paul is speaking about what happens apart from trusting in Jesus's righteousness-achieving substitutionary sacrifice. A person's deeds won't actually be judged if that person accepts Jesus, since Jesus's merit or accomplished work will count instead. Since none are righteous, Paul is speaking hypothetically to encourage his audience to cling by faith alone to Jesus's perfect righteousness rather than to their own deeds.

On the surface this hypothetical solution sounds plausible. But accepting it is a dangerous theological gambit. *The hypothetical solution takes Paul to be saying the opposite of what he actually says.* Paul says each person will be judged for eternal life by his or her *own* works. The hypothetical solution says Paul is trying to help everyone see that they will *not* be judged by works but purely on trusting Jesus and his work alone. If we accept the hypothetical solution without adequate warrant, we make Scripture speak backwards.

In the following section, I'll begin with the primary reason why the hypothetical solution fails, and then supply four additional reasons. The primary reason is the Bible's consistent teaching that the final judgment will be based on works. The importance of this observation goes far beyond settling how to best interpret Romans 2:5–8, because it shows that we cannot appeal to Paul's all-have-sinned argument in order to treat Romans 2:5–8 as a special hypothetical case.

Judgment according to Works

The Bible consistently teaches that we will be judged by works. It is well known that the Old Testament affirms this (e.g., Job 34:11; Ps. 62:12; Prov. 24:12; Jer. 17:10; Ezek. 18:30). But it is also what Jesus and other New Testament writers repeatedly stress. *We will be judged for final salvation according to our own works, what we have done*. Consider the words of Jesus:

> For the Son of Man is going to come with his angels in the glory of his Father, and then he will repay each person *according to what he has done*. (Matt. 16:27; cf. Matt. 19:28–29; 25:31–46)

> Do not marvel at this, for an hour is coming when all who are in the tombs will hear his voice and come out, *those who have done good* to the resurrection of life, and *those who have done evil* to the resurrection of judgment. (John 5:28–29)

And Paul:

> For we must all appear before the judgment seat of Christ, so that each one may receive what is due for what *he has done in the body*, whether good or evil. (2 Cor. 5:10)

> . . . knowing that *whatever good anyone does*, this he will receive back from the Lord, whether he is a bondservant or is free. (Eph. 6:8)

> Why do you pass judgment on your brother? Or you, why do you *despise* your brother? For we will all stand before the judgment seat of God. (Rom. 14:10)

> Alexander the coppersmith *did* me great harm; the Lord will repay him *according to his deeds*. (2 Tim. 4:14)

And the description of the final judgment in Revelation:

> And I saw the dead, great and small, standing before the throne, and books were opened. Then another book was opened, which is the book of life. And the dead were judged by what was written in the books, *according to what they had done*. And the sea gave up the dead who were in it, Death and Hades gave up the dead who were in them, and they were judged, each one of them, *according to what they had done*. . . . And if anyone's name was not found written in the book of life, he was thrown into the lake of fire. (Rev. 20:12–13, 15)

In Revelation, although the Lamb's book of life is ultimate, nothing in context suggests that the books of deeds are totally irrelevant to eternal life. On the contrary, they seem to explicate or supplement the Lamb's book in some way. Consider: If *allegiance* to Jesus the king determines individual listing in the Lamb's book, then it makes sense that books of deeds recording the *quality of allegiance* for each would be present at the final judgment to serve as evidence for the presence or absence of each name. Final judgment includes deeds.

Not Hypothetically Speaking

Jesus, Paul, and the rest of the Bible consistently state that the final judgment will include our works (see also 1 Pet. 1:17; Rev. 2:23). Paul repeatedly says that we will be repaid according to what we have done, and he does so not merely in those places where he is making an all-have-sinned argument (Rom. 14:10; 1 Cor. 3:12–15; 2 Cor. 5:10; Eph. 6:8; 1 Tim. 5:24; 2 Tim. 4:14). This is why it is invalid for those favoring the hypothetical solution to argue that Romans 2:5–8 is a special case in which Paul means the reverse of what he actually says. It is not a special case. This is the primary reason why the hypothetical solution should be rejected, but four others are weighty too.

1. *Immediate context*. There is nothing in the immediate context of Romans 2 to suggest that Paul is speaking hypothetically. In fact there is evidence that he is *not* doing so in 2:25–29 (see below). It is true that the none-are-righteous overarching context of Romans 1:18–3:20 must be considered in interpreting 2:5–16, but it is not true that this *uniquely* favors the hypothetical solution, because other solutions are possible. The even-nearer context in Romans 2 must be prioritized, and it points at *life in the Spirit*, making this the more probable overall solution.

2. *Not marked as hypothetical*. Elsewhere in Romans, Paul marks his statements that are not to be taken at face value. For example, in Romans 3:5 he says, "I speak in a human way" (see also Rom. 6:19). But he does not do this in 2:5–8, nor should we pretend that he has. We must take seriously Paul's statement that each will be judged for eternal life according to (and on the basis of) works (2:5–8) and will be justified on the basis of law-doing (v. 13).

3. *Positive verdict*. Paul speaks of the possibility of both a *positive* and a negative verdict in Romans 2:5–16. If Paul were speaking hypothetically only about the grim prospect of condemnation by works so as to motivate us to flee to Jesus, we would expect him to speak only of a guilty verdict against all humanity—because that is the only possibility. But Paul indicates that the judgment can go either way. Why would Paul announce a possible *positive* verdict—"God will render to each one according to his [or her] works: to those who by steadfastness in *well-doing* seek for glory and honor and incorruptibility, *eternal life*" (Rom. 2:6–7

AT)—in the judgment according to deeds if he is really trying to tell everyone that only a guilty *negative* verdict can result? The hypothetical solution cannot account for a possible positive verdict, but the life-in-the-Spirit solution can.

4. *The Holy Spirit empowers good works*. The Holy Spirit empowers holy living. Paul says in near context (Rom. 2:25–29) and later on in the letter (Rom. 8:1–4, 12–13) that the Holy Spirit enables us to perform good deeds and fulfill the law in the Christ. "A Jew is one inwardly, and circumcision is a matter of the heart, *by the Spirit*, not by the letter. His praise is not from man but from God" (2:29). Such a person is praised by God when judged because he "*completes* [*telousa*] the law" (2:27 AT). Note the connection to Romans 2:13: "it is not the hearers of the law who are righteous before God, but the *doers* of the law who will be justified." In both cases doing or completing the law results in righteousness or praise before God. Thus we are encouraged to see the Holy Spirit as the key in both. A better solution than the merely hypothetical lies ready to hand in Romans 2 itself. *Good works are saving when they are part of faith because the Holy Spirit empowers us to perform them.*

The gospel-allegiance model shows that the gospel, grace, faith, and works can cohere without the need to treat Paul's words as merely hypothetical. We are not permitted to make Paul say the opposite of what he actually says just because we find his words inconvenient for our systems. Although it still has a purchase in free-grace circles, the hypothetical view is rightly rejected by most biblical scholars today.

Congruent with Works?

A different solution for how to read Romans 2:5–8 is more popular among those anxious to safeguard justification by faith alone today. But their solution is equally problematic. Let's call it the *congruent* solution. John Piper, for example, rejects the hypothetical view while putting forward this alternative:

> I believe it is actually true, not just hypothetically true, that God "will render to each one according to his works . . ." (Rom. 2:6–7). I take the phrase "according to" (*kata*) in a sense different from "based on."[9]

For Piper, Paul is not speaking hypothetically but is instead describing *judgment according to works* not *judgment based on works*. Piper is attempting to draw special significance from Paul's exact language in Greek in Romans 2:6: "God will repay each person *according to his works* [*kata ta erga autou*]." Piper notes, correctly, that when the Bible elsewhere on occasion disavows works, slightly different language is sometimes featured: that we are justified by faith and not *ex ergōn* (by/from works) or *ex ergōn nomou* (by/from works of the law).[10] Piper thinks the use of the word *kata* (according to) in Romans 2:6 rather than *ex* (by/from) is highly significant for understanding the role of works in salvation.

Piper says that the final judgment for eternal life will *accord with* (*kata*) works but not *derive from* (*ex*) works. He takes faith as the sole instrument or medium while saying that faith alone is invariably accompanied by good works that *accord*, or are *in harmony*, with saving faith. He excludes works as any foundation, or basis, for salvation but nevertheless says that the good works that come in the wake of saving faith are necessarily *congruent* with it—and if congruent, then works serve as required evidence for faith's genuineness.

Yet even Piper himself notes that his desire to make distinctions of this sort cannot consistently be supported by the Bible. Scripture does not overtly speak of justification by *pistis* alone, but famously speaks positively of justification by works (*ex ergōn*) three times (James 2:21–25).[11] And it is used by James to *deny* justification by *pistis* alone ("you see that a person is justified *by works and not by faith alone*," James 2:24). The distinction that Piper has made is unstable and forced.

Justification Is Based in Part on Works

Beyond these reasons, the congruent solution of Piper, Thomas Schreiner, and others does not stand up to scrutiny for three reasons.[12]

1. *False restriction of "according to."* The congruent solution wrongly restricts the meaning of *kata* to *accordance apart from basis*. It is not constrained in this way in ordinary usage. Accordance or congruency typically *includes* rather than excludes basis in English and in Greek. For example, consider the following sentences:

> *According to* Iowa's state law, the police officer issued a speeding ticket.
>
> *On the basis of* Iowa's state law, the police officer issued a speeding ticket.

In ordinary usage we do not find one of these sentences to mean something appreciably different than the other. It is assumed that Iowa's state law is *included*, not excluded, as part of the foundational reason why it is valid to issue the ticket. Accordance ordinarily includes basis.

The same is true in Greek as in English. For example, the first uninflected use of *kata* in the New Testament indicates that Herod killed the infants *kata ton kronon* (according to the time) he learned from the wise men. It would be absurd to say that Herod's actions were merely congruent with the time but not based on it. Learning the time was foundational to his actions. *Kata* ordinarily assumes *basis* as part of its meaning, so Piper's attempt to exclude it is invalid.

2. *Context discourages congruency and promotes basis.* The context of Romans 2:5–8 suggests not mere correlation but also basis. Paul follows up his words "God will repay each *kata* his works" (2:6) with a further description of how this judgment will be made. The further description suggests the verdict will be based upon performed actions, such as "well-*doing*" and "*obeying* the truth" rather than "*obeying* unrighteousness" (2:7–8). This qualitative language makes it difficult to escape the conclusion that Paul regarded performed works as part of the basis.

3. *Other examples in the Bible involve basis.* Other judgment-by-deeds passages in the Bible that use *kata* do not have in view

correlation to the exclusion of basis. For example, Paul says, "Alexander the coppersmith *did* me great harm; the Lord will repay him *according to his deeds* [*kata ta erga autou*]" (2 Tim. 4:14). Paul clarifies that Alexander "vigorously opposed" his teaching. Context suggests that Alexander's actual deeds will be the basis for repayment at the judgment. See also Job 34:11; Psalm 62:12; Proverbs 24:12; Jeremiah 32:19; Matthew 16:27; John 7:24; 8:15; 1 Peter 1:17; Revelation 2:23 (cf. Sirach 16:12). In all of these examples congruency and basis appear to coincide, as in ordinary language. So the contention of Piper, Schreiner, and others that Paul has congruency but not basis in view is special pleading.

The conclusion is that *good works form part of the basis of judgment for final salvation* in Romans 2:5–8. This is reinforced subsequently when Paul says, "For it is not the hearers of the law who are righteous before God, but *the doers* of the law who will be *justified*" (Rom. 2:13). The most straightforward interpretation of this verse is to accept that *the actual doing or performance of the law forms part of the basis for justification.* This is because justification is not a mere declaration of innocence but involves a change in a person's very being (liberation from bondage to sin's power)—"For one who has died *has been justified* [*dedikaiōtai*] from sin" (Rom. 6:7 AT). That is, justification itself includes the kind of personal ontological change frequently associated only with sanctification. Works cannot be excluded from the basis of justification according to the witness of both Paul and James. These saving good deeds are able to happen because the Holy Spirit allows us to fulfill the true intention of God's law in our actions, as Romans 2:25–29 suggests and 8:1–17 indicates.

The proposed solution of merely *congruent* saving works must be rejected as unbiblical. The consistent witness of both the Old and New Testaments is that we will be judged for eternal life at least in part on the foundation of our own works. Although Luther may have been right to identify good works as dangerous in some fashion, they are not the ultimate enemy. *Works have a positive saving role within allegiance as part of the basis for our justification and final salvation.* How then can faith, grace, and works fit together without contradiction? The so-called new perspective on Paul reassesses works so as to better understand the Bible's vision of salvation.

The New Perspective on Paul

It is not always worthwhile to enter into the history of scholarship. In this case it definitely is. In 1977, *Paul and Palestinian Judaism*, written by E. P. Sanders, was published. It has been enormously influential, opening up productive new conversations about salvation. This is true whether Sanders's ideas are right, wrong, or (more likely) a mixture of both.

Saving Works in the New Testament Era

Sanders went back to the Bible and other ancient sources in an attempt to recover how Jews in Jesus's day understood grace, works, and forgiveness in relationship to salvation. In so doing, Sanders recovered what he regarded to be the true pattern of religion held by nearly all Jews during the New Testament era. We must remember that Jesus, Peter, Paul, and the other apostles were all Jews, even if unusual ones. Sanders called this pattern *covenantal nomism*.

By "covenantal" Sanders was signaling that Jews in Jesus's day didn't think that they needed to perform works to earn salvation. They were already born into covenant membership. They did not regard themselves as born into a situation in which they already stood condemned by sin, or even a neutral setting, so that they needed to earn salvation. Even when acknowledging their innate evil inclination and their sin, they were convinced that they had been born "saved." They were saved *by race by grace* by being born into the covenant family. They didn't have to earn God's favor via works to "get in." Nor must an individual's good deeds outweigh the bad at the final judgment.

Why then do any good works? With the second word, "nomism," Sanders sought to describe how deeds were believed to save. He contended that works were purposed toward *maintaining* the covenant, the law of Moses. The Greek word for the law is *nomos*, hence "nomism." One needed to keep the Sabbath, obey kosher laws, maintain holiness codes, pilgrimage to the temple for festivals, offer sacrifices, and the like. *Works were necessary not to earn initial salvation but to maintain a saved status for final salvation.*

Perfect obedience was not necessary since God graciously provided provisions for forgiveness within the old covenant. Forgiveness was found in bringing offerings (Lev. 1–7) and participating in the Day of Atonement (Lev. 16). Specific works were required, indeed commanded, in order to maintain the status of forgiven in the Old Testament.

Covenant maintenance by good works was both individual and collective. God would punish or rescue the whole nation (or large groups therein) together. If an individual disregarded God's law, God would punish the individual and the nation as a whole. Salvation was not focused on heaven. Rather, God would bring about a blessed new era, the age to come, likely through a future Messiah. This communal element intensified the social pressure to keep the Mosaic law among the Pharisees in Judea and among the Essenes living at Qumran (where the Dead Sea Scrolls were discovered). Individual sin affected everyone's collective future salvation.

Changes in Understanding over Time

Sanders argues that Catholics and Protestants alike in the Middle Ages largely misunderstood how Jews during the New Testament era conceptualized salvation. For Luther, the Catholic Church's insistence on ceremonial works (such as penance and indulgences) was basically the same as Jewish insistence on obedience to the law of Moses. But Luther misunderstood the true role of good works in Judaism, which were purposed toward not earning initial salvation but instead maintaining it. For Sanders, Luther imposed a faith-versus-works scheme on the Bible in questionable ways.

If Sanders is right, then the classic Protestant fear of works—that works lead to mistaken attempts at earning salvation through works righteousness or legalism—is mostly beside the point. That is, if Paul was not combating the idea that a person could earn salvation by doing good deeds (works righteousness) or attempting to prevent individuals from trying to be saved by keeping God's commands (legalism), then much Protestant energy and theology has been misdirected.

Appraising the New Perspective

The million-dollar question is, of course, is Sanders right? The scholarly assessment of the new perspective on Paul has been overwhelming and mixed. There is no monolithic new perspective on Paul since literally thousands of scholars have weighed in with their varying stances. It is meaningless to say that one is for or against the new perspective on Paul, as there is no single "it." Good resources exist that chronicle the discussion and analyze its many aspects.[13]

Most agree that Sanders is right about crucial matters and wrong about others. His basic proposal for *covenantal nomism* is almost certainly correct in its broad outline, but not in some of its details. Jews did believe that they were born by grace into God's covenant family, so that they could expect to participate in God's final salvation (not primarily "heaven" but rather a new epoch) if they maintained the Mosaic covenant. He is also almost certainly right when he affirms that most Jews did not believe that perfect obedience to the law of Moses was required for salvation, since the law itself contains provisions for forgiveness. Moreover, by showing that Jews in Jesus's day affirmed God's saving grace, Sanders corrected caricatures of Judaism and performed a major service to the church and the world.

Problems in the New Perspective

The plight existed. Yet Sanders overreaches. For instance, he famously contends that Paul had no real problem with Judaism except inasmuch as it had failed to recognize Jesus as the Messiah. Sanders asserts that Paul invented an all-are-guilty thesis for humanity, and that he did so by beginning with the Christian solution to that plight. Although doubtless it is true that Paul, in coming to the conviction that Jesus was the Christ, was able to think in sharper ways about the true nature and depth of the human predicament, Sanders underplays the degree to which Jews were already aware of fundamental human problems.

Limited works righteousness. Additionally it can be demonstrated that some Jews living at the time of Jesus believed that they needed to accrue sufficient good deeds in order to attain final salvation (e.g., Tobit 4:9–10; 4 Ezra 6:5; 7:77; 8:33–36; 2 Baruch 14:12; 51:7; Psalms of Solomon 9:3–5). Even if Sanders is right that good works were performed as a response to an established covenant, nonetheless the need to accumulate sufficient good deeds might have been an anxiety for some. A *limited works righteousness* for final salvation was at the very least still in view in Judaism. Thus Luther's polemic against it was not entirely misguided.

Grace mistakes. Moreover, although Sanders correctly affirms that Jews believed in grace, he overemphasizes grace's prior timing and its unmerited quality in Second Temple Judaism. He fails to see that Paul's view of grace as *unmerited* was unusual among his Jewish contemporaries.[14]

Perfect obedience mattered to Paul. Finally, though most Jews did not believe that perfect obedience to the Mosaic law was required, Paul might have veered from that course after accepting Jesus as the Messiah. Regardless of what Paul believed before his conversion, in light of the Christ events he came to the conviction that, apart from the Christ, *perfect* obedience to the law was now required if final salvation were to result (see Rom. 2:25; Gal. 3:10; 5:3; cf. James 2:10). Paul probably believed that previous provisions in the old covenant for forgiveness (the atonement system) were now void because God had made a new covenant with the people rooted solely in the Messiah's death, resurrection, and enthronement as priest and king. Minor grievances with Sanders and the new perspective could be multiplied, but some critiques have been more productive than others.

Rethinking Works

Works as works of the law. Scholarship has critiqued Sanders while building on aspects of his project. James D. G. Dunn (followed by N. T. Wright and others) has made the intriguing observation that when Paul is speaking about justification, "works of the law" (*erga nomou*) rather than just "works" are usually in view.[15] Moreover, it can be shown that in several passages Paul intends "works" as a shorthand for "works of the law." For example, in Romans 9:32, Paul says merely "works," but since Israel's pursuit of the covenantal law is in view (9:31), "works" is an abbreviation for "works of the law." Likewise in Romans 3:20 and 3:28 Paul uses the full expression "works of the law." But in 3:27 he certainly intends "works of the law" as is proven by the broader context (and the verse itself) but abbreviates it to "works":

> Where then is boasting? It is excluded. Through *what sort of law*? Of ***works***? No, but through the law of *pistis*. For we reckon a person is justified by faith apart from *works of the law*. (Rom. 3:27–28 AT)

In contexts pertaining to justification, Paul at least sometimes intends "works of the law" (his preferred language) but abbreviates that to "works."[16] So we must be open to the possibility that "works of the law" rather than all "works" in general are Paul's real aim with regard to justification. This opens up new avenues for making sense of Paul's vision of salvation.

Works, justification, and boundary marking. That Paul says works justify (Rom. 2:6–8, 13) shows he did not place *all works* outside the purview of justification. Rather, just specific kinds of works that divide Jew and Gentile—*works of the law*. For Paul, "works" or "works of the law" refers to specific socioreligious boundary markers such as circumcision, Sabbath, kosher, and table-fellowship. Prior to the Messiah, these works of the law functioned to divide the people of God (Jews) from outsiders (Gentiles).

For example, when Paul for the first time in recorded history broached the topic of justification by faith rather than works, it was with regard to Peter's table-fellowship practices. Peter had been eating with both Gentile and Jewish Christians in Antioch, but under pressure from the circumcision group, he started to dine only with Jewish Christians (Gal. 2:11–14). In that time, when a Jewish Christian like Peter ate the wrong food (non-kosher) with the wrong people (Gentile Christians), he would be perceived to be violating or failing to perform specific "works of the law"—or abbreviating, "works."

Paul knew this was an extraordinarily serious matter. Peter's actions were a practical denial of justification by *pistis*. His actions had not compromised the gospel proper, but the one-new-humanity *result* of the gospel. Paul rebukes Peter, saying,

> We ourselves are Jews by birth and not Gentile sinners; yet we know that a person is not justified by *works of the law* but through the loyalty (*pistis*) of Jesus the Christ, so we also have given allegiance (*pistis*) unto the Christ, Jesus, in order to be justified by the loyalty (*pistis*) of the Christ and not by *works of the law*, because by *works of the law* no one will be justified. (Gal. 2:15–16 AT)

Works of the law, not good works in general, are in view in this episode. With his opening words, Paul himself suggests that his distinction between justification by *pistis* and justification by *works of the law* pertains to Jew and Gentile differences. Works of the law are predominately but not exclusively markers that separated Jew and Gentile.

In speaking about justification by *pistis* rather than by works of the law in Galatians 2:15–16, Paul is speaking to the Christian community, to those who have already acknowledged the Messiah. Therefore, Paul's words here are almost certainly *not* an attempt to tell his original hearers in Antioch (or later those in Galatia who were reading his letter) about how to become Christians in the first place.

Paul was *not* saying that if you want to get saved, have faith in Jesus and avoid trying to earn your salvation by doing good deeds. (Yet this is how Paul's words about justification by faith are often read today.) For it is indisputable that Paul was addressing those whom he already regarded as fully Christian—even if he is worried that some are falling away. It makes little sense that Paul would be telling them how to first enter salvation. In speaking of justification by *pistis* versus works of the law, he is describing how the truly righteous community is properly marked off from outsiders.

What we discover from Paul himself about works of the law is reinforced by very early church history. Works and works of the law are consistently understood by Paul's earliest interpreters to be circumcision, fasts, and the like, in association with the Mosaic law, not good deeds in general.[17] Unless Paul was uniformly misunderstood by all his earliest interpreters, this strongly suggests that works (of the law) for Paul are indeed predominately old covenant Jewish practices—and these cannot be generalized to all human moral effort, doing, or good works with regard to justification.

In sum, Paul is saying that *pistis* is the true boundary line between those who have been declared innocent (righteous) by God and non-Christians. Justification is not about moving into the saved people of God, but about being declared (or found) to be within the people of God. Justification should therefore not be seen as the first step in the process of entering salvation; it is *being declared as having status within the saved* (although entrance and status can never be entirely separated, because anyone identified as "in" must have entered through the singular *pistis* boundary). While Paul's Jewish-Christian opponents thought that works of the law, such as circumcision and table-fellowship practices, were valid for defining right standing before God, Paul was convinced that God is indifferent to such things. These works cannot successfully mark off the true people of God because they are not universally demanded for allegiance to the Messiah in this new-covenant era.

Not merely boundary markers. Yet in suggesting that works of the law are primarily socioreligious boundary markers, scholars such as Dunn and Wright left themselves open to the charge that these works were *merely* markers—and that Paul was not interested at all in them as *works that actually needed to be performed as part of the entire law*. Whether this charge was accurate or not, regardless I want to make the gospel-allegiance proposal clear: although I think Paul viewed works of the law as status-maintainers more than rules to be followed to earn initial salvation, nevertheless they were not mere markers. It was required that one *do* them as part of the Mosaic covenant for final salvation. And although Paul emphatically objected to this need to *perform* works of the law for salvation, we cannot extend this objection to all bodily activity, to doing any and every work. Paul excludes *works of the law* from justification but includes works of Spirit-led *law-doing* (e.g., Rom. 2:13; cf. 2:29; 8:4). Moreover he finds good works in general to be part of the basis for final salvation (e.g., Rom. 2:6; 2 Cor. 5:10). This is because *pistis* is necessarily embodied (as chap. 5 has shown). It therefore must include bodily doing—good works—as acts of obedient allegiance to the king.

Gospel Allegiance and Works

How, then, can prevalent Protestant fears about *legalism* and *works righteousness* be articulated more precisely within the gospel-allegiance model? First, Paul absolutely and emphatically rejects *legalism*, which is the attempt to find salvation by not breaking God's list of rules. Paul says salvation by legalism is impossible and results only in God's curse (Gal. 3:10; 5:3).

Yet Paul's true position on *works righteousness*—salvation by performing good deeds—is more complex. We have now established the following four points:

1. Even if Paul's aim was not to object absolutely to *works righteousness* in a universal fashion, he nevertheless certainly rejected a specific species of it with regard to *works of the law*.
2. Performance of *works of the law*, such as circumcision, absolutely cannot contribute to final salvation specifically because they are not by *pistis*. Paul says *pistis* alone avails.
3. Yet Paul does not reject the saving function of all works. Good works are not simply congruent with justification or final salvation but at least partially the *basis*.
4. The Spirit empowers us to be obedient to the law's deepest intentions in order to perform works that lead to life rather than death.

The tension between these points can be reconciled and Paul's view made consistent if we draw the following conclusion.

For Paul, works are saving only when they are an embodied outworking of genuine allegiance (pistis) to Jesus the king. But absolutely not otherwise. We can do nothing *to earn* our salvation. Jesus's death for our sins is completely *effective*. Effective how? Gospel benefits are supplied as a gift of the Spirit as allegiance unites us to the king and allows us to perform saving good works. The Spirit is necessary due to the weakness of human flesh on its own. Sin's colonizing power must be broken and the Holy Spirit must recolonize the flesh. This recolonization allows obedience to the king from the heart, as this is where the king's law has now been written. Accordingly, a list of required works of allegiance for salvation can never be produced. Such a list would be a denial of the Spirit's leading by *pistis*.

Yet although bodily deeds, as a facet of true *pistis*, are required for salvation, we can do absolutely nothing through these to *earn* it. Jesus's death for us is completely effective. Allegiance alone counts. Allegiance's genuineness and quality is relationally determined by Jesus the king as the Spirit leads us to serve him. The gospel-allegiance model objects to any form of *works righteousness* that seeks to operate as a salvation system independent from (or within) allegiance. It staunchly opposes any list of laws, rules, or deeds that must be performed by everyone in order to earn or maintain salvation, for such things ignore the way Jesus the king is making his allegiance demands known by way of the Spirit, written on the tablet of the individual human heart. The acts of allegiance that the king demands from specific individuals can differ (e.g., John 21:18–22). Salvation is therefore Spirit-driven by allegiance alone. It is not a matter of works righteousness.

Catholics, Protestants, and the Gospel

Protestants, Catholics, and Orthodox alike uphold the content of the one true biblical and apostolic gospel (see chap. 3). And this is true regardless of whether Protestants, Catholics, or Orthodox recognize its truth! Yet there are imprecisions since the gospel itself is often truncated, inaccurately described, and conflated with response and benefits.

Should Protestants break fellowship with or excommunicate Protestant leaders such as Chandler, Gilbert, MacArthur, Piper, and Sproul if it is true that they have made mistakes about the true content and boundaries of the gospel? Absolutely not. This would be wildly inappropriate because at the end of the day all uphold the ten events that constitute the actual gospel, even if they have confused the gospel itself with its benefits and our response. All happily profess allegiance.

Likewise Protestants should not excommunicate or break fellowship with Catholics or Orthodox Christians (and vice versa). They also uphold these ten events and profess Jesus as Lord—even though there is similar confusion about the gospel, its benefits, and our response. My remarks that follow pertain more to the Catholic-Protestant divide than Orthodox Christianity.

Although Catholicism upholds the one true gospel, it does partially compromise the only acceptable *response* to the gospel (*pistis*) in such a way that one of its *benefits* (justification) is jeopardized. Catholics do not uphold *pistis* alone. But nor do they simply believe that justification is faith plus works. Rather, justification is through something more specific—sacramental performance. Sacraments are believed to be effective through the sacramental action itself (*ex opere operato*—"by the work worked"), since this is how God's grace is felt to be ordinarily supplied. For Catholics, to be justified, participation in the sacraments must be combined with faith and additional good deeds.

Works of the Law and Catholicism

For Paul the law of Moses is a system of listed commands or rules. But in light of the turning from the old age to the new in the Messiah (Gal. 1:4; 4:3–4, 9), the previous distinctions between Jew and Gentile have been abolished (Gal. 3:28). The old order of things has passed on account of the cross of the Christ, and a new creation has been revealed (Gal. 6:15; cf. 1 Cor. 7:19). The law has lost its power to imprison because the era dominated by allegiance to the king has now been revealed (Gal. 3:23–24).

The law is powerless because it is part of the old order of things that has passed away. Any attempt to prop it back up and treat it as if it can justify alongside or within allegiance is a dreadful mistake. Paul puts it this way: "If I rebuild what I tore down, I prove myself to be a transgressor" (Gal. 2:18). Any suggestion that the law of Moses has justifying status in its capacity as written law is doomed. It has justifying status only when fulfilled not as written law but through the Spirit (Rom. 2:13; 8:4).

This inability of the law of Moses to justify extends to listed rules in general. It is not restricted to the old covenant per se. We know this because violations of listed rules had a deadly effect even *prior* to the institution of the old covenant (Rom. 5:13–14; 7:9–10). We also know this because the flesh itself was dominated by the *stoicheia* within the old order (see chap. 5 above). When read in conjunction with Paul's statements about the Spirit and the written code (e.g., 2 Cor. 3:6), this shows that a list of you-must-do-this or you-can't-do-that obligations can never define what is necessary for salvation; only the non-enumerable, non-quantifiable, Spirit-produced works can do this. Thus, Paul would vigorously object to Catholic claims that old-covenant works like circumcision are not saving, but that a list of mandatory works for salvation can be produced within the new covenant. Such regulations are not saving and we will violate them regardless, proving ourselves to be transgressors. Moreover, if we seek to be justified by even one single rule of such a system rather than by Spirit-led embodied allegiance to the king, then we become *violators of that entire code of rules*. The result is that one becomes debtor to the whole system of rules, "obligated to keep the whole law" (Gal. 5:3).

In issuing this warning, Paul is speaking to those who identified themselves as Jewish *Christians* (they expressed allegiance to Jesus the king). These Jewish Christians upheld a list of commands within the new covenant that had to be performed in order to maintain justification, suggesting that such is required for allegiance to the king. Paul calls this a turning away from the one true gospel (Gal. 1:6–9), because even though it is not a departure from the gospel's *content*, it compromises the only acceptable *response* (or *means*) to the gospel and its one-new-humanity *result*. Thus it jeopardizes a principal saving *benefit* that results from the gospel: justification (see "Objection 2" in chap. 3).

Official Catholic doctrine violates Paul's teachings. Even though Luther and other Reformers caricatured Catholicism in a variety of ways, on this vital point the parallel is exact. Just like Paul's Jewish-Christian opponents in Galatia, while acknowledging the necessity of faith (Catholics express allegiance to Jesus the king), Catholics uphold a list of mandatory practices that have to be performed within the new covenant in order to maintain justification, suggesting that such is required for allegiance to the king. Paul strenuously protests!

Mandatory Works for Catholics

What sort of must-be-performed-to-be-justified deeds are present within Catholicism? First, one must receive the sacrament of baptism. As the most authoritative statement on justification within Catholicism (the "Decree on Justification" issued by the Council of Trent) puts it, "The sacrament of baptism is the sacrament of faith, without which no man was ever justified."[18] This washes away the stain of original sin so that a person is justified before God. If a person subsequently commits a mortal sin (serious and intentional), then one must participate in the sacrament of penance or risk hell.[19]

Penance. Second, penance is mandatory. It is not possible to be restored by faith alone. Trent's "Decree on Justification" declares that if a person who has fallen after baptism says that he can "recover again the lost justice but by faith alone without the sacrament of penance," then "let him be anathema."[20] For Catholics, one cannot be restored to justification without performing penance (or, if impossible, desiring it). Anyone who thinks otherwise is declared cut off from Christ. One must go to a priest, confess, and agree to perform a voluntary action in relation to the sin (i.e., penance). If the priest is convinced that repentance is sincere, the priest—purportedly acting in the person of Christ—absolves the sin.

Obligatory holy days. Third, Catholics must not only perform penance but also attend holy days of obligation. Ordinarily failure to do so is to commit a mortal sin. Thus final salvation within Catholicism depends on legalism: not breaking listed rules. If broken, penance is required. Paul warns specifically against required holy days:

> But now that you have come to know God, or rather to be known by God, how can you turn back again to the weak and worthless elementary principles of the world [*stoicheia*], whose slaves you

> want to be once more? You observe days and months and seasons and years! I am afraid I may have labored over you in vain. (Gal. 4:9–11; cf. Col. 2:15–17)

Paul says that attempting to maintain justification by not violating commands within a system—like not missing holy days and fasts—has the opposite effect. Paul is speaking to new-covenant Christians in Galatia, warning that anyone who does this becomes a debtor to the entire law and comes under the curse attached to law breaking (Gal. 3:10; 5:3).

Paul rejects the necessity of observing holy days because in the Christ the enslaving power of sin—associated with the old order, its powers, and its elements (the *stoicheia*)—has been broken forever. Sin uses rule-based systems as a bridgehead to infect humanity (Rom. 7:5–13). Recolonization of the flesh by the Holy Spirit involves a new creation that has forever ended the ineffective rule of such systems over the flesh (see chap. 5 above).

Indulgences. Finally, within Catholicism, indulgences are not required for salvation but are considered a good idea to reduce the amount of time that you or your loved ones will spend being purged. Purgatory is purported to be an intermediate state for those on their way to heaven but who first require purification. An indulgence, then, reduces the time required for the purgation of nonmortal (venial) sins.[21] They can be attained for yourself or another. Luther was angered when Johann Tetzel was selling indulgences, with papal permission, to raise money for rebuilding St. Peter's Basilica in Rome.

Indulgences are still granted by the Catholic Church today. For instance, only considering the month of June 2018, the official US Conference of Bishops website indicates that a person can receive a plenary indulgence—a full erasure of time in Purgatory for all past venial sins—on June 3, 8, or 29.[22] This can be obtained by participating in a specified Eucharistic procession, or reciting *Jesu dulcissime* on a certain feast day, or making prayerful use of a crucifix, rosary, scapular, or medal during a specific solemnity.

Collectively, Catholicism falls afoul of what Paul says about *legalism* and *works righteousness*. If performing commands within an indisputably God-ordained system such as the law of Moses was not capable of providing the gospel benefit of justification for Jewish Christians in Paul's day, then how much more a disputed system like Catholicism? The issue is not the quality of the saving rule-based system. *Here's the fundamental problem with official Catholic teaching about salvation: saving rule-based systems cannot exist in the Messiah's new era of the Spirit.* Any system that makes use of mandatory obligations to dictate the terms of true saving allegiance is not compatible with Spirit-led allegiance in this new era of the Messiah's reign.

How Does Gospel Allegiance Point Forward?

In this chapter we have explored classic articulations of the faith-works problem in salvation. Popular Protestant articulations should be reconsidered in light of the biblical evidence, for they run counter to the following truths:

1. *Pistis*, though not devoid of interiority, is not primarily inward trust (or an inward feeling of confidence) but rather outward facing and relationally enacted.
2. *Pistis* is not mental first apart from the physical—it requires a body from start to finish and is implicated in the flesh.
3. The final judgment for eternal life will be based at least in part on the allegiance-based quality of the works we perform with our bodies.
4. Certain behaviors apart from repentance will result in exclusion from eternal life.
5. Scripture excludes *works of the law* from salvation (and all such rule-based systems), but does not exclude *moral effort or good deeds in general*.

6. It is "the *doers* of the law who will be justified" (Rom. 2:13), and performing Spirit-led deeds with the body fulfills the law, leading to eternal life.
7. Biblically speaking, justification may not be distinguishable from so-called sanctification within an order of salvation.

Allegiance does not exclude inward trust in Jesus's atonement. Yet it refocuses faith's aim. Allegiance stresses that saving faith (*pistis*) in the Bible is above all outward facing, embodied, and relationally directed toward a crucified, risen, ruling *king*. Good works are not simply the result of a prior inward faith. Nor is *pistis* mind first and then body. *Pistis* can never be anything other than an embodied happening. Good works are not merely congruent with justification or its fruit-bearing result; they form part of its basis within *pistis*.

Yet gospel allegiance rejects Catholic sacramentalism. Catholic sacramentalism correctly allows good works within faith as part of the basis of justification but wrongly demands that a list of actions be performed (works righteousness) and rules not be broken (legalism) for justification to be maintained and completed. According to the Bible, works are saving only when they are acts of embodied allegiance to the king as facilitated by the Holy Spirit, not when embedded in a system that demands rule performance. This is why saving faith is best regarded as allegiance to Jesus the saving king.

More about Protestant-Catholic disagreements can and should be said. Interesting questions could be pursued regarding justification and so-called sanctification within the *ordo salutis* (order of salvation). Imputed versus imparted righteousness is vital, especially as it relates to complex controversies surrounding "the righteousness of God." *Theosis* could be discussed, in conversation with the Orthodox tradition. I treated these topics in a preliminary fashion in *Salvation by Allegiance Alone* (chap. 8), and plan to extend this work in a future book. My task here has been to articulate the core gospel-allegiance model, so that the gospel might be better proclaimed in the church.

Gospel, Benefits, and Response

The way the gospel is preached and taught in the church today must change. The conflation of the gospel's *content* with its *benefits* and the required personal *response* to it has caused an incalculable amount of damage for Protestants and Catholics alike. Our justification by faith is certainly not the center of the gospel. Neither our justification nor our faith are even part of the gospel's content! Gospel allegiance clarifies Protestant-Catholic dialogue by making biblical distinctions. The true relationship of *justification by faith* to the gospel can be summarized this way:

Jesus's justification by his faith is part of the gospel's *content*.
Our justification is not gospel content but one of its leading *benefits*.
Our faith is not gospel content but the only effective *response* to it.
Saving faith (*pistis*) is externalized, embodied *allegiance* to Jesus the saving king.
Baptism is the premier initial way to *embody* allegiance.

Contrary to the basic Protestant model, the gospel is not "you only have to trust that Jesus died for your sins and was raised in order to be forgiven." And contrary to Catholicism, it is not "you only have to perform the sacramental actions of baptism and reconciliation to be forgiven." The gospel-allegiance model shows that the biblical gospel is best described as ten Christ events. Protestants and Catholics agree about *the content of the true gospel*—even when this agreement is not recognized. Accordingly, Protestants and Catholics should welcome one another as full brothers and sisters when allegiance to Jesus the king is confessed and present (that is, under ordinary circumstances).

The content of the gospel should not be mixed up with the realization of the gospel's special saving benefits or the required response. The gospel's content includes the offer of special saving benefits, like personal justification and forgiveness, but not their realization. Similarly trust (faith) and sacramental actions are not the gospel's content but typical Protestant-Catholic responses that may or may not reflect the one necessary response—*allegiance alone* to the forgiving king.

By differentiating the gospel from response and benefits, gospel allegiance may help Protestants and Catholics find new common ground. On a personal level, it also helps protect us from spinning endlessly in a faith-works vortex. Doug's personal hell was caused by the inadequate theology he was imbibing. It wrongly turned any genuine act of allegiance he performed into a work that could dangerously lure him to trust in it rather than Jesus alone. So his faithful labor in the Lord kept causing him to doubt his salvation. Now Doug no longer feels any desire to get resaved. Instead he is frequently preaching about Jesus's kingship in his local church.

A similar tailspin can occur when we are overwhelmed by intellectual doubts about Christianity's truth. At such times we must remember that we are not saved by emotional or intellectual certainty. Faith as allegiance faces bodily outward and embraces saving good deeds from the ground up. If we have enough intellectual confidence in the truth of the gospel that we continue to yield imperfect bodily allegiance to Jesus the forgiving king, we know that we are united to him.

7

Taking the Allegiance Challenge

This past summer my two teenagers and I went waterfall jumping. I grew up in a region in Northern California that has an abundance of waterfalls. Several have fifteen- to twenty-five-foot-high natural platforms overhanging deep pools. Waterfall jumping was a favorite pastime during my teen and college years.

My boys had never been before. So I had primed them for the challenge in advance. I repeatedly told them that from below it would look reasonably safe, but from above the prospect would be terrifying. They were ready. Even having done it a hundred times, my heart raced as I went first. With little hesitation they hurtled after me. I was impressed by their courage. We and others made the leap several times.

Meanwhile, a middle-aged man stood on the edge for an hour, trying to master his fear. He was obviously a tourist. He had just stopped at the waterfall, never considering a jump until he saw others doing it. When we left, he still hadn't made the leap.

This book has argued that the gospel in our churches needs to change. But not as an end in itself. For the gospel must change us. The gospel-allegiance model can help facilitate this transformation.

If you, your church, or your family are considering how to enact gospel allegiance more fully, it will be hard to launch if you are not prepared.

This chapter is themed around meeting the three most important challenges of gospel allegiance. The first is *doctrinal*: Can I explain gospel allegiance starting from the leading salvation passage in the Bible? The second is *pastoral*: How much allegiance is enough? The third is *missional*: Can I tell others why discipleship is the saving mission? And put that into action personally and in my church?

Teaching Gospel Allegiance

Let's say you are meeting with friends from church, or maybe having coffee with your pastor. You've read *Gospel Allegiance* and are convinced that a more nuanced understanding of the gospel and faith will improve your church's ministry. So you attempt to explain why saving faith is best understood as allegiance. There is some polite affirmation but equally polite pushback: we are saved by trusting in Jesus alone, not by works. Allegiance is too much like works.

It won't take long. Someone is going to quote Ephesians 2:8–10 as the showstopper. Once this passage has been uttered, perfectly articulating the proper relationship between grace, faith, and works within a framework of salvation, what more is there to say? The curtain drops.

If you've been prepared to meet the gospel-allegiance challenge, you'll know that serious conversation is just beginning. Walk through Ephesians 2:8–10 with your dialogue partners one key word at a time. I've made bold each word that you should be able to explain.

> For by **grace** you have been **saved** through **faith**. And this is not from ourselves; it is the gift of God, not by **works**, in order that no one may **boast**. For we are his workmanship, created in the Christ,

> Jesus, for **good works**, which God prepared beforehand, that we should walk in them. (Eph. 2:8–10 AT)

If you've read this whole book, you should be able to explain each word, however imperfectly, in light of gospel allegiance. I'd encourage you to try. Get out a piece of paper. See if you can do it. First evaluate the *context* of the passage, especially its relationship to the gospel. Then explain each word. Consider rereading portions of this book if you struggle. Then read my suggestions below.

Context

Paul's Christ language throughout Ephesians presupposes a royal framework. Paul contrasts our former dead condition with our new life united to the enthroned *king* (Eph. 2:1–10). More broadly Paul describes the blessings of the church in the Messiah as part of God's cosmic plan of redemption (1:3–14). Paul prays that the church will understand this fully (1:15–23). God's redeeming purpose is to unite Jew and Gentile into one humanity in the king (2:11–18).

Paul does *not* say that Ephesians 2:8–10 is the gospel. Your conversation partners will often assume that it is the gospel or a close approximation. Use Scripture to show why the actual gospel is different and bigger. Review chapters 1–3 as necessary.

Grace

What Paul meant by grace is not what everyone means by it. Saving grace is not an abstract principle that God gives us better than what we deserve, but pertains to the gospel. Contextually Paul has already explained what he means in 2:8 with "by grace you have been saved" by using this exact language in 2:5. It is gospel specific. Here grace means God made us alive together with the king, even when we were dead in transgressions. This refers to our union with the king's death and resurrection. It also means he seated us in the heavenly realms with the king. This refers to our union with the king's reign. Grace is not a generic principle in Ephesians 2:8, but refers to the central gospel events—death, resurrection, and enthronement—and the church's union with the king in sharing them. Saving grace is gospel defined.

Beyond this, six dimensions of grace may be differently emphasized by various interpreters of Scripture: (1) merit, (2) size, (3) desire to benefit, (4) timing, (5) effectiveness, and (6) return-gifting. Your conversation partners will usually package multiple meanings of grace together rather than disentangling them. The most typical package assumes that when Paul speaks of "grace" in Ephesians 2:8, he intends to say that God gave *individuals* the gift of salvation before time began, and so there is absolutely nothing we can do to deserve God's gift of salvation, nor anything we can do to return a gift to God bodily without violating grace. In other words, it is typical to stress (4) God's prior timing, (1) personal lack of merit, and (6) an individual's inability to give a bodily return gift back to God. But this must be corrected by pointing out (4) Paul's *corporate* understanding of prior timing, (5) grace's *effectiveness* for the individual, and, especially, (6) grace's demand for *a return gift of bodily allegiance*. Consider reviewing chapter 4.

In the context of Ephesians, the timing for this specific grace is not *before creation for individuals*. (Although it is *before creation for the church as a whole* in the Son—see 1:4–5; 2:10.) For Paul, grace, the Christ-gift, came at a specific time in the first century: when we were *collectively* needful. It came when we were dominated by evil spiritual powers, sensually indulgent, disobedient, and dead in transgressions. *Collective lack of prior merit* is in view. But lack of prior merit does not mean total lack of personal merit *after receiving the gift*—such a view is foreign to Paul. Paul's view is that saving grace (the Christ event) is *effective* in transforming individuals, but must be *reciprocated* by the return gift of allegiance. Effectiveness for the individual and the need to give back through bodily allegiance must be included in any personalized understanding of saving grace.

Saved

Even without specialized knowledge, we can observe the most vital points by simply paying attention to the context of Ephesians 2:8–10. Paul is *not* describing the process of individual salvation. He is *not* saying:

1. you *personally* were dead in sins;
2. but God is *gracious in general* because he gives *individuals* saving gifts that they can do absolutely nothing to deserve;
3. so you *personally* have now been saved once-for-all-time;
4. so now *you* can go to *heaven* when you die.

Rather Paul is addressing the church as a group as "you." He *is* saying:

1. *the church* as part of humanity as a whole was previously dead in sin;
2. in recent history God gave a *specific gift* (grace) to us as a *group* that we did nothing to deserve—the gospel of the king's death, resurrection, and enthronement;
3. so the true church's *collective* status past, present, and future in the king is "saved";
4. so *we*, in *the coming age*, can rule with him in our resurrected bodies.

In other words, group salvation is in view.

Yet specialized knowledge can clarify the word "saved." When Paul says, "It is by grace you have been *saved* by faith," we tend to see this "saved" as a static, one-time, past-tense event connected to the individual: "I was not saved, but then I became once-for-all-time saved when I put my faith in Jesus." But this is incorrect. In the Greek text, the "you" connected to the verb "saved" refers to more than one person. Moreover, it does not emphasize a static past-tense event, but *continued holistic status as saved*. The phrase *este sesōsmenoi* could also be translated "you are being saved," which brings out the *continual* aspect of the perfect participle, or "you are saved" which highlights a *holistic* perspective on the event, also intended.

Faith

If you are discussing "faith" in Ephesians 2:8 with other leaders or a friend, two things will nearly always be assumed. That in Paul's "For by grace you have been saved *through faith*," (1) he is speaking about *our* saving faith in Jesus and (2) faith primarily means *interior trust* that God's promise of salvation through Jesus's death and resurrection is true. Both of these assumptions are in doubt.

First, Paul may not even be speaking of *our* faith in Jesus in this passage at all. The Christ may be performing the faith action. Paul may intend, "through the faith [of the Christ]"—that is, "For by grace you have been saved through *the king's faithfulness or allegiant activity*." Support for this view comes from the next clause: "this is not from yourselves, it is the gift of God." Paul says the gift of salvation *does not come from us at all*. So he might be stressing that it has come *entirely through divine action*: God sent his Son, the king, and he demonstrated *his loyalty* to the Father and to us by bringing the divine plan to completion. The king demonstrated *pistis*.

Additional support can be found in passages where it is more likely that "faith of the Christ" (*pistis Christou*) refers not to "faith in the Messiah" but to the "faithfulness of the Messiah" (see chap. 5). In the end we cannot be sure if this is Paul's intention in Ephesians 2:8—and scholarship is split. For the sake of argument, let's assume he does intend the traditional view, our faith in the Christ.

Second, even if Paul does intend our faith (*pistis*) in the Christ, we have to ask what *pistis* actually means. This book has argued that saving *pistis* is best comprehensively understood as allegiance (see chaps. 2 and 5). The easiest way to demonstrate the plausibility of this claim quickly is Romans 1:5 or 16:26, where Paul speaks about the purpose of the gospel as "the obedience of *pistis*" in all the nations. Contextually the obedience characterized by allegiance to a king makes far better sense of *pistis* than attempts to reduce it merely to trust in a Savior. *Pistis* is not inward facing as emotive confidence. It faces outward relationally, is embodied, and can have the applied meaning of allegiance.

Works

Chapter 6 discussed works and works of the law extensively. Works of the law are different from good deeds in general. Works of the law were required by Jews for covenant maintenance. They were especially important for showing who was and was not a faithful Jew. For example, circumcision, table-fellowship practices, kosher laws, and ceremonial washings are works of the law. They were not mere boundary markers, because they still needed to be performed amid the other laws—although boundary separation was a primary function.

When Paul says "works" he often intends not good deeds or moral effort in general but "works of the law" (see discussion in chap. 6). It is most likely that Paul has done this in Ephesians 2:9 with his "not by works, in order that no one may boast." Paul probably intends "works of the law" although he has written "works" in Ephesians 2:9. There are two considerations. First, Paul abbreviates in this way in other places. For example, in Romans 3:27 and 9:32 it is virtually certain that "works" is an abbreviation for "works of the law"—and these occur in contexts pertaining to faith and boasting, similar to what we find in Ephesians 2:8–10.

Second, Paul signals contextually that in Ephesians 2:9, works of the law are intended rather than works in general. Paul mentions violations of the law ("trespasses," 1:7) and twice stresses it in the immediate context ("transgressions," 2:4, 5). Yet the decisive proof is that immediately after Ephesians 2:8–10, Paul uses the word "therefore" and begins to speak about how God has abolished the significance of circumcision (2:11–18).

Because of Paul's "therefore," we know that "works" in 2:9 must have implications for what Paul says about the erasure of circumcision's significance in 2:11–18. Galatians and Romans indicate that Paul regarded circumcision as premier among the "works of the law" (e.g., Gal. 2:16; Rom. 3:28). In Ephesians 2:14–15, Paul generalizes beyond circumcision to the law's regulations in general when he says, "He nullified in his flesh the law of commandments in decrees" (AT). Paul says much the same in Colossians 2:13–14 and applies that imagery to "works of the law" in Galatians 3:10–14. What he describes as "works" in Ephesians 2:9–15 he describes as "works of the law" elsewhere.

In sum, it is highly probable that "works" in 2:9 are "works of the law" in light of Paul's description of "works of the law" in other places in his letters. Paul intends, "For by grace we are saved through allegiance, not by works of the law, in order that no one may boast." The implication is that Paul is not trying to exclude all good deeds from salvation, but is affirming an allegiance-based approach to salvation while condemning a rule-based approach.

Boast

Paul's exact concern about the "boast" is clarified when we read "works" as Paul's abbreviation for "works of the law" in Ephesians 2:9. Paul is indicating that there is no criterion of worth in which a human can glory or brag in conjunction with "works of the law" of Moses. Whether a person would boast of possessing the law as an ethnic privilege or in excellence in performing works of the law to maintain the covenant—all such things have been proven to be of no value. The Christ-gift (gospel) was not given to humanity as a whole or any subset thereof on the basis of possession or performance of "works of the law." It is an unmerited grace that came at a specific time in human history. Any system with enumerated rules (e.g., Catholicism) cannot contribute to justification (righteousness), because such systems have been abolished in the age of the Spirit. We are justified by *pistis* alone as we perform good works through the assistance of the Holy Spirit.

Good Works

Paul's words, "For we are God's workmanship, having been created in the Christ, Jesus, for *good works*" (Eph. 2:10 AT), make sense in light of the full gospel-allegiance model. Paul has no problem with Spirit-based saving good works. His target in Ephesians 2:8–10 is works of the law and the way in which they create an alternative worth system that denies the unmerited nature of the Christ-gift as given to humanity collectively. Good works are required for final salvation (Rom. 2:6–8) and are even part of *the basis* of justification (Rom. 2:13). This does not violate grace. Saving grace is the specific Christ-gift, the gospel. This gospel gift from God requires a return gift to ratify its acceptance, a reciprocating response. This response is faith (*pistis*) and includes good works within its purview. This is possible because saving faith (*pistis*) is primarily outward-facing, embodied *allegiance* to Jesus, the saving king announced in the gospel. The Holy Spirit has colonized human flesh, so that humans can actually perform good deeds that fulfill the law's deepest intentions (Rom. 8:1–17).

The "How-Much" Challenge

Explaining the gospel-allegiance model from Scripture is the most basic challenge. But a second challenge arises on the pastoral front: *Can you explain how much allegiance is enough?* Given what is at stake—eternal life—it is understandable that we crave absolute assurance of our status as saved.

This question is acute because we know that we are disloyal to Jesus the king in small and sometimes significant ways every day. Plus, doesn't allegiance throw us onto the treadmill of fear and works, where we must earn salvation? Our allegiance to Jesus and our good deeds are far from perfect, so surely it cannot depend on us.

How would you address these concerns in light of what you've learned so far? My own conviction is that allegiance doesn't destroy assurance any more than does the traditional faith-as-interior-confidence model. Nor does it promote works righteousness or legalism, because genuine allegiance can only be Spirit-led. Allegiance is about loyalty toward the king, which includes bodily doing (good deeds) but excludes rule performance. There is no way to measure objectively how much allegiance is enough by using a universal standard. That's part of the point.

How much is the wrong question entirely because it isn't about *quantity* or *conforming to written rules*. It is about *relational quality* as the Spirit leads each person within the king's corporate body. You can't earn it. Jesus has paid it all for you. But in response to his grace, he demands your Spirit-led *bodily loyalty*—and you'll be judged (in part) by what you have done with your body as part of your trusting allegiance as a relational quality. The king will call individuals to different tasks, so allegiance is personalized.

In considering assurance, above all we must remember that God via the Son will be the final judge regarding eternal life for each individual. The Lord Jesus himself relationally determines the legitimacy of our allegiance, and he will not be hoodwinked by lip service. Some who say "Lord, Lord" are told by Jesus, "I never knew you!" precisely because they are habitually doing evil ("workers of lawlessness," Matt. 7:21–23). Doubtless King Jesus will prove to be more fair and more merciful than we can imagine. Beyond this the gospel-allegiance model suggests four tips for embracing the how-much challenge.

Perfect "Faith" Not Required, However Defined

First, traditional models of "faith" as interior confidence in God's promises do not escape the same how-much-is-enough concern. No one ever thinks perfect faith is required under traditional ideas about faith. Why would anyone think perfect allegiance to be required either? Jesus says that *pistis* the size of a mustard seed can avail with God in prayer (Matt. 17:20). So we have good reason to believe that even our small *pistis*, whether conceived as interior confidence or outward-facing allegiance, suffices to create a saving union with the king.

Blessed, Not Perfect, Assurance

Second, because we can be self-deceived, it is doubtful whether anyone could or should have perfect assurance in any case, only firm assurance. Even though Christians dispute whether those in genuine union with the king can subsequently fall away, there is virtually zero disagreement that we must persevere in *pistis* to attain final salvation. Just because we desperately want perfect personal assurance doesn't mean that we have it. Maybe it is to our advantage *not* to have it, as this helps us persevere.

Paul warns and encourages, "If we endure, we will also reign with him; if we deny him, he also will deny us; *if we are faithless, he remains faithful—for he cannot deny himself*" (2 Tim. 2:12–13). Even when we are faithless (disloyal), we are still part of his body if we have not decisively rejected or denied him as our true king. If we *endure* in our imperfect allegiance to him, the king cannot deny himself. So we will reign with him.

Guidelines Give Assurance or Warning

Third, Scripture gives guidelines in 1 John to help us weigh whether we are truly in saving union with the king so that we can have blessed yet imperfect assurance. John speaks of keeping Jesus's commandments, not loving worldliness, practicing righteousness, not continually sinning, the Spirit's witness, and loving rather than hating brothers and sisters (2:3, 9, 15–16, 23, 29; 3:6, 9, 14; 4:2–3). Yet the most important "test" is his final one, since it reflects John's purpose in writing:

> The one who gives *pistis* unto the Son of God has the testimony in himself. . . . God has given us eternal life and this life is in his Son. The one who has the Son has life; the one who does not have the Son of God does not have life. (1 John 5:10–12; cf. 5:13)

This final guideline clarifies ambiguity in the others. If our eternal life truly hinged upon not continually sinning, we would have every right to be concerned. We don't just have one-off failures. Repeated failures and sinful addictions plague us. But we see that not continually sinning is placed within a framework that prioritizes giving *pistis* to Jesus as the ultimate test that trumps all others. If we have declared and enacted allegiance, albeit imperfectly, we have eternal life.

Jesus Is the Forgiving and Empowering King

Fourth, when assailed by doubts, we should remember the kind of king we serve. He wore a crown of thorns. This Jesus is the forgiving, empowering king. He is radically *for us*. Jesus's entire gospel career—incarnation, life, death for sins, resurrection, sending of the Spirit with the Father, enthronement—is purposed toward fostering allegiance. The good news is effective for personal transformation. God's urgent desire is for us to be in allegiant union with the forgiving Son. God is on our side.

The Challenge of the Disciple-Making Mission

What does "getting saved" look like under the gospel-allegiance model? What about growing up in our salvation—that is, Christian discipleship? There can be no separation between discipleship and salvation. The final challenge is embracing disciple-making as God's way of salvation for ourselves and others: *the path of discipleship is the path of salvation.*

We are saved from death in the exact same way that Jesus was, by allegiance alone. *Except.* Except his allegiance was *perfect.* Ours is *imperfect.* But *our imperfect allegiance is perfectly saving* when it unites us to him. And we must be united to all of him.

Embodied discipleship into his pattern of life, death, resurrection, and enthronement is not optional. Saving allegiance includes doing what our Lord commands.

Jesus's instruction to take up the cross and follow him is not a suggestion (Mark 8:34). It is *not* as if he were saying, "You are saved by faith that my sins cover you, but if you want to take your Christian life to a higher level, here's a pro tip: try being less selfish." Dying to your current self for the sake of Jesus and the gospel is the *only* way to obtain a life that is suitable for the resurrection age to come (Mark 8:35–38). Discipleship is how we actualize saving allegiance throughout our lives.

Sent by the King

Because a cross-shaped life is nonnegotiable for salvation, Jesus tells the apostles not to go out and save souls, but instead to do something different—to make disciples.

> And Jesus came and said to them, "All authority in heaven and on earth has been given to me. Go therefore and make disciples of all nations, baptizing them in the name of the Father and of the Son and of the Holy Spirit, teaching them to observe all that I have commanded you. And behold, I am with you always, to the end of the age." (Matt. 28:18–20)

The Great Commission becomes fully comprehensible within a gospel-allegiance framework. Jesus speaks not about atonement but enthronement. Since the gospel can be summarized as "Jesus has been installed at the right hand of God as the saving king," we know that Jesus's statement "all authority in heaven and on earth has been given to me" is not incidental to the mission. It is the very foundation. In light of Jesus's enthronement, we are sent out as the king's emissaries to tell people about it. Let's go!

Disciple-Making Is Gospel Purposed

In this book we have emphasized the importance of the apostle Paul's description of the purpose of the gospel for understanding its allegiance demands. Jesus's Great Commission parallels Paul's description in interesting ways. In the Great Commission, in light of Jesus's kingship, we are

1. to make disciples
2. of all nations, baptizing them and
3. teaching them to observe all of Jesus's commandments.

Consider how this corresponds to Paul's description of the purpose of the gospel: "the obedience of *pistis* in all the nations" (Rom. 1:5; cf. 16:26). If *pistis* (allegiance) is coordinated with discipleship, we have the same three elements in each:

1. discipleship / allegiance;
2. all the nations;
3. obedience / observing Jesus's commands.

Why is discipleship not optional for final salvation? The parallel suggests that "faith" (allegiance) and obedient discipleship function the same way within the saving mission. The gospel is purposed toward allegiance/discipleship in all the nations.

Any gospel that makes discipleship optional or additional is a false gospel. Gospel allegiance helps us to understand why faith in Jesus, discipleship, and obedience to his commands go hand in hand. In traditional articulations that place saving faith in opposition to works and the law, it is hard to find a positive place for Jesus's commands. Not so if saving faith is allegiance to the king. We are not saved by adherence to an enumerated list of commands that Jesus promulgates as king—as if we could be saved by perfectly keeping the Golden Rule, the principles of the Sermon on the Mount, or some other system, like the Ten Commandments. We are saved by allegiance to him as we are led by the Spirit (rather than rule systems) into obedience to his commands. For the Spirit allows us to produce good works pleasing to him. This is not salvation by works but by loyal discipleship or embodied allegiance.

Because discipleship is the one and only road to salvation, we should never separate evangelism from disciple-making. Here's a challenge for church leaders: *What changes can you make to your programming so that all evangelism activities reflect the necessity of discipleship and vice versa?* Break down the silos so that allegiance to Jesus the king is the integrative center of all church life.

Divine Boundaries to Disciple-Making

When sending us, why does Jesus command that we baptize in the name of the Father, Son, and Holy Spirit? This seems arbitrary if we think the gospel's center is our justification by faith. Or if we think the gospel is all about the cross and resurrection. If we don't have the full gospel in view (the ten events), we do not see that the incarnation and sending of the Spirit are fully gospel too. The expanded definition of the gospel (see chap. 3) reveals its trinitarian underpinnings:

> The gospel is the true story of how *Jesus the Son* was sent by *God the Father* to become the saving king who now rules forever at his right hand through the sending of *the Holy Spirit*, fulfilling God's promises in Scripture.

Baptism in the threefold name is commanded because this is the premier means by which allegiance to Jesus the king is initially embodied. Our bodies must give allegiance, however imperfect, again and again thereafter (with his assistance) to attain to final salvation, for this is what saving biblical faith intends. The threefold name delineates the divine boundaries that frame the one true gospel, preventing it from becoming an alternative non-gospel. The one and only gospel is the true story of how Jesus became king, but that story necessarily includes God the Father sending the Son to take on human flesh, the Son returning to the right hand of the Father, and the sending of the indwelling Spirit.

The gospel is not identical to the Trinity nor the Trinity to the gospel, but they are enmeshed and mutually defining. This is why the doctrine of the Trinity will always remain central to the church's authentic evangelistic mission. Here's another challenge: *memorize the Apostles' Creed or Nicene Creed as a summation that safeguards gospel allegiance*. Say it individually and corporately in your church not just as a statement of shared belief but as a rallying cry of missional allegiance to Jesus the king.

The Great Commission is Jesus the king's ultimate challenge for us. He received all authority when he was installed at the Father's right hand. *Therefore, let's go! Practice gospel allegiance*. Teach others how to be loyal disciples to the king too. Let's do it with fresh energy, remembering that salvation depends upon it. Enact loyalty to the king by baptizing in the name of the Father, the Son, and the Holy Spirit. *For the good news is that King Jesus is the Son sent by his Father. He reigns with him. They have sent us the Spirit*. Teach others to remain allegiant to him by obeying all that he has commanded. He will be with us always, empowering our allegiance, to the end of the age.

Appendix 1

Gospel-Allegiance Summary

The gospel-allegiance model is consolidated into the following chart in order to facilitate preaching, teaching, evangelism, and discipleship. The point of this summary is to disentangle the gospel itself from closely related concepts.

The Gospel

The *gospel* is that Jesus the king

1. preexisted as God the Son,
2. was sent by the Father,
3. took on human flesh in fulfillment of God's promises to David,
4. died for our sins in accordance with the Scriptures,
5. was buried,
6. was raised on the third day in accordance with the Scriptures,
7. appeared to many witnesses,

8. *is enthroned at the right hand of God as the ruling Christ,*
9. has sent the Holy Spirit to his people to effect his rule, and
10. will come again as final judge to rule.

Short Gospel Summary

Jesus is the saving king.

Expanded Gospel Summary

The gospel is the true story of how *Jesus the Son* was sent by *God the Father* to become the saving king who now rules forever at his right hand through the sending of *the Holy Spirit*, fulfilling God's promises in Scripture.

The Purpose of the Gospel

The purpose of the gospel is allegiance to Jesus the king in all the nations.

Our Response to the Gospel

Allegiance alone. Allegiance is expressed in repentance, trusting loyalty, and baptism. Repentance from sins means revoking other allegiances so as to live in the way Jesus commands. Saving faith is loyalty to Jesus as the forgiving king and includes good deeds done through the power of the Holy Spirit. Baptism embodies allegiance.

Benefits of the Gospel

We must not confuse the gospel itself with its *saving* benefits. The gospel proper announces *possible* saving benefits. But only those who respond to the gospel by giving allegiance *actualize* these special benefits. These include forgiveness of sins, righteousness (justification), adoption, glory, and so on. *Special* saving benefits are received personally only when we give allegiance and receive the Holy Spirit. This unites us to others who already possess these benefits—the true church. There are also *general* social and political gospel benefits—for example, healing, liberation from oppression, and poverty relief—that will be experienced even by the nonallegiant when the gospel is proclaimed.

Backdrop of the Gospel

The gospel assumes God's creation of the world, human disobedience with cosmic consequences, and the rest of the Old Testament story. There is a special emphasis on God's promises to Israel via the covenants with Abraham and David. These backstories are not the gospel proper. Select portions of the Old Testament story become gospel when fulfilled and brought to a climax in Jesus the saving king.

Appendix 2

Guide for Further Conversation

We want to grow in our ability to live and proclaim the gospel of Jesus the king. The purpose of this guide is to stimulate individual and group growth through suggested questions and activities. It is organized by chapters and sections. For activities designed for a group or pairs, those studying solo can benefit by role-playing each part separately. Reflect, personalize, share, apply.

Introduction

1. What do you hope to gain by reading and discussing this book?
2. What concerns you most about salvation? About discussing salvation with others?
3. Why do Christians like to use labels like Catholic, Reformed, and Arminian? What ideas or feelings do you associate with each? What is the good and bad in using such labels?
4. Share two key moments in your own salvation story.

5. How do you think it would have been different to be a Christian in Pliny's province? How would it have been like and unlike our circumstances today?
6. Identify two or three challenges in the coming week about which you hope Jesus will one day say to you, "You did not deny your *pistis* (faith or allegiance) unto me" (Rev. 2:13). What steps could you take *now* to stay allegiant this week?

Chapter 1: Getting the Gospel Right

Opening

1. What's your funniest or most embarrassing meal story? Who responded in a gracious way in that incident? Who did not?
2. Show gospel-related hospitality by inviting a friend or acquaintance to join you in studying this book. Do not delay. Pick at least one person. Text, call, or email this very minute.

A Better Gospel?

1. Why is a "better gospel" both possible and impossible?
2. Who first told you the gospel? Were there deficiencies in the presentation? Why was it effective nonetheless (for both practical and theological reasons)?
3. Identify a specific situation in which you can practice "downward mobility" this week. What's the first step downward you'll need to take?

The Gospel Is Not

1. Why talk about what the gospel is *not*?
2. Why is proclaiming the gospel with actions but not words insufficient? How is it equally problematic to share it with words and no actions?

3. Which topic listed in this section do you think is most dangerous for the church if confused with the actual gospel?
4. Is the gospel cross-centered? What factors need to be weighed to answer this question?
5. Split into two teams. Team 1: Prepare and present the gospel according to the Romans Road. Team 2: Prepare and reply why the Romans Road is not actually the gospel.

Gospel Basics

1. Why is it helpful to know that the Greek words for "gospel" and "gospeling" are used outside the Bible?
2. Tell about the last time you shared the gospel with a non-Christian.

Jesus Proclaims the Gospel

1. What is the principal subject of the gospel proclaimed by Jesus? How does its timing and manner of unfolding relate to the gospel?
2. While Mark and Luke use "the kingdom of God," Matthew prefers "the kingdom of heaven." Write down ideas you associate with "kingdom" and also with "heaven." If final salvation is less about going to heaven than about Jesus the king's heavenly rule on earth, should this change how you share the gospel?

The Gospel according to Paul

1. What is the difference between "Jesus of Nazareth" and "Jesus Christ"?
2. Why is "raised from among the dead ones" preferable to "raised from the dead"?
3. What is the significance of "came into being" in Romans 1:3? Of "was appointed Son-of-God-in-Power" in 1:4?

4. I suggest using "Jesus *the* Christ." Why? List other ways of speaking about Jesus that could achieve a similar effect.
5. How does the use of formal titles (Mr., Mrs., Ms., Rev., Dr., Prof.) change the tone of a story? (As an experiment, you might even share yesterday's events using formal titles.)

Presenting the Purified Gospel

1. Perhaps the only thing more urgent than getting the gospel right is sharing it, however imperfectly. Identify three friends, neighbors, or coworkers who you think have not accepted the gospel. Pray now and each day that God will give you motivation and opportunity to share, and that the Spirit will prepare the way.
2. Describe an imaginary but realistic first few lines of conversation with each of those three persons. Describe a point of gospel contact—that is, how the good news could be relevant to the conversation.

Chapter 2: Not Faith but Allegiance

Opening

1. How would you respond to someone who said that Christians shouldn't say the Pledge of Allegiance?
2. Whose loyalty or allegiance do you admire? Why?
3. We associate the word "allegiance" with pledging allegiance to the flag. Create a short "Pledge of Allegiance" that features Jesus the king and distills his kingdom principles. Refine it, then commit to saying it at a specific time each day. (Don't like yours? Consider using the Apostles' Creed.)
4. List the major differences between being loyal to a friend, a spouse, the government, or a king. The Bible invites us to consider Jesus as all of these, but kingship is emphasized most.

Faith Problems

1. What meanings of "faith" seem most prevalent today among non-Christians? What about among Christians? What about "belief"?
2. What is common to our concepts of "faith in" and "fidelity toward" that allowed the ancients to use the single word *pistis* to actualize both meanings?
3. Brainstorm a list of English words that have changed meaning over time (e.g., "tablet" or "gay"). Why do they change? What could result if a person was unaware that a word had changed meanings?

Faith as Allegiance

1. Why is it misleading simply to say, "In the Bible, *faith* means *allegiance*"? What's a more accurate phrasing?
2. How do words mean things? Why is this important for *pistis* (faith) as allegiance?
3. In Romans 3:21–26, how would the meaning change if you substituted "faith in" or "believe" with "allegiance to" or "give allegiance to"?
4. Discuss these uses of the word "safe": (1) The child is *safe*. (2) That toy is *safe*. (3) This website is not *safe*. (4) He is *safe* at first base. (5) The jewelry is in the *safe*. What's the same and what's different in each instance?
5. With regard to the question above, how does our cultural background information about children, baseballs, toys, websites, and jewelry affect the applied meanings of "safe"? What's the lesson here for *pistis*?

Gospel Purpose

1. How is the purpose of the gospel understood in popular Christian culture?

2. What does it mean to obey the gospel (e.g., Rom. 10:16; 2 Thess. 1:8; 1 Pet. 4:17)?
3. Why did God give the gospel? Why does Paul speak of "the obedience of faith (*pistis*)" (Rom. 1:5; 16:26) rather than just "faith"?

The Gospel Is God's Saving Power

1. In your own words, answer each of the five questions about Romans 1:16–17 from this section.
2. How does "the righteous will live by *pistis*" (Rom. 1:17) apply both to Jesus and to us?
3. Tell about a time when you personally understood God's saving power.
4. List three ways the saving power of the gospel can change the way you go about work or school this week.

Moving from Faith to Allegiance

1. In what *specific* situations at home, work, or school do you find yourself discussing topics relevant to salvation? What's a concrete *action* to help pave the way for an allegiance shift?
2. Read 2 Corinthians 4:3–6. What would we tend to emphasize if we made this the first and primary passage for learning about the gospel? How do vv. 5–6 inform vv. 3–4? Why might Mark 1:14–15; 1 Corinthians 15:3–5; or Romans 1:1–5 be a better starting point?

Chapter 3: The Full Gospel of the King

Opening

1. What are some advantages and disadvantages to summaries of the gospel?

2. Give your best gospel in a phrase. Write it down.
3. With regard to the US Constitution (or other national charter), what's the difference between its content, purpose, required response, and benefits? What happens when we mix them up? How does this relate to the gospel?

The Gospel Itself

1. Review the ten Christ events. What are some other important Christ events? Should they be considered gospel too? Why or why not?
2. Although each of the ten events is irreducibly essential to the gospel, nevertheless some have more theological heft than others. Reorder these events, placing the most theologically weighty first, the least last. Why did you choose this order?

Expanding on the Gospel Content

1. Why is it vital to establish that *Jesus is the saving king* is the overarching framework for the ten gospel events?
2. Why is the incarnation essential to the gospel and to our salvation?
3. What do you think Christianity's largest problem is today? Does this relate to Christian salvation?
4. Work through Peter's Pentecost speech (Acts 2:14–41) or Paul's speech in Pisidian Antioch (13:16–41). Each time you find one of the ten elements of the gospel, write it down.
5. Create a mnemonic to help you remember all ten Christ events that constitute the gospel. (E.g., Preexisted. Sent. Incarnation. Died for sins. Buried. Raised. Appeared. Enthroned. Spirit. Return. "Penguins steal ice. Dogs bite rabbits. Ants eat sticky rice.") Surely you can do better than that. The more oddly memorable the better.

Objections to the Royal Gospel

1. Do the words of the thief on the cross show allegiance?
2. If you have a winning lottery ticket, do you get the money if you never claim the prize? Is this a good or bad analogy for the "died for our sins" part of the gospel?
3. Read the Priene Calendar Inscription (see p. 105–6). List five points of contact between it and early Christian ideas of salvation. How is its vision similar to but different from Christianity's?

The Gospel and the Trinity

1. An acquaintance says, "I think Jesus taught good things, and I think we should be good people. But I'm not convinced he was God. It's just not for me." She gives you space to reply. What should you say?
2. Is it necessary to give all ten parts of the gospel when sharing it with others? How should you choose which parts to share and emphasize in a given setting?
3. How is the Trinity important to the royal gospel?

One Gospel for All Christians

1. Read 1 Corinthians 11:17–22. What in the text indicates that the Lord's Supper must eliminate, rather than reinforce, divisions if it is actually to be the Lord's Supper? How can you eliminate such divisions in your local church? What can your church do in relationship to other churches in your city?
2. Which of the ten gospel events are mentioned or strongly implied in the Apostles' Creed? What does the Apostles' Creed emphasize that the gospel as outlined here does not?
3. What are the advantages and disadvantages of saying a creed together during a church service?

4. What are several ways the church can be unified without a single leader (such as the pope)? What are some advantages and disadvantages to each different model for unity?

Bridge: Gospel Clarified—Gospel Mobilized

1. In your own words, summarize the difference between the gospel's content, purpose, response, benefits, and backdrop.
2. Are there limits to saying that the gospel is not the gospel unless it is helping the poor or disadvantaged?
3. Jesus should receive our unconditional but not exclusive allegiance. Make a flowchart to diagram your allegiances. Jesus goes at the top. Arrange underneath him your other relationships. Consider those to whom you owe allegiance and those who owe it to you: family, spouse, company, bosses, coworkers, employees, classmates, friends, relatives, acquaintances, nation, local government, world, church, elders, pastors, neighbors. Where do you fit?
4. Do you tend to overcommand or undercommand loyalty from others? Do you tend to overplay or underplay the allegiances you rightfully owe to others? Why?
5. How would you preserve allegiance to Jesus if you were asked to do something financially dishonest by someone to whom you owe allegiance (e.g., your boss)?
6. How could you enhance allegiance to Jesus if you were a teacher and your students were gossiping?
7. Tell about a time when you *almost* shared the gospel with someone but didn't. What stopped you?

Chapter 4: Grace in Six Dimensions

Opening

1. In the song "Amazing Grace," what definitions of grace are assumed? Think of a contemporary song that features the word "grace." How is it used?

2. When a pastor encourages the congregation to model God's grace with one another, what's the usual intent?
3. Discuss how "grace" is used differently in the following contexts: (1) It is about *grace* not rules. (2) He caught me cheating on the test but extended *grace*. (3) That dancer exhibits such *grace*. (4) This marriage needs more *grace*. (5) You are saved solely by God's *grace*.

Grace Problems

1. A friend says, "Grace means a free gift. Therefore what I do after accepting Jesus can have no bearing on my salvation. Otherwise the gift is no longer free." How do you respond?
2. Compare the free-grace movement's and the gospel-allegiance model's definitions of "gospel," "faith," and "grace." What are the principal differences? What's the common ground?

The Gospel Is Saving Grace

1. How do you feel when someone gives you a gift? What are some typical ways you respond after receiving it?
2. What happens when we fail to see that the gospel itself (given in history) is God's preeminent saving grace?

Six Dimensions of Grace

1. It is often said, "It is not the gift but the thought that counts." Is this always true? Usually true? Ever true? How does this apply to God's grace?

Merit

1. Tell about a time you received something you did not deserve.
2. How is it that grace could be considered grace by the ancients *and it could only be for the deserving*?

3. You have $10,000 to give to a person, group, or charity. Where are you going to give? On a scale of zero to ten, rate how much merit will factor into your decision about whom you'll grace with the money.

Size

1. What's the largest gift you have ever received?
2. Is the size of a gift or grace better measured in terms of *quantity* or *quality*? And where should we measure: in the feelings of the giver or the receiver, or objectively when we appraise the gift itself?
3. How is it, according to Scripture, that saving grace can be growing in size?

Desire to Benefit

1. Tell about a time when you gave a devious gift—perhaps you were truly being malicious or perhaps it was a practical joke. Who benefited? Why?
2. What was the most thoughtful gift you've received in the last several years? What made it special?
3. If God is perfect, how can his grace fail to benefit perfectly?

Timing

1. Describe a gift that you received too early or too late.
2. When did God's grace begin? Why is this question difficult to answer?
3. Is faith (*pistis*) always a gift from God? In what ways?
4. A boss says to her employees, "You are going to receive a bonus this year!" What might cause someone to *not* receive it? What are points of similarity and difference when we apply this analogy to what the Bible teaches about the gospel, grace, and salvation?

Effectiveness

1. Last Christmas you doubtless received several gifts that you've never used. Describe. Why did you never use them?
2. Describe a gift you received that has proven super helpful. What makes it such?
3. If God is perfect, why is grace, as described in the Bible, not always perfectly effective?
4. Why is grace's effectiveness inextricably bound to purpose?
5. Why must we consider grace's effectiveness for individuals and groups separately?

Return-Gifting

1. Why does our present-day culture tend to think perfect gifts are given with no strings attached?
2. Describe a recent memorable gift. How did you acknowledge acceptance of the gift? (Think beyond repayment in kind or size to emotional or social repayment.)
3. If we must respond to God's gospel gift with allegiance, then what does allegiance look like for you presently? What habits or practices encourage allegiance? Which encourage disloyalty?
4. Identify one act of allegiance to Jesus that you want to perform this week. What's the first practical step toward making that happen?

Chapter 5: Faith Is Body Out

Opening

1. Describe your baptism. Whose allegiance did it highlight and encourage? Do you think this was the proper emphasis? (If you're not yet baptized, repent, confess allegiance to Jesus as king, and get wet!)

2. Why do you think God commands us to do something bodily as part of our initial profession of faith?

Faith and Works Today

1. What's one area of life in which you struggle to make your faith work? How would you describe the disconnect?
2. How have you heard others (e.g., friends, family, pastors) describe the relationship between faith and works in Christian salvation? What's usually emphasized?
3. What's the standard view of the faith-works relationship among Protestants?

Faith as Outward Facing

1. This book has claimed, "Faith is generally relational and outward facing rather than psychological or emotional" (p. 153). What is meant by relational? By outward facing?
2. For each of the following expressions, choose which label best fits—outward, inward, relational, or individualistic. Then rank which are closest to saving faith as described in the Bible. (1) You're worried, but you need to have faith. (2) He belongs to the Islamic faith. (3) I'm not sure about evolution; I operate on faith. (4) Sometimes you need to take a leap of faith. (5) We're a faith-based organization. (6) The coach showed faith in me by letting me start. (7) I wish I could believe in God, but I don't have faith. (8) I don't go to church because my faith is personal.
3. When you think of Jesus relating to you, what are the most prominent visual images or scenes? How do these impact your ideas of faith or trust in Jesus? Now, think about Jesus as a mighty king on a throne, and visualize yourself preparing his banquet, cleaning his hall, or supplying his firewood. Listen! He is speaking to you, sending you on a quest. Imagine your prompt allegiance. Now

imagine him as king telling you how to treat a specific family member this week. Change your images of Jesus to foster greater allegiance.

The Faith of Abraham

1. What is wrong with the claim that Abraham was justified (counted righteous) by trusting God's promise *in general*?
2. Galatians 3:13–14 reads, "Christ redeemed us . . . so that in Christ Jesus the blessing of Abraham might come to the Gentiles, so that we might receive the promised Spirit through faith." What specifically is said to be the blessing of Abraham? How is it received? How does this passage relate to the gospel and its purpose (see Rom. 1:5; Gal. 3:8)?
3. How was Abraham's faith externalized bodily? How did it face relationally outward?
4. What is God calling you to trust him about this week? How does that relate to God's very specific gospel and its purpose or result?

Outward Became Inward

1. Why does it matter that faith has gradually become less outward and more inward throughout Christian history?
2. Make a bookmark for your Bible about allegiance. Let it remind you that reading your Bible is an embodied act of allegiance.

Faith as Embodied

1. How does the mind relate to the brain? (This is an enormously complex question, and there are many theories, to say the least.)
2. Why is Docetism, the denial that Jesus had a genuine physical body, such a dangerous false teaching?

3. What is a colony? How does it relate to *pistis*?
4. A friend says, "I am saved by faith, not by anything I do afterward." How could you turn this into a productive conversation?

The Christ Embodies Faithfulness

1. Explain in your own words the two basic options for the meaning of "faith of Christ." How does this matter for understanding salvation?
2. Read Psalm 116. Imagine that the psalmist (presumably David) was speaking this psalm from the person of the future Messiah. (That is how it appears the apostle Paul read this psalm.) How would you summarize the psalm's story line? How many points of correspondence can you find between the psalm and Jesus's life story? You could also try this with Psalms 16, 22, and 69.
3. How does Paul's use of Psalm 116:10 in 2 Corinthians 4:13 relate to Romans 1:17?
4. How is Jesus's salvation the same as yet different from yours?

Faith Is Unique

1. Why do we need to establish the degree to which faith (*pistis*) is uniquely saving?
2. One person claims that faith alone is saving. Someone counters that faith must be shaped by love for it to count, quoting Paul's words, "If I have all faith, so as to remove mountains, but have not love, I am nothing" (1 Cor. 13:2). You decide to chime in. What do you say?
3. What's the logical link between faith alone and life in the Spirit for salvation?
4. Open your Bible to Exodus 20. Why is it impossible for you to be saved by keeping these commandments *as listed*

commandments? Why might you nevertheless be required to *fulfill* these commandments for salvation?

Chapter 6: How Works Are Saving

Opening

1. Have you or has anyone you've known been "resaved"? Or baptized more than once? Describe what you think motivated this.
2. Do you see Christian salvation as a definitive, one-time event or a process? Why? Can you support your view from multiple passages in the Bible with consistency?
3. Identify a time when you refrained from doing something good because you were afraid it was for the wrong reasons. How much should the purity of our motives factor into what we do?

Works as the Problem

1. What is legalism? Where in your Christian walk do you struggle with it? Why?
2. Do you identify yourself more as a rule-follower or a rebel? How much does the image you want to project to others affect you in this regard? How has this affected your walk with the Lord?
3. What is *works righteousness*? Have you personally ever believed in it? Can you name specific people or groups ("Christian" or otherwise) that you think truly do believe in it?

Works Are Not the Problem

1. What arguments does this chapter give for why it is foolish to see works as entirely problematic?

2. Classic Protestantism (e.g., Luther and Calvin) disagrees sharply with the free-grace movement regarding whether good works are required for salvation. How so?
3. List three good things you have done this month. How do you think God was involved? How were you involved? What about when you sin? How do you think God's agency coordinates with your own?

More Reasons Works Are Not the Problem

1. It has been claimed that even for those in the church, certain actions or behaviors (apart from repentance) will result in exclusion from eternal life. What is the leading biblical evidence for this view?
2. Read Romans 2:5–8. Identify all the words that describe the criteria by which God will judge. How would you summarize?

Attempts to Avoid Works within Justification

1. What is the basic meaning of justification? How does it relate to righteousness?
2. Describe the hypothetical approach to Romans 2:5–8. Why do you think this view has been so influential within Protestantism in the last five hundred years?
3. This book gives five reasons why the hypothetical view should be rejected. Which of the five did you find most and least convincing? Why?
4. What is the congruent view of the relationship between faith and works?
5. What is at stake in the proper interpretation of the Greek word *kata* in Romans 2:6?
6. Read Romans 2:13. Why do you think this verse is extraordinarily important within disputes about how salvation

happens? What evidence in Romans 2 itself must be considered when interpreting Romans 2:13?

The New Perspective on Paul

1. Explain both words in the phrase "covenantal nomism." What is the significance of the entire phrase when the words are joined?
2. What does it mean to say that most Jews in Jesus's day believed they were already saved by race by grace?
3. What's a sin that self-evidently affects others? How about one that *appears* to affect only you? How do private sins hidden from others actually harm more than just the self?
4. Do you think public or private sins are worse? What are different ways to measure "worse"? And "worse" with respect to whom?

Appraising the New Perspective

1. What portions of the initial articulation of the new perspective on Paul by E. P. Sanders have most scholars affirmed? Which parts have been widely rejected?
2. Do Paul's expressions "works of the law" and "works" include any and every good deed that a person might do or strive to do? Try arguing both for and against this position.
3. If Paul saw "works of the law" as predominantly socio-religious practices that separated Jew and Gentile, why is it vital to recognize that they were still commands that had to be performed?
4. If a congregation splits over contemporary versus traditional worship, is it fair to consider adherence to traditional music "works of the law"? How, if at all, should Paul's view of "works of the law" inform our church's practices today?

Gospel Allegiance and Works

1. What does it mean that Paul rejected a specific species of works righteousness?
2. An acquaintance expresses puzzlement: "I don't understand the whole faith-works relationship." How does the role of the Spirit help us nuance?
3. In seeking to be Spirit-led, do you tend toward individual or communal practices? How does this affect the quality of your discipleship? List three practices that help you most.

Catholics, Protestants, and the Gospel

1. What are common stereotypes about Catholics among Protestants? Vice versa? Orthodox Christianity tends to be less known in the West. What do you know about it?
2. Do you agree that the gospel should be the principal theological standard for Christian unity? What other standards need to be considered? Why?
3. In your judgment, what's the difference between a sacrament and a ceremony?
4. What's penance? An indulgence? Why are they believed to be effective for salvation by Catholics?
5. What's identified in this book as the fundamental problem within Catholicism? Do you agree with this analysis? Why or why not?

How Does Gospel Allegiance Point Forward?

1. How would you summarize the main gospel confusion within Protestantism? Within Catholicism?
2. Biblically speaking, what's the best way to describe the true relationship between justification, faith (*pistis*), and the gospel?

3. Describe a time (perhaps even now) when you struggled with doubts about the truth of Christianity. How have you managed to renew yourself and persevere at such times?
4. How intellectually certain do we need to be about the gospel in order to be saved? How might allegiance help define a boundary?

Chapter 7: Taking the Allegiance Challenge

Opening

1. Tell about when you were underprepared to meet a challenge, and so you (mostly) failed.
2. Which of the three gospel-allegiance challenges do you think will be hardest for you to meet in the future? What are two practical steps you can take to prepare right now?

Teaching Gospel Allegiance

1. Can you explain each word in bold in Ephesians 2:8–10 (see p. 212–13), using one or two sentences per word?
2. How does the wider context before and after Ephesians 2:8–10 supply vital information about the applied meaning of grace, faith, and works? Read all of Ephesians 1 and 2 with a pencil in hand and note any connections.
3. How is Ephesians 2:8–10 understood differently when we recognize it is addressed to a group and to individuals only as part of that group? List three possible misunderstandings that could occur if readers today individualize Ephesians 2:8–10 carelessly.
4. Do you think Jesus's faith (faithfulness) or our faith in Jesus is more likely in view in Ephesians 2:8? Why?
5. Ephesians 2:8–10 has been put forward as a helpful passage for learning how to teach the gospel-allegiance

model. But James 2:14–27 is also helpful. Underline key salvation terms in James 2:20–24. See if you can explain each.

The "How-Much" Challenge

1. How much allegiance to Jesus the king is necessary for salvation?
2. Why is the difference between quantity and relational quality important to maintain? Who ultimately determines relational quality? How?
3. Paul says, "**If** we **endure**, we will also **reign** with **him**; if we **deny** him, he also will deny us; if we are **faithless**, he remains **faithful**—for **he cannot deny himself**" (2 Tim. 2:12–13). Explain the bold terms and the overall point of the passage.
4. Read 1 John 2. Identify all the verses that give necessary warning or assurance about salvation. Which do you think are most pertinent in our current Christian culture?

The Challenge of the Disciple-Making Mission

1. Tell about one or two others who have helped disciple you. What was effective? Ineffective?
2. Have you ever helped disciple someone? If no, why not? If yes, share the resources you used, your pattern of interaction, and something about your successes and failures.
3. If your pastor were to say that "the path of discipleship is the path of salvation," what objections do you think members of your congregation might raise? Can these be answered?
4. What are the points of similarity between Jesus's Great Commission and Paul's description of the gospel's purpose in Romans 1:5? What are some implications?

5. Name five regular activities or programs in your church. Do they lean more toward evangelism or discipleship? On a scale of one to ten, rate the degree to which "Jesus is the saving king" is the integrative center of each activity. Choose a program and brainstorm how you could help move it closer to ten.
6. What is the relationship between the gospel and the doctrine of the Trinity?
7. *Be a disciple-maker.* We can be confident that this is the best way to make a deep, long-term impact in service to Jesus the king, for it is what Jesus tells us to do. Identify individuals who may be ready for Christian discipleship. Invite. Create an intentional discipleship group and lead six to twelve others in seeking to be a disciple of Jesus. Speak into one another's lives for a couple years. Then send these people out as disciple-makers to lead their own groups. Repeat. Outstanding free resources for how to do this exist (e.g., www.discipleship.org, www.renew.org).

Notes

Introduction

1. See Hiroo Onoda, *No Surrender: My Thirty-Year War*, trans. Charles S. Terry (Annapolis, MD: Naval Institute Press, 1974), 197–204, esp. 197–98.

2. Onoda, *No Surrender*, 11–16.

3. For this retelling of Graham's conversion, I rely upon Bob Paulson, "Jesus Saves an Ordinary Farm Boy," *Decision Magazine*, October 1, 2009, https://billygraham.org/decision-magazine/october-2009/jesus-saves-an-ordinary-farm-boy.

4. Tony Bravo, "Grace Cathedral's Beyoncé Mass Draws Faithful Crowd of 900-Plus," *San Francisco Chronicle*, April 25, 2018, https://www.sfchronicle.com/news/article/Grace-Cathedral-s-Beyonce-Mass-draws-faithful-12865544.php.

5. Sometimes I supply my own translation (as here) to highlight precise features of the Bible's original languages, but my translations (marked as AT) generally remain close to the ESV.

6. Pliny the Younger, *Letters* 10.96, in J. Stevenson, *A New Eusebius: Documents Illustrating the History of the Christian Church to AD 337*, rev. W. H. C. Frend, new ed. (London: SPCK, 1987), 18–20. I draw from this source throughout this section of text.

7. Rev. 2:13 reads *ouk ērnēsō tēn pistin mou* ("You did not deny *pistis* of me"). The *mou* is probably an objective genitive: "You did not deny allegiance *to me*." See G. K. Beale, *The Book of Revelation*, New International Greek Testament Commentary (Grand Rapids: Eerdmans, 1999), 245–48.

Chapter 1: Getting the Gospel Right

1. Matt Chandler, with Jared Wilson, *The Explicit Gospel* (Wheaton: Crossway, 2012).

2. Greg Gilbert, *What Is the Gospel?*, 9Marks Series (Wheaton: Crossway, 2010), 18–20.

3. Scot McKnight, *The King Jesus Gospel* (Grand Rapids: Zondervan, 2011), chap. 2.

4. E.g., see Luther, *Commentary on Galatians* 1:1; *Preface to the New Testament* (1522); *Commentary on Romans* 1:17.

5. John Piper, *God Is the Gospe*l (Wheaton: Crossway, 2005), 44.

6. R. C. Sproul, *Faith Alone* (Grand Rapids: Baker, 1995), 19.

7. R. C. Sproul, *Getting the Gospel Right* (Grand Rapids: Baker, 1999), 100–103.

8. John MacArthur, *The Gospel according to Paul* (Nashville: Thomas Nelson, 2017), 55, 60.

9. Gilbert, *What Is the Gospel?*, chap. 7.

10. John Piper, *The Future of Justification* (Wheaton: Crossway, 2007), 82.

11. Scot McKnight, *King Jesus Gospel*, chaps. 6–7; N. T. Wright, *How God Became King* (New York: HarperOne, 2012); Matthew W. Bates, *Salvation by Allegiance Alone* (Grand Rapids: Baker Academic, 2017), chap. 3.

12. For evidence that Jesus proclaimed this about himself, see Bates, *Salvation by Allegiance Alone*, chap. 3.

13. On the Messiah's theological significance for Paul, see Joshua W. Jipp, *Christ Is King* (Minneapolis: Fortress, 2015).

14. See Matthew V. Novenson, *Christ among the Messiahs* (Oxford: Oxford University Press, 2012).

15. For a full scholarly presentation, see Matthew W. Bates, "A Christology of Incarnation and Enthronement," *Catholic Biblical Quarterly* 77 (2015): 107–27. See also Joshua W. Jipp, "Ancient, Modern, and Future Interpretations of Romans 1:3–4," *Journal of Theological Interpretation* (2009): 241–59.

16. It is well known that Joseph descended from David (e.g., Matt. 1:20), but it was also remembered that Mary did too (Luke 3:23 probably intends Mary rather than Joseph); Ignatius, *To the Trallians* 9.1; Justin Martyr, *Dialogue with Trypho* 100.3.

17. See *ruach qodesh* ("spirit of holiness") in Ps. 51:11; Isa. 63:10–11. In the Dead Sea Scrolls *ruach qodesh* is common (fifty-four times according to my BibleWorks search)—e.g., 1QS 8.16; 9.3.

Chapter 2: Not Faith but Allegiance

1. "Civil War Battle Flags," American Civil War Story, accessed January 19, 2019, http://www.americancivilwarstory.com/civil-war-battle-flags.html.

2. Richard Dawkins, speech at the Edinburgh International Science Festival, April 15, 1992, published as an editorial, "A Scientist's Case against God," *Independent* (London), April 20, 1992, 17. See also https://en.wikiquote.org/wiki/Richard_Dawkins. I have been unable to confirm this source independently.

3. More precisely, I would translate: "Now faith [*pistis*] is the underlying substance [*hypostasis*] toward which hope is directed, the conviction of things

not seen" (Heb. 11:1 AT). The author of Hebrews' definition of *pistis* is clarified by the examples in Heb. 11. Faith (*pistis*) is a willingness to act on God's more certain underlying reality (*hypostasis*) that is invisible yet visible through the manifestation of God's revealed word.

4. Frederick W. Danker, ed., *A Greek-English Lexicon of the New Testament and Other Early Christian Literature*, 3rd ed. (Chicago: University of Chicago Press, 2000), 818–20.

5. See Dennis R. Lindsay, *Josephus and Faith: Pistis and Pisteuein as Faith Terminology in the Writings of Flavius Josephus and in the New Testament* (Leiden: Brill, 1993), esp. 78–80.

6. For those working with the Greek, the phrase is *tēn pistin Iēsou* ("allegiance of Jesus"). Most commentators correctly consider *Iēsou* an objective genitive, hence "allegiance unto Jesus."

7. For additional examples, see Matthew W. Bates, *Salvation by Allegiance Alone* (Grand Rapids: Baker Academic, 2017), 78–89.

8. See Vyvyan Evans, *How Words Mean* (Oxford: Oxford University Press, 2009), from which the title of this section derives.

9. Matthew J. Traxler, *Introduction to Psycholinguistics*, 3rd ed. (West Sussex: Wiley-Blackwell, 2012), 79–128, esp. 82, 119–28. Although brain-image scanning does show that monosemy is the norm, Traxler indicates that polysemy is more prevalent than we might realize—perhaps as high as 40 percent of words (p. 116). On neuronal differences for polysemous words, see also Stanislas Dehaene, *Consciousness and the Brain* (New York: Viking, 2014), 66. I am grateful to David J. Downs, *Alms* (Waco: Baylor University Press, 2016), 37–38; and Benjamin Lappenga, *Paul's Language of* ζῆλος (Leiden: Brill, 2015), for alerting me to the pertinence of single-meaning bias for biblical studies.

10. See Teresa Morgan, *Roman Faith and Christian Faith* (Oxford: Oxford University Press, 2015), 5–15, for the history of scholarship affirming that "trust/trustworthiness" is the semantic core of the *pistis* word family.

11. Morgan, *Roman Faith and Christian Faith*, 86–95.

12. Morgan, *Roman Faith and Christian Faith*, 77–85.

13. J. D. Greear, *Gospel* (Nashville: B&H, 2011), 10.

14. For Greek readers: the underlying assumption in this argument is that even if a more precise genitival relationship might be in view, its specific categorization is speculative. A qualitative or descriptive genitive ("the obedience characterized by *pistis*") is the most exegetically responsible option because at its most basic level the genitive is *qualitative* and *descriptive*. See Daniel B. Wallace, *Greek Grammar beyond the Basics* (Grand Rapids: Zondervan, 1996), 76–79. I would especially caution against labeling "the obedience of *pistis*" as a genitive of product ("the obedience produced by *pistis*"), for this is a rare category. It is invoked by those who are convinced by their theological presuppositions that faith simply must be prior to and causative of obedience. But such a reading lacks contextual support and is theologically tendentious.

15. N. T. Wright, "Romans," in *New Interpreter's Bible*, vol. 10, ed. Leander E. Keck (Nashville: Abingdon, 2002), 423.

16. For these glosses and the lexical data, see Ludwig Koehler and Walter Baumgartner, *The Hebrew and Aramaic Lexicon of the Old Testament*, trans. M. E. J. Richardson, 2 vols. (Leiden: Brill, 2001), 1:62.

17. Rom. 5:8; 8:3, 32; 2 Cor. 5:21; Eph. 5:2; Titus 2:14; Heb. 9:28; 1 Pet. 3:18; 1 John 3:16.

18. E.g., see Acts 7:52; 22:14; 1 Pet. 3:18; 1 John 2:1; 1 Clement 16.12; Barnabus 6.7; Diognetus 9.2, 9.5 (cf. 1 Enoch 38:2).

Chapter 3: The Full Gospel of the King

1. Alistair Begg, "An Innocent Man Crushed by God," in Nancy Guthrie, *Jesus Keep Me Near the Cross: Experiencing the Passion and Power of Easter* (Wheaton: Crossway, 2009), 21–25, here 25. Adapted by Guthrie with permission from Alistair Begg, "Jesus Our Substitute" (sermon, Parkside Church, Chagrin Falls, Ohio, July 13, 2003). Greg Gilbert, *What Is the Gospel?*, 9Marks Series (Wheaton: Crossway, 2010), 18, first brought this quote to my attention. He cites it without attribution or approval/disapproval.

2. This list of ten slightly modifies the eight in Matthew W. Bates, *Salvation by Allegiance Alone* (Grand Rapids: Baker Academic, 2017), 52. It makes explicit two events that were implicit in my previous list. The main difference is the isolation of the sending of the Son and the sending of the Holy Spirit as distinct gospel-events in their own right.

3. On the preexistent Messiah as a speaker of Old Testament passages, see A. T. Hanson, *Jesus Christ in the Old Testament* (London: SPCK, 1965); and Matthew W. Bates, *The Birth of the Trinity* (Oxford: Oxford University Press, 2015).

4. See especially John 4:34; 5:23–24; 6:29, 38–39, 44, 57; 11:42; 12:44–45; 13:20; 14:24; 17:3, 8.

5. It is probable that Paul received the foundational gospel events, Jesus's resurrection and enthronement, directly from Jesus (Acts 9:3–8; 22:6–10; 26:12–18; Gal. 1:11–12; 1 Cor. 9:1) and the rest through the other apostles (cf. Gal. 1:18).

6. E.g., Pss. 16–18; 22; 69; 116; Isa. 42:1–7; 49:1–12; 50:5–10; 52:13–53:12.

7. On Jesus's words and actions as a proclamation of his death for sins in the Gospels, see Matt. 8:17; 20:28; 26:28; Mark 10:45; 14:24; Luke 22:20, 37; 24:47; John 20:23.

8. "Foundation Documents," The Gospel Coalition, accessed January 19, 2019, https://www.thegospelcoalition.org/about/foundation-documents/#confessional-statement.

9. Cf. Matt. 10:23; 24:27; Mark 8:38; Luke 9:26; 18:8.

10. John Piper, *The Future of Justification* (Wheaton: Crossway, 2007), 86.

11. Piper, *Future of Justification*, 88.

12. I have drawn texts and translations in this section from Glen Davis, "Pre-Christian Uses of 'Gospel,'" February 25, 2010, http://glenandpaula.com/wordpress/archives/2010/02/25/pre-christian-uses-of-gospel.

13. On the trinitarian structure of the gospel, see Fred Sanders, *The Triune God* (Grand Rapids: Zondervan, 2016), esp. chaps. 4–5. On its biblical foundations, see Bates, *Birth of the Trinity*.

14. E.g., see Justin Martyr, *First Apology* 31.7 (expanded in chaps. 31–52); Irenaeus, *Demonstration of the Apostolic Preaching* 3.

Chapter 4: Grace in Six Dimensions

1. Philip Yancey, "Grace," accessed January 19, 2019, https://philipyancey.com/q-and-a-topics/grace.

2. As an example of the tendency to reduce faith to mental appropriation of the saving facts, see Zane C. Hodges, *Absolutely Free! A Biblical Reply to Lordship Salvation* (Dallas: Rendención Viva, 1989), 38–39, 40–42.

3. On the naivete, consider Hodges, *Absolutely Free!*, 28–29: "Let it be clearly stated here that English words like 'believe' or 'faith' function as fully adequate equivalents to their Greek counterparts. There is not some hidden residue of meaning in the Greek words that is not conveyed by their normal English renderings." Hodges's claim entirely discounts ancient evidence and modern language theory.

4. Ken Yates candidly acknowledges the sharp decline: "Free Grace seminary professors are few and far between." Yates, "Taking Free Grace Overseas," Grace Evangelical Society, November 1, 2017, https://faithalone.org/grace-in-focus-articles/taking-free-grace-overseas.

5. Carl R. Trueman, *Grace Alone—Salvation as a Gift of God* (Grand Rapids: Zondervan, 2017), 24.

6. R. C. Sproul, *Grace Unknown: The Heart of Reformed Theology* (Grand Rapids: Baker, 1997), 141.

7. Words other than *charis* are pertinent to "grace." See John M. G. Barclay, *Paul and the Gift* (Grand Rapids: Eerdmans, 2015), 575–82.

8. Barclay, *Paul and the Gift*, 331, in reference to Paul's grace greeting (Gal. 1:3) and the statement that Jesus "gave himself in behalf of our sins" (Gal. 1:4 AT). Barclay shows throughout that grace, for Paul, mainly intends the specific Christ events of the gospel. See his summary on p. 451.

9. Barclay, *Paul and the Gift*, 70–75, lists these as (1) incongruity, (2) superabundance, (3) singularity, (4) priority, (5) efficacy, (6) and noncircularity. I've renamed these rubrics for ease of discussion. In what follows, the categories are Barclay's but the scriptural examples and explanations are my own except when noted.

10. See Barclay, *Paul and the Gift*, esp. 360, 566–69.

11. Louis Berkhof, *Systematic Theology*, 4th ed. (Grand Rapids: Eerdmans, 1979), 427.

12. Barclay, *Paul and the Gift*, 316.

13. Philo, *On the Special Laws* 1.43, in Barclay, *Paul and the Gift*, 227 (slightly modified). For additional evidence that unmerited grace was atypical although attested (e.g., 4 Ezra, 1QHoyadoth in the Dead Sea Scrolls, and Pseudo-Philo's *Liber antiquitatum biblicarum*), see Barclay's pp. 24–51, 189–318 (esp. 315), 565–66.

14. E.g., Gregory A. Boyd, *The Crucifixion of the Warrior God*, 2 vols. (Minneapolis: Fortress, 2017). Boyd argues that God, in punishing the wicked in the Old Testament, deliberately allowed himself to be misrepresented as violent because it is part of his very nature to absorb evil violence—and God intended to correct this view later by revealing himself as nonviolent in Jesus. For a critique, see Matthew J. Lynch's four-part review, "Crucifixion of the Warrior God, by Gregory A. Boyd—Review Part 1," Theological Miscellany, August 30, 2017, http://theologicalmisc.net/2017/08/crucifixion-warrior-god-gregory-boyd-review-part-1.

15. John Piper, *God Is the Gospel* (Wheaton: Crossway, 2005), 118; Sproul, *Grace Unknown*, 147.

16. Paul has drawn his quote "Jacob I loved, but Esau I hated" (Rom. 9:13) from Mal. 1:2–3. In it Jacob and Esau refer to *entire* nations, not individual men. This shows that although Paul refers to Jacob and Esau as individuals in Rom. 9:10–13, he is doing so to speak about their corporate role as national figureheads in salvation history. This passage is not about predestination of individuals to eternal life or damnation.

17. The apocalyptic school is associated especially with J. L. Martyn's analysis of Paul's theology. The quotes are from Douglas A. Campbell, *The Deliverance of God* (Grand Rapids: Eerdmans, 2009), 100; and the title of Philip G. Ziegler's *Militant Grace* (Grand Rapids: Baker Academic, 2018).

18. E.g., Acts 20:32; 2 Cor. 6:1–2; Eph. 1:6–9; Col. 1:6; Titus 2:11–14.

19. Barclay, *Paul and the Gift*, 52–63, esp. 53.

20. Hodges, *Absolutely Free!*, 72.

Chapter 5: Faith Is Body Out

1. Zane C. Hodges, *Absolutely Free! A Biblical Reply to Lordship Salvation* (Dallas: Rendención Viva, 1989), 172.

2. Hodges, *Absolutely Free!*, 31.

3. John F. MacArthur Jr., *Faith Works: The Gospel according to the Apostles* (Dallas: Word, 1993), 99.

4. MacArthur, *Faith Works*, 89–91, 98. MacArthur regards justification as distinct but inseparable from sanctification. For problems with this view, see Matthew W. Bates, *Salvation by Allegiance Alone* (Grand Rapids: Baker Academic, 2017), 172–75.

5. MacArthur, *Faith Works*, 50.

6. MacArthur, *Faith Works*, 51.

7. See John Piper, *The Future of Justification* (Wheaton: Crossway, 2007), esp. 103–16; R. C. Sproul, *Faith Alone* (Grand Rapids: Baker, 1995), esp. 67–91, 135–71; Matt Chandler, with Jared Wilson, *The Explicit Gospel* (Wheaton: Crossway,

2012), 13–15, 56–59, 135–54, 203–22; Thomas S. Schreiner, *Faith Alone: The Doctrine of Justification* (Grand Rapids: Zondervan, 2015), 97–143, 191–206.

8. Plutarch, *Precepts of Statecraft* 805B.

9. Josephus, *Antiquities of the Jews* 9.145.

10. Josephus, *Jewish War* 2.135.

11. Josephus, *Jewish War* 2.341.

12. Josephus, *Antiquities of the Jews* 12.396.

13. Josephus, *Antiquities of the Jews* 11.217.

14. Plutarch, *On the Fortunes of Alexander* 344e.

15. Teresa Morgan, *Roman Faith and Christian Faith* (Oxford: Oxford University Press, 2015), 14.

16. Morgan, *Roman Faith and Christian Faith*, 29.

17. While *pistis* is widely (and questionably) regarded as primarily interior confidence by the Reformers and by pastor-scholars like MacArthur, Piper, and Sproul (as this chapter shows), at the same time they correctly recognize that "believing" or "trusting" is not devoid of objective, external Christian content. So I am not critiquing the standard view on this point.

18. I treat the question of Abraham in more detail in *Salvation by Allegiance Alone* (chap. 5). What follows sharpens what I say there. Portions of this section were first published at Tavis Bohlinger, "Abraham's 'Allegiance' to King Jesus? Part 4 of the Matthew Bates Interview," Logos Academic Blog, June 22, 2017, https://academic.logos.com/abrahams-allegiance-to-king-jesus-part-4-of-the-matthew-bates-interview. I have adapted and reworked the wording.

19. Morgan, *Roman Faith and Christian Faith*, 29–30, 224–30, 444–72.

20. Martin Luther, *Preface to Romans*, in *Martin Luther: Selections from His Writings*, ed. John Dillenberger (Garden City, NY: Anchor, 1961), 24.

21. John Calvin, *Institutes of the Christian Religion* 3.2.7, trans. Ford L. Battles, ed. John T. McNeill, 2 vols., LCC 20 (Philadelphia: Westminster, 1960), 1:551.

22. Calvin, *Institutes*, 3.2.15; 3.2.16–18; 3.2.37.

23. Calvin, *Institutes*, 3.2.2–5; 3.2.8; 3.2.13; 3.2.6–7, 13, 29–36.

24. Philip Melanchthon, *Commonplaces*, trans. Christian Preus (St. Louis: Concordia, 2014); Francis Turretin, *Institutes of Elenctic Theology*, 3 vols., trans. George M. Giger, ed. James T. Dennison Jr. (Phillipsburg, NJ: P&R, 1994), 2:561–63. See discussion in Sproul, *Faith Alone*, 75–91, esp. 89.

25. David J. Downs, *Alms* (Waco: Baylor University Press, 2016); Gary A. Anderson, *Charity* (New Haven: Yale University Press, 2013); Joshua W. Jipp, *Saved by Faith and Hospitality* (Grand Rapids: Eerdmans, 2017).

26. Susan Grove Eastman, *Paul and the Person* (Grand Rapids: Eerdmans, 2018), 95. For the discussion of colonization and the embodied self, I am indebted to her large-scale arguments in chaps. 3–6.

27. Richard Hays, *The Faith of Jesus Christ*, 2nd ed. (Grand Rapids: Eerdmans, 2002). For recent discussion, see Michael Bird and Preston Sprinkle, eds., *The Faith of Jesus Christ* (Grand Rapids: Baker Academic, 2009).

28. The Scripture quotations in this paragraph are my own translation.

29. Including Anthony Hanson, Richard Hays, Thomas Stegman, Kenneth Schenck, and Douglas A. Campbell, among others. For a full exposition, see Matthew W. Bates, *The Hermeneutics of the Apostolic Proclamation* (Waco: Baylor University Press, 2012), 304–25.

30. The crisis-unto-death language of Ps. 116:3 has precise correlations to other texts in which the Messiah was understood to be the true speaker of Old Testament passages—e.g., Acts 2:24–31 (citing and interpreting Ps. 16:8–11 as truly spoken by the Messiah); Rom. 15:9 (citing Ps. 18:49 [cf. Ps. 18:4–6]; cf. Heb. 2:12). I translate from the Greek version of the Old Testament here because this was Paul's practice.

31. For Greek readers: *energoumenē* is a present middle or passive participle. Middle is more probable than passive since the middle voice is frequently observed when the verb *energeō* has an impersonal subject (e.g., Rom. 7:5; 2 Cor. 1:6). The significance of the middle voice is that it casts attention reflexively back on faith as the subject of the verb—that faith *itself* is working through love. See BDAG, s.v. ἐνεργέω; J. Louis Martyn, *Galatians*, Anchor Bible 33A (New York: Doubleday, 1997), 474; F. F. Bruce, *The Epistle to the Galatians*, New International Greek Testament Commentary (Grand Rapids: Eerdmans, 1982), 232.

Chapter 6: How Works Are Saving

1. Martin Luther, *Preface to the New Testament*, in *Martin Luther: Selections from His Writings*, ed. John Dillenberger (Garden City, NY: Anchor, 1961), 17.

2. Martin Luther, *The Freedom of a Christian*, in *Martin Luther's Basic Theological Writings*, ed. Timothy F. Lull and William R. Russell, 2nd ed. (Minneapolis: Fortress, 2005), 403.

3. Luther, *On Councils and the Church*, in Lull and Russell, *Martin Luther's Basic Theological Writings*, 365.

4. Luther, *Preface to the New Testament*, in Dillenberger, *Martin Luther: Selections from His Writings*, 28 (emphasis added).

5. Luther, *Preface to Romans*, in Dillenberger, *Martin Luther: Selections from His Writings*, 17 (emphasis added).

6. Both quotes are from John Calvin, *Institutes of the Christian Religion* 3.16.1, trans. Ford L. Battles, ed. John T. McNeill, 2 vols., LCC 20 (Philadelphia: Westminster, 1960), 1:797, 798.

7. Calvin, *Institutes* 2.3.9 (trans. Battles, 2:302).

8. The word *phthoran* pertains to decay, perishability, and destruction. Situated opposite eternal life, it is best rendered "destruction" (NIV) or "corruption" (NRSV).

9. John Piper, *The Future of Justification* (Wheaton: Crossway, 2007), 110.

10. Piper, *Future of Justification*, 109–10, esp. 109n8.

11. Piper, *Future of Justification*, 109–10, esp. 109n8.

12. Thomas Schreiner, "Justification apart from and by Works," in *Four Views on the Role of Works at the Final Judgment*, ed. Alan P. Stanley (Grand Rapids: Zondervan, 2013), 71–98, esp. 78, 97.

13. For a brief introduction, see Michael B. Thompson, *The New Perspective on Paul* (Cambridge: Grove Books, 2002). For advanced treatment, consider Stephen Westerholm, *Perspectives Old and New on Paul* (Grand Rapids: Eerdmans, 2004), 3–258; N. T. Wright, *Paul and His Recent Interpreters* (Minneapolis: Fortress, 2015), 64–131; Garwood P. Anderson, *Paul's New Perspective: Charting a Soteriological Journey* (Downers Grove, IL: IVP Academic, 2016); Stephen J. Chester, *Reading Paul with the Reformers* (Grand Rapids: Eerdmans, 2017).

14. For these categories of grace, see chap. 4. For how this relates to Sanders specifically, see John M. G. Barclay, *Paul and the Gift* (Grand Rapids: Eerdmans, 2015), 151–58, 318–21.

15. Justification is not contrasted with "works" in general but more specifically "works of the law" in Rom. 3:20, 28; Gal. 2:16; 3:2, 5, 10. See James D. G. Dunn, *The Theology of Paul the Apostle* (Grand Rapids: Eerdmans, 1998), 354–71; N. T. Wright, "4QMMT and Paul: Justification, 'Works' and Eschatology" (2006), reprinted in Wright, *Pauline Perspectives* (Minneapolis: Fortress, 2013), 332–55.

16. We find "works" rather than "works of the law" in Rom. 4:2, 5–6; 9:11, 32; 11:6; Eph. 2:9–10; Titus 3:5. See Dunn, *Theology*, 354–71, for why such passages probably refer to works of the law, not all works in general.

17. E.g., Barnabas 2.1; 4.11–12; 10.11; 13.7; Justin Martyr, *Dialogue with Trypho* 23.4; 28.4; 92.3–5; 95.1; Irenaeus, *Against Heresies* 4.16.1–3; Irenaeus, *Demonstration of the Apostolic Preaching* 35; Matthew J. Thomas, *Paul's "Works of the Law" in the Perspective of Second Century Reception*, WUNT 468 (Tübingen: Mohr Siebeck, 2018), 211–30.

18. Council of Trent, "On Justification," §7, in *Canons and Decrees of the Council of Trent*, trans. H. J. Schroeder (St. Louis: Herder, 1941). This document is also available at http://www.thecounciloftrent.com/ch6.htm. On contemporary ecumenical dialogue, including whether sixteenth-century anathemas still apply and the *Joint Declaration on the Doctrine of Justification* (1999), see Anthony N. S. Lane, *Justification in Catholic-Protestant Dialogue: An Evangelical Assessment* (Edinburgh: T&T Clark, 2002), 87–126, esp. 100–107 and 119–26.

19. See *Catechism of the Catholic Church* (Liguori, MO: Liguori Publications, 1994), §1420–70.

20. Council of Trent, "On Justification," canon 9, in *Canons and Decrees of the Council of Trent*.

21. On indulgences, see *Catechism of the Catholic Church*, §1471–84.

22. United States Conference of Catholic Bishops website, http://www.usccb.org.

Scripture and Ancient Writings Index

Acts (of the Apostles)

Romans

1 Corinthians

2 Corinthians

Galatians

Ephesians

Philippians

Colossians

Other Ancient Writings